Industry, War and Stalin's Battle for Resources

Industry, War and Stalin's Battle for Resources

The Arctic and the Environment

Lars Rowe

BLOOMSBURY ACADEMIC
LONDON • NEW YORK • OXFORD • NEW DELHI • SYDNEY

BLOOMSBURY ACADEMIC
Bloomsbury Publishing Plc
50 Bedford Square, London, WC1B 3DP, UK
1385 Broadway, New York, NY 10018, USA
29 Earlsfort Terrace, Dublin 2, Ireland

BLOOMSBURY, BLOOMSBURY ACADEMIC and the Diana logo
are trademarks of Bloomsbury Publishing Plc

First published in Great Britain 2021
This paperback edition published in 2022

Copyright © Lars Rowe, 2021

Lars Rowe has asserted his right under the Copyright, Designs and
Patents Act, 1988, to be identified as Author of this work.

For legal purposes the Acknowledgements on p. ix constitute an
extension of this copyright page.

Cover design by Adriana Brioso
Cover image: View of the Kola GMK Pechenganickel plant at Nikel, Murmansk
Oblast, Russia. (© Jason Koxvold)

All rights reserved. No part of this publication may be reproduced or transmitted in any form or by any means, electronic or mechanical, including photocopying, recording, or any information storage or retrieval system, without prior permission in writing from the publishers.

Bloomsbury Publishing Plc does not have any control over, or responsibility for, any third-party websites referred to or in this book. All internet addresses given in this book were correct at the time of going to press. The author and publisher regret any inconvenience caused if addresses have changed or sites have ceased to exist, but can accept no responsibility for any such changes.

A catalogue record for this book is available from the British Library.

A catalogue record for this book is available from the Library of Congress.

ISBN: HB: 978-1-7845-3795-1
PB: 978-0-7556-3761-4
ePDF: 978-0-7556-0044-1
eBook: 978-0-7556-0045-8

Typeset by Deanta Global Publishing Services, Chennai, India

To find out more about our authors and books visit www.bloomsbury.com
and sign up for our newsletters.

For Elana and Sammy

Contents

List of illustrations		viii
Acknowledgements		ix
Abbreviations, acronyms and Russian terms used		x
1	Introduction	1
2	In the Finnish corridor	13
3	War	35
4	Sovietization: Rebuilding a company town	67
5	Finland builds Soviet power	105
6	Conclusion	149
Notes		159
Sources		202
Index		211

Illustrations

Figures

1. The nickel plant in Kolosjoki — 33
2. Kolosjoki with nickel works seen from vantage point along Arctic Highway — 34
3. The sight that met advancing Soviet troops. The Kolosjoki nickel plant was demolished by retreating German soldiers in October 1944 — 68
4. German soldiers atop the river bank shortly before dam in Niskakoski is destroyed, October 1944 — 68
5. The dam in Jäniskoski destroyed by retreating German troops, October 1944. Cascades of water push through the breaches — 92
6. The power plant and dam in Jäniskoski before demolition, 1944 — 92
7. The Jäniskoski power plant shortly before demolition in October 1944 — 106
8. Construction work in Jäniskoski — 116

Maps

1. The Pasvik valley and surroundings — 2
2. Finnish–Soviet border in 1939 and 1944 — 19
3. Industrial network in Pechenga 1944 — 72
4. Sea voyage Murmansk–Pechenga — 94
5. The Jäniskoski area — 107

Table

1. Production of Nickel Ore and Nickel Matte in Nikel 1948–53 — 98

Acknowledgements

Several people have assisted me in the completion of this book. First, I would like to express gratitude to my previous employer, the Fridtjof Nansen Institute, and more specifically colleagues Geir Hønneland and Claes Lykke Ragner. Thanks to Geir for unfailingly and patiently supporting me, also through less productive periods, and to Claes for providing the original maps of Pechenga and surroundings. Rune Rautio has generously allowed me to pick images from his photo archive. I am indebted to Anne-Kristin Jørgensen, Jan Sørensen, Frode Nilssen and Pavel (Pasha) Golovin for making stays in Moscow a lot easier and more enjoyable than they could have been. I have been professionally and efficiently assisted by the staff at RGAE and RGASPI. The author of an early reference work on Petsamo, Professor H. Peter Krosby, welcomed me in his home at an initial stage of this project. His advice and authorship have guided my studies. Professor Helge Pharo has alerted me to references and contexts that were obvious to him, not me. The text is much richer for it.

My mentor and good friend Professor Sven Holtsmark calmly but relentlessly pushed me to make additional investigations when something in the text seemed off to him. He never counts the substantial number of hours he devotes to improving my work. I always come away from my conversations with Sven feeling inspired, bolstered and better prepared. For all this, I am deeply obliged.

Most of all, I am thankful for the support of my wife and companion Elana. Not knowing how to express the full extent of my gratitude, I simply dedicate this work to her and our first-born, Samuel.

Hølen,
winter 2020, Lars Rowe

The research for this book was funded by the Norwegian Ministry of Defense.

Abbreviations, acronyms and Russian terms used

BRIZ	Byuro ratsionalizatsii i izobretatelstva (bureau of rationalization and development – a standard component in Soviet enterprises)
d. (in notes)	delo (Russian archival unit (file))
ed.khr. (in notes)	edinitsa khraneniya (Russian archival unit, same as delo (file))
Glavalyuminstroi	Glavnoe upravlenie po stroitelstvu predpriyatii alyuminievoi i magnievoi promyshlennosti (Directorate for Construction of Aluminum and Magnesium Enterprises)
Glavnikelkobalt	Glavnoe upravlenie nikelevoi i kobaltovoi promyshlennosti (Directorate for Nickel and Cobalt Industries)
GKO	Gosudarstvennyi Komitet Oborony (State Defense Committee)
Gosplan	State Planning Agency
GULag	Glavnoe upravlenie ispravitelno-trudovykh lagerei, trudovykh poselenii i mest zaklyucheniya (Directorate for Administration of Labor Camps)
INCO	International Nickel Company of Canada, Limited

ITR	Inzhenerno-tekhnicheskie rabotniki (engineering-technical staff)
l. (in notes)	sheet number in Russian file
MID	Ministerstvo innostrannykh del (Ministry of Foreign Affairs)
Minelektrostantsii	Ministerstvo stroitelstva elektrostantsii (Ministry for Power Station Construction)
Mintsvetmet	Ministerstvo tsvetnoi metallurgii (Ministry for Non-ferrous Metallurgy)
MVD	Minsterstvo vneshnykh del (Ministry of Internal Affairs)
navedenie kultury	'bringing culture'. A normative Soviet way of expressing the need for raising the workers' standards for tidiness in the workplace and in living quarters
oblast	Soviet/Russian administrative unit, county
orgnabor	organizatsionnyi nabor (organized recruitment – form of forced placement of labourers)
osvoenie severa	'settling of the North', the drive in the 1930s to explore northern areas of Soviet Eurasia
PNO	Petsamon Nikkeli OY (Petsamo Nickel Company, subsidiary to Mond Nickel/INCO)
prikaz	order issued by minister or ministry
propusk	personal permit to enter (a territory, building etc.)

raion	Soviet/Russian administrative unit, municipality
raskulachivanie	'de-kulakization', campaign to eradicate the class of landowning farmers (the kulaks)
RGAE	Rossiiskii Gosudarstvennyi Arkhiv Ekonomiki (Russian State Archive of the Economy)
RGASPI	Rossiiskii Gosudarstvennyi Arkhiv Sotsialnoi i Politicheskoi Istorii (Russian State Archive for Socio-Political History)
Torgpredstvo	trade representation (often at embassies)
Ushossdor	Upravlenie shosseinykh dorog (highway management)
VLKSM	Vsesoyuznii Leninskii Kommunisticheskii Soyuz Molodezhi (All-Union Leninist Communist Youth Organization, also known as Komsomol)
Vneshtorg	Ministry of Foreign Trade
vozhd	'chieftain', the Soviet informal but honorific title for Stalin as the General Secretary of the Communist Party
zakazchik	customer
zamtorgpred	deputy trade representative (Soviet diplomatic post)
zemlyanki	earth dugouts
zhilaya ploshchad	'living space' – Soviet term used to denote number of square metres available per inhabitant.

1

Introduction

What seemed completely impossible before – in a no-man's-land to where only exiles were banished in tsarist times – now, by the will of the Bolsheviks and based on the half-tundra's natural riches, where no human had until recently set foot, a new and rapidly growing industrial center along the Arctic Circle has been created.

Sergei Mironovich Kirov, 1934[1]

To the far north of Europe, well above the Arctic Circle, in the northwestern corner of the Russian county (*oblast*) of Murmansk on the Kola Peninsula, we find the municipality (*raion*) of Pechenga. Neighbour to the Norwegian county of Finnmark to the west, and Finnish Lapland to the southwest, Pechenga's landmass stretches along the eastern banks of the Pasvik River (*Reka Paz* in Russian; *Paatsjoki* in Finnish),[2] which forms most of the border between Russia and Norway. The Pasvik River flows from the vast Lake Inari in Finnish Lapland to the northeastern section of the Atlantic Ocean – the Barents Sea. It provides energy to no less than seven hydroelectric power plants, two Norwegian and five Russian, along its 145-kilometre course (see Map 1). Most of the electricity produced here is consumed by the local power-intensive nickel industry in the valley, the Pechenganikel combine. With its undulating hills and abundant wildlife, the area can at first glance seem like one of the quietest corners of Europe. Its history, as will be demonstrated in this book, suggests otherwise.

In this book the Pechenga territory, whose fate has been intertwined with the local industrial activity, is at the centre of attention. Throughout the investigation, albeit with varying emphasis, the dynamics and

Map 1 The Pasvik valley and surroundings.

interaction between commercial ambitions and state security will be highlighted. Specifically, I analyse Soviet security concerns and economic thinking as these became evident in Pechenga. With this study, I intend to contribute towards contextualizing today's political and academic hyperbole surrounding Arctic regions: the Arctic has a past, and Pechenga was one of the places in the European north where security and economic interests were not only balanced against each other but forged. Only through a deep understanding of the dynamic history of places like Pechenga can the Arctic of today truly be understood.

The present study will also inform our knowledge about wider historical processes. While Pechenga and its nickel resource figure as the sole constant in the narrative, its development touches on a range of high-impact historical events: this book will shed light on Soviet–Finnish relations after the Russian Revolution, Soviet motives and strategies before and during the Second World War and the nature of the Stalinist economy in the first post-war years. While having no pretensions of (re)interpreting all these widely studied historical phenomena, I hope this book will provide some new insights pertaining to them.

The significance of Petsamo

Petsamo, as Pechenga was called while under Finnish sovereignty from 1920 to 1944, was not merely a piece of real estate. It represented much more. Firstly, and most importantly, the ice-free Petsamo fjord gave Finland access to the world oceans, thus rendering the country's dependence on passage through the Danish straits in the Baltic Sea less crucial. The Petsamo route did prove itself extremely important in periods of high tension, most notably from May 1940 to June 1941, when Sweden and Finland's only access to world markets went through the port of Liinahamari. In this period, Petsamo also provided an outlet for Jewish refugees. More prosaically, Finland's traditional fisheries in the Barents Sea were bolstered through national control over a section of the Arctic coastline, and in the latter part of Finnish sovereignty, the area was being developed as a tourist destination.[3]

But it is the industrial aspect of Petsamo that will be this book's main concern. Quite soon after gaining possession of the territory, Finnish authorities set about mapping its geology. As we shall see in Chapter

2, a rich vein of nickel ore was discovered and would gradually be developed for industrial purposes. I will throughout this book argue that it was this geological feature that would be at the forefront when Petsamo's destiny was shaped by several interested parties, such as the Finnish state, Canadian and German industrialists, the German *Wehrmacht* and the Soviet government. It was to a large degree the local resource, nickel ore, that attracted non-Finnish actors to the area and turned it into not only an industrial asset, but also a political bargaining chip for the Finnish government to make use of in its never-ending quest for security. The main reason for this international preoccupation with Finnish nickel lay in the ore's application: Nickel is counted among the 'strategic metals', as it has since the late 1800s been a pivotal ingredient in war important war materiel, most notably ammunition and armoured plates.

The nickel in Petsamo was from the mid-1930s a constant in Helsinki's foreign and trade policies. Prolonged negotiations with various industrial actors over its development took place. The nickel resource was not only to be exploited in and of itself, but also made to contribute towards the welfare of the Finnish population. The Finnish government always kept a keen eye on factors such as employment for the northern workforce in these negotiations, obviously in addition to demanding taxation arrangements that would bolster their coffers. Crucially, Helsinki only leased the concession rights, but preserved Finnish ownership over the land.

As the world progressed towards conflict in the latter years of the decade, security concerns became an increasingly important aspect of the Petsamo property. A repository of a strategic metal, the area now became an object of German and Soviet desires. As such, it could be – and was – used as an element in Finland's self-defence against the soon-to-be warring powers. This self-preservation, combined with aspirations for territorial advances in the east, led Finland to side with Europe's main aggressor Germany in the upcoming Great-Power struggle.[4] What did Hitler gain from the arrangement? Of course, Finland constituted the northern flank in his megalomaniac Barbarossa plan, but there was also the Petsamo nickel, a resource he himself described several times as pivotal for the German war industry.

At that time, the Soviet approach to Petsamo had already developed from seemingly disinterested to aggressively pursuant. The underlying shift in Moscow's assessment of Petsamo, the reasons of which will be discussed in detail in Chapter 3, came suddenly and surprisingly to Finland in June 1940. After that, the Soviet desire to annex the area to the socialist realm never abated. Towards the end of the war, as Finland capitulated and agreed to shed its brotherhood in arms with the Nazi forces, Petsamo was no longer Finnish, but became Soviet Pechenga.

Thus, the area entered into a new phase in its dramatic history, which gives us an opportunity to study how the local industry fared in a production system alien to the one in which it had first been established, namely the Soviet planned economy. As part of the socialist homeland, this former Canadian property would be 'Sovietized'. By this is meant a process different to the political upheaval experienced in Eastern European countries, the so-called People's Democracies, at the end of the Second World War. Instead, Pechenga and its nickel industry, now a part of the Soviet Union, was organizationally and economically transformed to become an integral part of the Soviet production system.

Studying this period in Pechenga's history, which was heavily influenced by the fervent rebuilding effort during Stalin's fourth five-year-plan (1946–50), will render insight into the inner workings of Soviet industrial production and the everyday life of administrators and factory workers in Soviet enterprises. Ultimately, we will study the means by which the socialist state attempted to accomplish the grand economic expansion that would by design bring it up to par with, and eventually past, Western capitalism. In other words – Chapter 4 provides a regional history of late Stalinism.

But Pechenga was still not brought to complete Soviet isolation. Yet another period of international engagement in the area, this time by Finnish and later Norwegian hydropower specialists and construction workers, would soon commence. The first hydropower station on the Pasvik River was partly rebuilt, partly constructed by the Finnish firm

Imatran Voima on a patch of land that until early February 1947 was still Finnish property. However, through shrewd combined negotiations on various fronts, Soviet representatives were able to not only acquire even more Finnish territory, but also have the main power supply to Pechenga's nickel industry built by Finnish hands – for free, so to speak.

In Chapter 5, we will follow this process towards the completion of the Jäniskoski hydropower plant in 1951. This entrepreneurial venture, which involved Soviet industrialists getting to grips with reality in capitalist Finland, constituted at times a veritable clash of cultures. Interestingly, however, the story also illustrates how shared ambition across the political divide could trump ideological inhibitions. The main protagonist of the chapter, Boris Mefodievich Kleshko, can serve as the embodiment of the apolitical industrious spirit, result-driven ambition and personal brilliance that even the immense bureaucratic hurdles posed by the Stalinist system and the same system's widespread infighting could not quite quench.

Following its inclusion in the Soviet realm in 1944, the Pechenga nickel industry underwent a profound transformation. The privately owned industrial operation, severely damaged after the war, was hastily rebuilt and reinvented as a Soviet enterprise. To provide the context for discussing Soviet strategic and industrial thinking of that time, and how the then Finnish–Soviet border territory figured in it, we will in the following examine several aspects of the Stalinist system that turned Finnish Petsamo into Soviet Pechenga. The insights presented here will be revisited and discussed on the basis of the intervening chapters in the concluding chapter of the book.

Settling of the Soviet North, and Stalinist totalitarianism

The 1930s are a thoroughly examined period in Soviet history. With Stalin at the height of his powers, it was the decade of such brutal historical processes as forced collectivization, involving the completion of the ruthless de-kulakization campaign (*raskulachivanie*) that had started in the late 1920s, the political transformation and unifying of Soviet cultural life and later the Great Terror. Another aspect of Stalin's staggering 'revolution from above'[5] was the expansion of the industrial resource base, prompting the exploration and subsequent incorporation of the Soviet Arctic into the socialist production system. This highly romanticized 'settling of the North' (*osvoenie severa*) was in a way the Soviet response to American pioneers' westward push to the Pacific coast in the 1800s. In the spirit of the words uttered by Leningrad Party boss Sergei Kirov – 'there is no land that Soviet power cannot transform for the good of mankind' – the resources of the North were to be explored and exploited for the benefit of the Soviet fatherland.[6] Of course, the Soviet North was by no means settled solely by willing and enthusiastic pioneers; among the many hands that unearthed precious metals such as nickel were prisoners within the system of correctional labour camps (GULag).[7]

The Kola Peninsula, with most of its territory north of the Arctic Circle, was among the targets for Soviet pioneering. Striving for resource autarchy, the Stalin regime began eagerly mapping the mineral riches in these northwestern outskirts. Throughout the 1930s, the region was industrialized on a massive scale.[8] When Petsamo (from then on Pechenga) was annexed by the Soviet Union in the fall of 1944, the previously Finnish territory was therefore a logical appendix to an already substantial industrial expansion. However, the industrial capacities on the Kola Peninsula had, like the nickel industry in Petsamo/Pechenga, been severely damaged during the war. Also, the unity of the wartime alliance gave way to increasing animosity between former co-belligerents. The Soviet Union spared nothing in its attempts to overtake the West. There ensued a period not only of recovery, but of frantically trying to catch up with ideological foes in the West.[9] The Pechenganikel combine, as the formerly Canadian-owned nickel industry was called as a Soviet state enterprise, was hastily enlisted among the industrial entities that were to contribute to this effort.

Preoccupied with fervent industrial production and ideological competition, the Soviet post-war rebuilding efforts were in many ways reminiscent of the large-scale industrialization that had started some fifteen years earlier. In his groundbreaking study of Stalinist civilization as expressed through the early history of the steel-producing company town Magnitogorsk in the southern Urals, Stephen Kotkin describes those times as follows:

> In the 1930s, the people of the USSR were engaged in a grand historical endeavor called building socialism. This violent upheaval, which began with the suppression of capitalism, amounted to a collective search for socialism in housing, urban form, popular culture, the economy, management, population migration, social structure, politics, values, and just about everything else one could think of, from styles of dress to modes of reasoning. Within a steadfast but vague noncapitalist orientation, much remained to be discovered and settled.[10]

In Kotkin's interpretation, these values, however distorted they became, constituted the foundation for the Stalinist civilization of which Magnitogorsk was a prime example.

Kotkin's in-depth study of the discourses and behavioural practices of Stalinist society was made possible by the opening up and subsequent dissolution of the Soviet Union.[11] When Western scholars gained access to primary sources in Russian archives in the early 1990s, new interpretations of Soviet history followed. To a large extent, these manifold new readings of the Soviet past have contributed to the repudiation of the totalitarian paradigm that was the dominant post-war Western understanding of the Soviet state, and Stalinism in particular. Thus, they seem to support some of the earlier revisionist critique levelled against proponents of totalitarian models.

From the mid-1980s, these revisionist scholars insisted that Stalinism was not merely upheld through coercive means, but also enjoyed the backing of a large portion of the Soviet population. Many Soviet citizens, they argued, adopted and accepted the values and ideals of the Stalin revolution.[12] With the opening up of Soviet archives, not only could the notion of Stalin's unlimited involvement in all matters of state (or all matters Soviet) be modified, but the newly available source material also allowed historians to study Soviet society 'from below', if not, as the radical revisionist Sheila Fitzpatrick called for, to write the social history of the Soviet Union 'with the state left out'.[13]

Although Kotkin's analysis falls short of fulfilling Fitzpatrick's programme,[14] it can be seen as a logical continuation of her and other revisionists' critique of totalitarianism models. Examining sources about lower-level Soviet entities – industrial enterprises in Magnitogorsk, the Magnitogorsk city administration and even the lives of common Soviet citizens in the steel town – Kotkin provides new analytical perspectives: a view 'from below'.

Though no historian will argue against the overwhelming evidence that supports the image of Stalin as an obsessive workaholic who sought total control of all Soviet matters big and small,[15] the sheer magnitude of human activity in the mammoth Soviet state precludes the possibility of one man, even one as frantically busy as Stalin, seeing, understanding and deciding everything. Of course, in a system that portrayed the ruling party and its chieftain (Soviet *vozhd*, or *Führer* in the Nazi version of totalitarian rule)[16] as omniscient, and accordingly presented all matters to the *vozhd* for his perusal, top-level intervention always existed as a fear-provoking possibility.

That said, a more imminent threat for Soviet citizens, workers and officials, most notably lower-level administrators, came from the 'smaller Stalins' placed immediately above them. Interpreting the Soviet command economy as a 'nested dictatorship', in which each administrative echelon mimicked the control mechanisms of its immediate superior level in the vertically organized command structure, historian Paul R. Gregory describes the Stalinist system as follows:

> The Soviet administrative-command system had many jockeys, not just one. The jockey was not simply Stalin or the Politburo, but the hundreds or thousands of 'smaller Stalins' that populated the 'nested dictatorship'. The superior at each level behaved as a despot relative to subordinates as did the superior's own 'dictator'. The administrative-

command system consisted of layer upon layer of dictators, each harassing subordinates.

And he continues,

> The dictators (note: plural) imposed coercive orders on their subordinates based on incomplete and inaccurate information, and the subordinate was confronted with a mass of confusing, ill-devised and apparently arbitrary instructions for which he was personally responsible.[17]

Thus, Gregory argues that, although embedded with a coercive and perpetually reproduced method of supervision, Stalinism was far from the unified system it depicted itself as. Amidst all its grandiose achievements, it was in fact a highly dysfunctional and fragmented tool for day-to-day management.

Similar observations – that Stalin was neither omnipotent nor omnipresent – have been made in the study of Stalinist foreign policy.[18] Claiming, however, that diffusion of power precludes the existence of totalitarian rule would be tantamount to throwing the baby out with the bathwater. Especially when studying the history of the Stalin years, completely omitting the interpretative framework provided by totalitarianism models seems unwise. On a very basic level, and in the words of historian Ian Kershaw, '[t]he fundamental value of the totalitarianism concept resides in its ability to recognize the primary distinction between democracy and dictatorship.'[19] Essentially different from say, the discrepancy between democratic and quasi-democratic (which might be applied to analyses of present-day Russia's 'Putinism'), this distinction is vitally important to grasping the motivations of power. Totalitarian rule, one may argue with Richard Sakwa, is more easily identified by looking at intent rather than result: '[t]otalitarianism … should be defined more as the aspiration to obtain total control rather than its achievement.'[20]

That what we may call 'totalitarian intent' was present in Josef Stalin's leadership is obvious. It is very likely that this intent came close to being realized, through the mechanisms of 'nested dictatorship' and the all-pervasive discursive manipulation by means of organizational methods and state propaganda which was both reflected and reproduced by the Soviet citizenry. However, once we recognize that even a group of leaders so obsessed with control as Stalin and his henchmen in the Politburo could not effectively oversee the myriad goings-on among their Soviet subjects, we see that the intent of total domination could never be fully attained. This position opens up to the existence of a playing field where institutional differences between various agencies in the compartmentalized Soviet ministerial structure could play out.[21] It also acknowledges the possibility of certain, albeit constricted, individual freedoms for actors within the oppressive system to further their own interests and pursue their own ideas, whether or not these interests and ideas converged with those of the Kremlin.

* * *

This brief discussion of autarchic ambitions and limitations to Stalin's totalitarian rule will be put in high relief throughout Chapters 3, 4 and 5: Was the Soviet annexation of Petsamo in 1944 a result of geopolitical realities – a function of Moscow's wish to provide infrastructure in the Murmansk area with a wider buffer zone – or was it a logical continuation of the Kola industrialization that had begun a decade earlier? Or – was it both? And how did Soviet authorities approach this property when it finally came under Moscow's control? Was it temporarily abandoned while other areas of the socialist realm underwent post-war rebuilding or was its industrial capabilities hastily resurrected? Did the Petsamo industry, with its foreign technology and non-Soviet organization, conform to Soviet production imperatives? And finally, can the sovietization of Petsamo teach us anything new about the class of industrial workers and administrators that negotiated the Stalinist system? Before we look closer at these questions, we shall trace the development of Petsamo under Finnish rule, and the process that transformed the area from a mostly uninhabited wilderness to an object of Great-Power contention.

2

In the Finnish corridor

For almost twenty-four years, from October 1920 until September 1944, Petsamo was part of Finland. During these years, the primary reason for the subsequent significance of the area – the nickel industry – was established, developed and fought over. In this chapter, we follow the transformation of Petsamo, from being a quiet corner of the Arctic inhabited mainly by eastern Saami reindeer herders, via the discovery and planned industrial exploitation of the local nickel ore, to an object of Great-Power contention.

The area became part of Finland through a treaty with the newly established but still very shaky and conflict-ridden socialist Russia, a treaty that later did not seem to sit well with the Soviet leaders. Their discontent was perhaps due to the subsequent Finnish exploration of Petsamo's geology, which revealed rich deposits of nickel ore and attracted financially powerful investors to the area. When the world again was headed towards war in the late 1930s, control over the nickel became of utmost strategic significance. Let us begin, however, with a brief review of the creation of the Finnish state, which was forged through the same processes that came to place Petsamo in Finnish hands.

Finnish independence and civil war

The emergence of the modern Finnish state is closely connected to revolutionary developments in Tsarist Russia from 1917 onwards. Finland had been under Tsarist rule from 1809 and was, consequently, affected by any major political development in the Russian empire. When political turmoil stirred in Petrograd,[1] this inevitably created commotion in the Finnish capital of Helsinki, only a day's journey away.

The revolutionary year of 1917 introduced a period of upheaval also for the Finnish nation, although the exact nature of the ensuing changes was for a long time uncertain. Whereas independence was a shared goal for the whole of the Finnish political spectrum, future relations to Russia were more disputed. The main schism in Finnish politics, which would later manifest itself in a violent and traumatic (albeit brief) civil war, was – somewhat simplistically put – one that Finland shared with much of a Europe polarized by the First World War: Should the country align with liberal democratic forces, or jump onto the bandwagon of the emerging socialists? Soon that choice would have to be made, under conditions heavily influenced by developments in Russia.

The February revolution of 1917 was championed by the fourth Duma, Russia's national assembly. Although progressive in the context of the Tsarist Empire, the Duma, as well as the provisional government that was based on its majority, tended to want to keep the borders of the Russian realm unchanged[2] and the Grand Duchy of Finland was then to remain within the realm. When Tsar Nikolay II abdicated in March, Finland found itself stripped of its Grand Duke, however. Contrary to initial expectations in the Finnish national assembly, the *Eduskunta*, this did not automatically entail Finnish independence. The provisional government in Petrograd in principle assumed the powers of the former Tsar.[3] In effect, instead of the Grand Duke (the Tsar), the supreme power in Finland was now the provisional government, headed by Prime Minister Georgi Lvov. During Lvov's brief reign (February–July), the provisional government did not revoke the Tsarist principle of the 'one and indivisible Russia'.[4] The provisional government's stance on Finnish independence did not change significantly during Aleksandr Kerensky's leadership from July 1917 till the Bolshevik seizure of power in October the same year.

Thus, a period of unresolved uncertainty ensued after the February 1917 revolution. The *Eduskunta*'s attempts to work out a solution for

Finnish self-government were repeatedly rejected by the provisional government. Parallel to exchanges between the Finnish national assembly and Lvov's and later Kerensky's cabinets, a gradual shift in power took place in the chaotic Russian capital. Spring/summer 1917 was a time of 'dual power' in the mid-revolutionary struggle. On the one hand, the provisional government derived its authority from the only lawfully elected body – the state Duma. On the other hand, the revolutionary parties and workers' unions organized the Soviets (councils), which together formed a structure that would soon wield enough power to threaten the provisional government's supremacy. Moreover, within the Soviets, the Bolsheviks gained ground relative to their Menshevik and Socialist Revolutionary competitors, and by late summer 1917 had begun to emerge as the leading political force in Russia.[5]

The Bolshevik rise to power was a key factor in the future of modern Finland. Lenin and his party held a favourable view on the right of *some* countries to independence, in line with Marxist dialectics and Lenin's concept of 'the uneven development of capitalism'. Finland was, as part of the Russian empire, fortunate enough to be grouped by Lenin among countries where the tasks of the proletariat could not 'be carried out without championing the right of nations to self-determination'.[6] A specialist on Lenin, Neil Harding, has paraphrased the Bolshevik leader's strategic approach to national self-determination as follows:

> [I]t would do the proletarian revolution no good at all to be seen putting down the aspirations of nations that had never enjoyed autonomy. Better by far, strategically speaking, to allow them to taste the illusory benefits of political independence and let experience teach them the larger economic benefits of voluntarily rejoining a much more extensive economic entity.[7]

The 'more extensive economic entity' was, of course, what Lenin saw as the future socialist union of the world proletariat. With the Bolshevik takeover in October 1917, the first building block of a worldwide socialist state was, in Lenin's eyes, put in place, and Finland would, the Bolshevik leader hoped, be one of the first nations to follow suit.[8] Thus, Finnish independence was to be seen merely as a transitional arrangement, not a permanent one.

To the extent they were known to the Finnish political camps, Lenin's views on the future of the nation were hardly shared by many Finns themselves. Even the socialists, who at the time were supportive of the Bolsheviks in their fight in Russia, did not necessarily concur with Lenin's aspirations for Finland. The divide between the Finnish political camps later known as the 'Whites' and the 'Reds' – analogical to the camps in the Russian civil war – was not on the issue of independence. Rather, the split concerned whether to align independent Finland with forces of the political left or the political right, with the new Bolshevik state or with Western powers, ranging from Germany to Great Britain and the United States. In the *Eduskunta*, the bourgeois parties from late November took the lead in advocating national independence and severance of all ties to Russia, whereas the socialist camp, which was also striving for Finnish independence, were ideologically akin to the new power in Petrograd and tended to favour a stronger Russian connection.[9]

The *Eduskunta* declared Finland independent on 6 December 1917. The bourgeois coalition government (Senate) headed by Pehr Eivind Svinhufvud now had its tasks clearly laid out: to gain Western recognition of independent Finland, and then break with Russia.[10] This was easier said than done. When Svinhufvud approached Western states, it became clear that they preferred to let events in Russia play out before making any commitment to independent Finland. In effect, they wanted to wait for the emergence of a grouping powerful enough in the still unstable Russia to grant Finland recognition of its independence, before giving their own.[11] Svinhufvud was therefore obliged to present Lenin's government, the Council of People's Commissars, with a letter requesting Russian acquiescence to Finnish independence. In the event, Lenin willingly approved, and Svinhufvud was given official Russian recognition in writing on the last day of 1917. In fact, however, as mentioned above, Lenin's decision was founded in a far greater scheme than just to giving a helping hand to a small neighbouring country. It was part and parcel of the plan to let the wheels of history turn in favour of the future federation of socialist republics, giving free rein to what Lenin saw as the unstoppable dialectics of the class struggle, which would finally lead to the new Finland voluntarily joining the avant-garde of socialist states.[12]

That was not to be. The first major experience of independent Finland was a traumatic civil war that would create an abyss between the political right and the political left that endured for many years. The fall of the Russian Tsar had left Finland without an actual police force or an army. To fill this vacuum, both sides of the political spectrum organized their own armies in anticipation of the unrest that was to come; the socialists activated labour union-led Red guards, and the right wing established 'defensive corps', also known as 'civil guards' (*skyddskårer*).[13] Fighting between the camps started in January 1918, and continued throughout the spring. Not until 16 May 1918, when Carl Gustav Emil Mannerheim, a former officer in the Russian Tsarist army and leader of the Finnish Whites, celebrated victory in Helsinki, did the hostilities abate. Through combat, Red and White terror and subsequent acts of vengeance, Finland suffered an estimated death toll of 30,000, of which 25,000 were Reds. Although neither Russia nor Germany participated in a way considered decisive for the outcome of the war,[14] their mere presence by way of supporting opposing camps gave a strong signal of the essence of this internal conflict, and also a premonition of Finland's nature given squeeze between the world powers. Situated on the outer rims of the vast Russian empire and later bordering on the Soviet Union, Finland would always be under the watchful gaze of its great neighbour, while at the same time seeking Western support.

The victorious Whites would see the Finnish civil war as a struggle for liberation from Russian dominance, whereas the Reds perceived the conflict as a failed revolution.[15] In the end, Finland secured its autonomy as a result of the war, with Western powers recognizing Finnish independence at differing times and for varying reasons.[16] However, de jure independence did not mean an end to Finland's problematical relationship with its eastern neighbour. There were still territorial issues, and Finland wanted a peace treaty to put a formal end to Russian claims on the former Grand Duchy.

The Tartu Peace Treaty: Petsamo becomes Finnish

The borders between Finland and the new socialist regime in Russia were unsettled. With the dissolution of the multiethnic Tsarist Empire, various delimitation questions were bound to crop up, and this was also the case in its northwestern parts. As subjects of the Russian Tsar, Finns had not been confined to the territory of the Grand Duchy. Especially in eastern Karelia, there was a large Finnish diaspora, forming a cultural and linguistic community with strong ties to Finland proper. Many Finns were set on including these territories in their new state as part of a more comprehensive 'Greater Finland'-project.[17]

There was also the question of an ice-free harbour. As early as 1864, Tsar Aleksandr II had agreed to compensate the Grand Duchy for areas ceded to Russia on the Karelian Isthmus. Although this compensation was specified only as 'areas on the Arctic Ocean',[18] geographic realities would suggest that the promise involved Finnish access to the Arctic port of Liinahamari through the Petsamo area. That pledge had never been fulfilled. During the winter of 1917–18, Finnish interests had tried to promote their demands through German negotiators in Brest-Litovsk, but to no avail.[19] This was a task the Finns had to take upon themselves. And so they did. Finnish forces ventured into Russian territory to seize land that they saw as rightfully theirs. The Repola area, parts of Karelia and the Petsamo corridor were targets for Finnish military expeditions in 1918 (see Map 2).

Despite the troubled relationship, Bolshevik leaders were apprehensive about conceding that an actual war had been waged between Russia and Finland. It seems to have been important for the Bolsheviks to emphasize that their intervention on the Red side during the Finnish civil war had not amounted to full participation – a

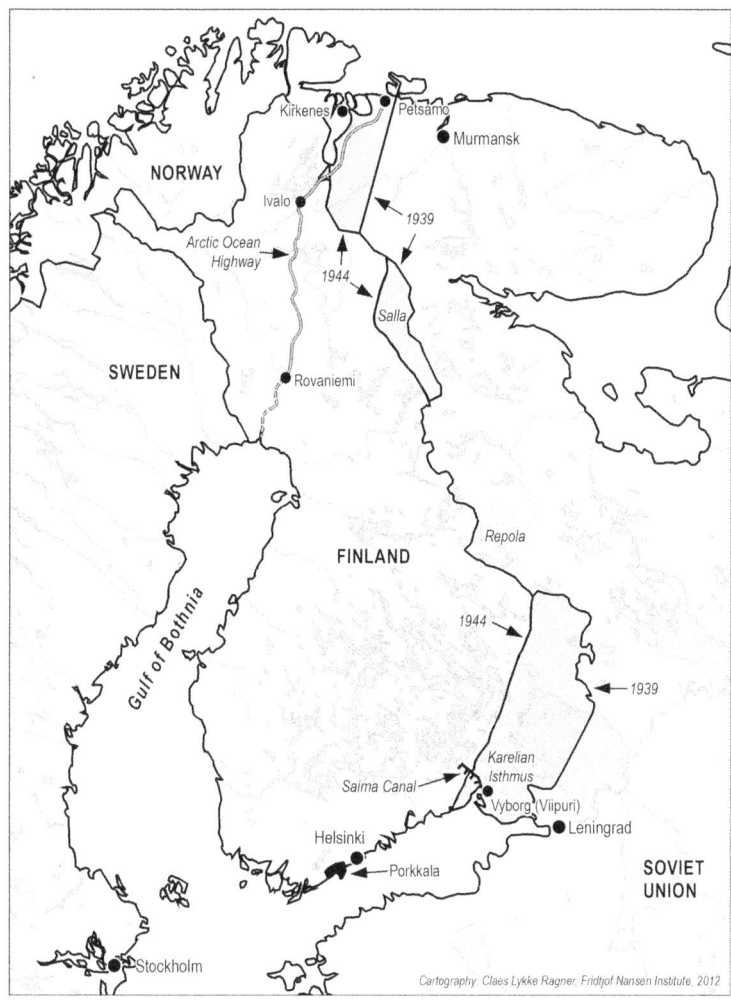

Map 2 Finnish–Soviet border in 1939 and 1944.

participation that then would have had to be interpreted as a Russian defeat by White Finland. Possibly, such a Soviet admission could deal the Finns a better hand in the negotiations. In the summer of 1918, the Soviet side did invite a Finnish delegation, with Germany as an intermediary, to negotiate a treaty to resolve the economic and financial disagreements that had arisen after the Tsar's abdication. This failed to yield results, presumably due to Russia's unwillingness to admit to having been at war with Finland, as well as due to unrealistic Finnish territorial claims.[20] In September 1919 skirmishes between Russian and Finnish forces in the border area put a halt to any rapprochement between the parties. The atmosphere between the two countries could hardly be seen as conducive for constructive negotiations at this point. Not until June 1920 could the Finnish and Soviet delegations sit down by the same table in the Estonian town of Tartu (Dorpat). Some five months later, an agreement would be reached.

That the agreement, concluded on 14 October 1920, was termed a 'peace treaty' clearly demonstrated that the Finnish view on the status of the bilateral relationship was now accepted by both parties. The two countries had in fact been at war. More importantly, the Finnish claim to access to the Arctic port of Liinahamari in Petsamo (Russian *Pechenga*) was also heeded. According to Article 4 of the treaty, '[t]he territory of Pechenga ... [s]hall, with its territorial waters, as soon as this treaty shall have come into force, be ceded by Russia to Finland in perpetuity, and placed under the unrestricted sovereignty of the latter.'[21] The parties agreed that Petsamo should be demilitarized, that fishing rights should be full and equal for nationals of both countries, and that Russian nationals would enjoy unhindered transit through the area (to and from Norway). Russian transit goods between Russia and Norway were to be exempt from taxes and duties.[22] These last two points may have been motivated by recent Soviet experience. Before and during the second Comintern Congress in Moscow earlier in the summer of the same year, the 'Murmansk crossing point' had proven very useful,[23] with many delegates and illicit communist literature passing through here.

Petsamo had a price. Against the better judgement of their envoys in Tartu Juho Kusti Paasikivi and Väinö Tanner, the government in Helsinki ordered their negotiators to accept the cessation of Repola and Porajärvi in a 'barter transaction' to gain the Petsamo territory.[24] Although the Petsamo portion of the treaty meant a substantial territorial gain for the Finns, Finnish reactions to the negotiation results from Tartu were mixed. The left side of the political spectrum was generally positive, whereas on the far right, and especially in circles that nourished dreams of a Greater Finland, the prospect of having to give up Repola and areas in eastern Karelia was devastating. One activist in Repola even committed suicide in an act of martyrdom for the Great-Finnish cause.[25] Nor did the Tartu Treaty bring an immediate end to Finnish–Russian border disputes. Several incidents followed in the years to come, with violations initiated from both sides of the border. The last of these, the 'pork barrel revolt',[26] took place in 1922.

In the longer term, the Tartu Peace Treaty would be seen as a historic mistake by the Soviet leadership. In a manner reminiscent of the German dismissal of the Treaty of Versailles, both Stalin and the Soviet commissar of foreign affairs, Vyacheslav Molotov, would later argue that the text had been forced upon a Soviet Union weak in its infancy.[27] This discontent, however, does not seem to have been caused by the loss of Petsamo, as the Soviet Union did not express any particular interest in reclaiming the territory between 1921 and 1940.[28] Rather, it was areas in southern Finland, close to the renamed Leningrad, that would attract the Soviet Union's interest a mere two decades after the Tartu Peace Treaty. As we shall see in the next chapter, Petsamo was, in that later instance, to become a pawn in the Soviet struggle for security on its western border.

Petsamo is explored

For Finland, then, a tangible result of the Tartu Peace Treaty was the acquisition of Petsamo. The prospect of an ice-free port on the Petsamo fjord, from which one could connect to the world oceans, was the main trigger of Finnish interest. Petsamo, it was felt, would also attract the interest of researchers as well as adventurous Finnish and foreign tourists.[29] The Arctic Highway from Rovaniemi via Ivalo to the port of Liinahamari on the Petsamo fjord was completed in the early 1930s, but also prior to that, the growth in tourism had required an increase in the very few lodgings in the new territory.[30] However, the corridor itself soon emerged as more than merely a conveyor belt to the sea. Covering some 10,000 square km and stretching almost 400 km along a North–South axis from the outlet of the vast Lake Inari to the northeastern corner of the Atlantic Ocean, the Petsamo area soon proved to be a potential Klondike of mineral riches.

When in 1921 the young geologist Alppi Talvia led a miniexpedition of two members into the newly won Finnish territories, it was in the hope of confirming that the iron ore deposits on the Norwegian side of the border extended into Petsamo.[31] The expedition did indeed find mineral deposits, but of a different kind than expected. The moment the first sample was taken by Talvia's companion, the young geology student Hugo Törnquist, has been described as a turning point:

> He [Törnquist] did not know it at the time, but he had made the biggest discovery of his life – in an economic and geopolitical sense. It was a find that would turn Petsamo into an arena of violent bloodshed, and that would direct the gazes of the Great Powers towards the Northern Cap. The ridge east of Svanvik [Norwegian settlement] did not contain iron. It contained nickel.[32]

This quote illustrates not only the level of drama involved: the description is also in fact quite accurate, as will become apparent in the next chapter. For the Finnish Geological Survey, Törnquist's find marked the start of a period of comprehensive studies of the Petsamo area, laying claim to nearly all the organization's funds for geological prospecting for the next decade.[33]

Analysis of Törnquist's sample the following winter showed a promising nickel content of 4.5 per cent,[34] which prompted a follow-up expedition. In the summer of 1922 geologist Hans Hausen, accompanied by the same Hugo Törnquist, attempted a comprehensive survey of the whole area. However, they did not have access to maps of Petsamo, which necessarily delayed their progress.[35] This is a reminder of how unexplored and undeveloped the unmapped terrain in Petsamo was at the time. There were few roads in the northern wilderness (the Arctic Highway was at this point far from complete) and harsh conditions rendered geological surveying impossible except during the short Arctic summer and early fall. When the next expedition, led by geologist and ethnologist Väinö Tanner,[36] arrived in Petsamo in 1924, weather conditions were rather different from the full summer enjoyed in southern Finland. Settling in for their Arctic stay from July to October 1924, expedition members had to pitch their base-camp tents amidst snow drifts.[37] The cold welcome, however, seems not to have dampened their enthusiasm. They set about systematically mapping the highland moors (in Finnish *tunturi*) stretching eastward from the Finnish–Saami settlement of Salmijärvi. At the end of the season, the expedition could report of finding two new sites of nickel ore.

This moved the head of the Finnish Geological Commission, Jakob Johannes Sederholm, to a cautiously optimistic description of the potential in Finland's newest territory: 'There is a region where, in relation to Finnish conditions, ore occurs over a remarkably broad area. Future surveys must decide whether the region can also fulfill the hopes with regard to its significance to industry that have been raised in many quarters.'[38] As Sederholm hinted, another decade of prospecting lay ahead before the anticipated industrial exploitation of Petsamo ore could commence.

By 1934, at the end of a period of intensified geological surveys, it had become clear that Petsamo boasted at least ten deposits of nickel ore. Electrical measurements and extensive drilling had revealed the hidden riches, and the content of the Kaulatunturi ore was estimated at a minimum of 5 million tons. From 1932 onwards, access to aerial photos of Petsamo had made mapping of the terrain and, consequently, pinpointing of observations substantially easier.[39] The stage was set for a new phase in the life of this remote wilderness: the modern era in its history soon would commence with the transformational industrialization carried out by Canadian nickel magnates.

INCO, Mond Nickel and Petsamon Nikkeli

While there was little doubt that the deposits in Petsamo were sizeable enough to justify investments, a much more complicated question remained to be answered: Which company was to operate the field? The Finnish authorities recognized that a project of this magnitude – constructing an industrial site complete with power supply, infrastructure and living quarters in a virtual wilderness area – could be realized only by a financially strong company with experienced management and staff. A central requirement also was that mineral resources on Finnish soil should not be handed over to foreign ownership.[40] However, domestic companies had neither the skill nor the financial muscle to develop a grand mining scheme in the north. The only serious Finnish candidate, state-owned Outokumpu, did not enjoy the necessary trust among the country's decision makers due to its financial problems in the 1920s and the poor record of its copper mines.[41] That Finland had been hard hit by the Great Depression from 1929 onwards further complicated matters. The *Eduskunta* was pursuing a prudent economic policy to get the country back on its feet by curtailing expenses in order to balance a state budget in deficit.[42] In such a financial environment, the investments needed in undeveloped Petsamo were simply out of the reach of Finland's private and public sectors alike. At the same time, an increasingly unemployed labour force needed new industrial activity to better their situation. In the case of Petsamo, the preferred solution was to attract foreign investments, while making sure that the workers would be mostly Finnish citizens and that the property stayed in Finnish hands.[43] It took some persuasion, though, before a suitable operator emerged.

The nickel ore in Petsamo did stir some interest abroad. In February 1930, the French firm *Coframent* had tried to obtain a mining concession for Petsamo, without success.[44] The Finnish government was not going to rush the matter and wanted to await the completion of the Petsamo surveys as well as the arrival of more suitors before deciding on an agreement. Of course, Finland was not alone in suffering by the downturn in world markets after 1929, and large investments were not easy to come by. However, when the global economy (including the world nickel market)[45] showed signs of picking up again in 1932/1933, a climate more conducive to constructive negotiations emerged.

Two German companies, Friedrich Krupp AG and Interessengemeinschaft Farbenindustrie Aktiengesellschaft (IG Farben), had up until that point shown only moderate interest in Petsamo. The latter was, however, possibly ready to embark on a role as a major actor in the nickel refining business. In chemical experiments, IG Farben researchers had developed a more efficient and less costly method for refining semi-manufactured nickel matte, a nickel ore concentrate. This meant that the company might be able to emerge at the forefront of world nickel production – if it could acquire sufficient supplies of raw material.[46] IG Farben's new technology and prospects would be a pivotal point in the upcoming negotiations about the Petsamo ore when the undisputed world leader in nickel manufacture and trade, International Nickel Company of Canada (INCO)[47], entered the playing field.

INCO officials had known of the Petsamo ore for some time. On 27 October 1930, the company's representative in Germany, Metallgesellschaft GmbH, reported to INCO headquarters in Toronto that an interesting nickel–copper ore had been identified in northern Finland.[48] For a company of INCO's stature and wealth, only very substantial ores would be deemed worth the time and effort necessary to exploit them. The company at the time enjoyed what was in effect a world monopoly on the nickel market, controlling the vast majority of known exploitable ore deposits.[49] In large measure, this position had been secured through INCO's 1904 cartel agreement with the two other actors on the relatively small world nickel market, the French *Le Nickel* and the British Mond Nickel Company. The First World War interrupted the cartel scheme (but also increased world nickel consumption dramatically)[50]. When the three companies re-established their common interests in 1923, they entered into a new agreement. Of the three partners, INCO would emerge as the strongest actor on the market. The next five years led to the demise of the French company and to INCO's takeover of Mond Nickel in 1928. As INCO consequently found itself in a position very close to a world monopoly, the company faced legal difficulties in the United States, where it had originally been based. To evade US antitrust laws, INCO simply let the Canadian subsidiary International Nickel Company of Canada stand as the formal top structure, thereby ensuring that the company came under the more lenient Canadian law.[51]

Given this dominant position and the possible threat from IG Farben's technological progress, INCO's approach to the Petsamo ore was initially defensively motivated. Controlling prospective occurrences was of the essence if the company was to be able to fend off any competition that might chip away at its monopoly. Based on INCO's own assessments of the ore, Petsamo operations were by no means a certain success. According to analysis made by J. C. Nicholls, the general manager of INCO's mines in Sudbury, Canada, in August 1933, neither the size nor the metal content of the ore indicated that the Petsamo property was especially promising. The assistant to INCO's president, Paul Mercia, in October 1933 expressed INCO's half-hearted approach:

> [I]n view of the present high price of nickel in Europe and the interest of Krupps and others, including IG [Farben], in deposits of this nature, we are inclined to feel that we should take some step at least to secure control over them for a few years.[52]

Aware of IG Farben's technological breakthrough, INCO could simply not sit back and let others take charge. This did not, however, imply that INCO would rush to a conclusion. Quite the contrary, the company was more than happy to keep negotiations with Finland running, while at the same time making sure that the competition was sidelined.

The Finnish government's priority was, as mentioned, to establish new industry that could employ as many workers as possible, as soon as possible. From that point of view, an expeditious negotiation process would be desirable. On the other hand, it was important that the ownership of the Petsamo nickel resources remained in Finnish hands and that the concession area was limited to where ore had been found.[53] This, combined with INCO's hope of stalling developments, made for lengthy negotiations. For the sake of convenience, and to draw on the good relations between Finland and Great Britain, INCO's side of the negotiations was taken care of by its British subsidiary, Mond Nickel Company. From November 1933, when the Finnish geological commission made it clear that it both supported the conclusion of an agreement and that INCO, represented by Mond, was the preferred partner, actual negotiations could start.[54] The further progress did not indicate any desire for a quick solution on either side of the table, and it was not until early 1934 that the talks began to gain momentum.

There were two reasons for this shift. Firstly, IG Farben was in the process of establishing a nickel refining plant based on the above-mentioned new technology and were now pressing for deliveries of nickel ore concentrate (nickel matte) to feed their production. This made it even more important for INCO to secure dominance on the raw material side of the nickel market. As a result, INCO entered an agreement with IG Farben which provided for the delivery of nickel matte (10 per cent of INCO's non-American sales) to the German company. This meant a break with INCO's long-standing policy of selling only refined nickel, not nickel ore or nickel matte. In return, INCO managed to contain the spread of German refining methods, as it was agreed that IG Farben would not share their technology with a third party.[55] This arrangement temporarily took care of INCO's defence of their monopoly position, but meant that the company required more nickel matte to make good their new obligations to IG Farben, which is where the future development of Petsamo came into play.

Even more important, however, was INCO's adjusted appraisal of the Petsamo ore's potential. In January 1934, company metallurgists reported new test results that showed that the previous figures were a grave underestimate. The nickel and copper deposits in northern Finland were indeed rich and highly promising. INCO kept this information tightly sealed. In a confidential memo, INCO's Sudbury manager Nicholls urged Mond Nickel's Edgar Pam, who was handling negotiations for INCO, to keep a lid on the new discovery, as revealing the secret 'would only increase their [Finland's] idea of the value [of the ore] and … make negotiations difficult'.[56] From the spring of 1934, INCO and Mond would push for a speedy conclusion to the negotiations.

Mond's counterpart was still in no hurry, however. Finnish objectives stood firm, and another five months of back and forth was necessary before the parties could put pen to paper. The Finnish reluctance to be rushed into an agreement shows the country's steadfastness when faced with an increasingly eager counterpart. According to historians Eloranta and Nummela, this bears witness to the strategic significance of nickel, and how even a small state could use that to its advantage. To them, the fact that the Finnish government succeeded in attracting INCO to the Petsamo ore seems to attest to the small nation's ability to navigate in waters fraught with Great-Power interests.[57] However, in the case of the agreement reached between INCO and the Finnish state, this seems a somewhat rash interpretation. True, the Finns had achieved their main objective already *before* the contractual negotiations started. It had been of the essence to engage the world's most powerful nickel company, INCO, in the development of Petsamo. Only a player of INCO's stature would be able to reliably carry the weight of a comprehensive industrial project in the northern wilderness, thereby creating much-needed employment in crisis-ridden Finland.

Eloranta and Nummela's theory of Finland's ability to use its ownership of the nickel ore to further its aims to an unexpected degree is weakened, however, by the actual content of the agreement between the Finnish government and INCO/Mond. Formally signed on 22 June 1934, the deal was extremely advantageous to INCO. It allowed for a ten-year period of exploration and preparatory work before the Canadians were required to produce nickel, and then only a relatively small quantity (1,000 tons the first year, 1,500 tons the two following years, and 2,000 tons annually thereafter). The royalty to be paid to the Finnish coffer was as low as 5 per cent, and the agreement was to run for forty years, with an option of a further forty years if so desired. The

Finnish state would, after the establishment of Petsamon Nikkeli OY (Petsamo Nickel Company) as the operational unit, tax the enterprise like any other Finnish company. Robert C. Stanley, president of INCO, was very enthusiastic:

> The property is the most promising from the standpoint of geology, surface sampling, and preliminary diamond drilling, that we have ever examined outside of Ontario. Should this property have gotten into German hands, with their low-cost refining processes, very serious inroads in our foreign business would have resulted. … From the standpoint of protecting the Company, I consider the negotiations just closed with Finland to be one of the most important the executives have undertaken.[58]

Of course, Stanley's assessment was made in light of sample test results unknown to INCO's Finnish counterparts. Nevertheless, the agreement reached at the end of lengthy negotiations must be seen as a very good result for INCO, and perhaps not equally advantageous to the Finnish state. As we shall see in Chapter 2, Finland was to sell its precious ore at a higher price the second time around, thereby demonstrating the country's growing ability to use its natural resources to enhance its position vis-à-vis the Great Powers. Nickel – since its recent introduction into the production of war materiel – had by then become an essential part of Great-Power industrial strategies.

The strategic metal

In the early 1900s, nickel was a new metal. Although known to Chinese blacksmiths and Saxon miners for centuries,[59] it was not until the Swedish mineralogist and chemist Axel Fredrik Cronstedt in 1751 isolated an unknown impure metal that this copper-like substance was given its status as an individual entity. With Antoine Lavoisier's new chemistry in 1789, nickel was recognized as an element. The name stems from the somewhat derogatory German word *Kupfernickel*, translated as 'the devil's copper' (Kupfer = copper; and Nickel = goblin, demon, devil). Over centuries, miners had attempted to refine the glowing ore, hoping to produce copper, but ended up with a useless mash, which led them to think that this metal was the work of the devil. Real progress – although not without initial difficulties – was not made until the late 1800s, after the discovery of vast deposits in the Canadian hinterland. The metal stubbornly resisted Canadian efforts at separation: 'Nickel was up to its old tricks. A perverse metal, it refused to be persuaded, or soothed, or driven into doing what engineers and furnacemen wanted it to do. It had always been that way.'[60] It took time, a lot of money and sustained efforts comparable to the stubbornness of the metal itself to transform it from a creature of the devil to a source of industrial success.

Several industrialists invested in refining the metal in the latter half of the 1800s, and experiments showed that nickel had properties that would radically change the metal business. Nickel-steel alloys were especially promising. With the addition of nickel, steel became not only stainless, but also considerably more durable and stress-resistant. Reporting on tests involving heavy firing on to a nickel-steel armour plate from a very short distance, US Navy secretary B. F. Tracy in 1892 clearly stated the military potential of the new alloy:

> Five Holtzer forged steel shells, weighing 250 pounds each, with a striking velocity of 1,700 feet per second, and each with an energy of 5,000 tons to the square foot, were fired at a distance of 30 [sic] yards.
>
> Never before these trials had any armor plate in the world been subjected to such a test as was represented by these five blows of a total energy of 25,000-foot tons.
>
> The result may be told in a word. All five of the projectiles were smashed upon the surface of the plate. The plate showed no signs of injury further than the opening of a slight temper crack four inches in length from one edge, and a wale less than one inch in thickness on the back of the plate opposite each point of impact.
>
> The striking ends of the projectiles appear to have been splashed on the face of the plate, filling the slight indentation made by the blow with new material which became welded to the substance of the plate itself

and left it as before a flush surface. The remainder of the projectiles could only be found in the shape of innumerable fragments.[61]

The military significance of nickel was both a blessing and a problem for the nickel industry. It secured demand from the armed forces around the world, which provided a first impetus for the new metal's position on the global metal market. In the Spanish–American War in 1898, armour plates made of nickel-steel alloys were seen as a central factor in the US Navy's victory, which led to a markedly heightened demand for the metal.[62] This trend was to continue, with nickel sales peaking before and during the two world wars, earning the 'devil's copper' a place among the 'strategic metals'.[63]

For INCO it was clear from the start that military demand alone would not be a sufficient foundation for a sound business. A company could not base its production and sales on international tensions and ensuing re-armaments. Especially the mining business was vulnerable to varying production intensity, as this would go counter to the necessity of thoroughly planning the extraction of ore from the mines. INCO therefore systematically broadened the market for nickel products by promoting the metal, first and foremost in alloys, for civilian purposes. By the 1930s, nickel was being used in a wide range of products in addition to armour plates, munitions and other war materiel. The peak in production and sales of nickel at the end of the First World War was surpassed ten years later, in 1928, when nickel was involved in the making of batteries, jewellery, coinage, bridges, automobiles, steel mills, ships, oil stills, roofing, electrical instruments, golf clubs, radio lines, various cables, telephone lines, kitchen utensils and objects made of or containing stainless steel – to name a few.[64]

Thus, we may say that when INCO and the Finnish government in 1934 agreed on the concession terms, the arrangement was primarily a civilian business venture. The output of the future mines would find a broad civilian demand in various branches. However, the military aspects of production and sales were always looming in the background. With the rising tensions in world politics that eventually led up to the outbreak of the Second World War in 1939, nickel became more and more of a war commodity and less and less of a commodity for civilian consumption. In the latter half of the 1930s, then, Petsamo and its mineral riches would become the object of intense international interest.

This was more due to the local ore's perceived potential than to the actual production of nickel from Petsamo. In the five years between 1934 and 1939, the local INCO subsidiary Petsamon Nikkeli OY (PNO) provided no new nickel to the world market. This did not mean that the property was less promising than expected. Quite the contrary – test drilling during the two first years had shown that the ore was even richer than INCO already anticipated. INCO, which from November 1934 had taken over all shares in PNO from its subsidiary Mond, came to spend substantially more money on developing the site than required in the contract with the Finns. Between September 1934 and December 1936, INCO's Executive Committee approved expenditures of up to USD 550,000 in Petsamo.[65] By November 1939, INCO had spent USD 6,723, 908, and the Executive Committee planned for a further USD 3,500,000 before production could start.[66]

The money financed a wide range of developmental necessities in the northern wilderness. Among the more capital-intensive activities were the building of a dam and a power plant at the Jäniskoski rapids upstream on the Pasvik River and the construction of a mine entrance and shaft to the Kaulatunturi ore.[67] INCO did not hold back on expenditures in the development of Petsamo. Technologically, the Petsamo installations, which included the world's two largest furnaces and Europe's two largest converters, were of a very high standard. Even the smokestack rising to the sky from the smelter plant was, with a height of 150 metres, the tallest in Europe.[68] INCO's progressivism was appreciated by their Finnish hosts. For the young state of Finland, it has been argued, demonstrating vitality and expansionism in Petsamo was essential. Though realized with Canadian money, the industrial conquest of the Petsamo wilderness was a symbolically important achievement that signified modern Finnish dynamism.[69]

Figure 1 The nickel plant in Kolosjoki. Photo: Archive Rune Rautio.

Similarly, living quarters for executives and miners were constructed in line with the ideals of contemporary functionalistic modernity. The new company town of Kolosjoki was situated close to the mines at Kaulatunturi, next to the electric smelter plant. It was nestled in a sheltered valley at 120 metres above sea level, on the left bank of the river that gave the town its name.[70] The spot was already partly inhabited, but only seasonally, as it had been an eastern Saami winter dwelling since the early 1600s. Kolosjoki was connected to the mines 240 metres above by a 2.6 km long tunnel, or adit, through which the nickel ore could be transported for processing in the smelter plant. The town itself had developed rapidly since the pioneer years, although in the early building period the residents did live under what have been referred to as 'bachelors' conditions'.

Curiously, the first building to be erected was a grand three-story club building for company officials, before an additional three buildings containing dwellings for the labourers and a workers' canteen. By the end of 1938, Kolosjoki was able to open up to a more diversified population, with the construction of a full eight new apartment buildings that would house forty-two families. However, that was not nearly enough

Figure 2 Kolosjoki with nickel works seen from vantage point along Arctic Highway. Photo: Archive Rune Rautio.

accommodation for the anticipated population of Kolosjoki, and 1939 saw another big leap towards elevating the still small hamlet to the status of a town. That year the biggest subdivision of Kolosjoki came, with the construction of a group of three-storey apartment buildings that would house up to 148 families. This subdivision came to be called Shanghai by the locals, supposedly for its city-like maze. Kolosjoki apartments were fitted with indoor plumbing, heated by a central heating plant, and the residents had access to a public laundry and bath. All these amenities were suggestive of how the young Finnish state embraced modernity and secured that living standards in the little town compared favourably to similar settlements, both in Finland and elsewhere.[71] In 1939, Kolosjoki boasted a total population of 2,000, with an additional 1,000 people working at the Jäniskoski hydroelectric power plant some 110 km further south. Although by no means large, Kolosjoki was, on the eve of the Winter War, a sprawling place, and totally transformed since the Finnish geologists had pitched their tents in the snowy wilderness fifteen years earlier.

3

War[1]

When INCO's Finnish subsidiary, Petsamon Nikkeli OY, was about to start mining operations, relations between Finland and the Soviet Union had deteriorated to the point of war. The Red Army crossed the border to Finland on the morning of 30 November 1939, supported by Soviet air strikes on major Finnish cities and naval bombardment of strategic coastal points. After 105 agonizing days – during which the Finnish forces proved surprisingly resilient – the Finnish government finally made the necessary concessions for a peace treaty with the Soviet Union.

However, it was not long before the country again found itself in a state of war. Squeezed between the Soviet behemoth and an aggressively expanding German war machine, Finland found its fragile neutrality increasingly difficult to maintain. When Hitler's armies broke the Soviet–German non-aggression pact by violating Soviet borders on 22 June 1941, Finland became involved in yet another war with the Soviet Union. For the next three years, its armed forces would collaborate with Germany, fighting what in the Finnish tradition is called the Continuation War. Gradually, the position next to Hitler's Nazi forces became untenable as the Germans began suffering massive defeats at the hands of Soviet forces from early 1943, and Finland once again entered into a separate armistice agreement with the Soviet Union. Signed in September 1944, this agreement marked the start of the Lapland War, as it was contingent on Finnish expulsion of all German troops from northern Finland. The Finns turned against their former brothers-in-arms – thereby also securing a modicum of post-war goodwill from the Allied powers.

One might argue that there is little reason to operate with three different wars in describing the Finnish experience from 1939 to 1945. The various phases, and especially the final two, can be seen as different chapters of the same war, the Second World War. They are all connected to developments following Nazi Germany's expansionism from 1938 onwards, via a short-lived Soviet–German non-aggression pact, to the failing fortunes of Hitler's *Lebensraum* project towards the end of the war. Nevertheless, the three phases did present themselves as distinctly different to the young Finnish state. The sole threat to Finland's position as an independent nation had been the Soviet Union, and Finland's wartime choices must be seen in the light of the country's deeply rooted mistrust of its powerful neighbour. That said, the exact nature of Finland's war history has remained an object of sometimes heated debate.[2] The complexity of this debate has filled volumes of historical works and is not covered here.

Instead, we will concentrate specifically on how the Petsamo area fared in the five years between 1939 and 1944. During the first war, in the winter of 1939/40, the Soviet Union took the opportunity for a closer look at Kolosjoki and the mines. In-between the two Finnish–Soviet wars, an intense diplomatic game was played over Petsamo by Finland and three great powers. The game, which illustrates the various and intertwining geopolitical and economic interests at stake, was to end with the demolition of Kolosjoki, and with subsequent Soviet control over the Petsamo territory.

The Winter War: Soviet reconnaissance

The Tartu Peace Treaty of 1920 was soon branded a flawed arrangement by the Soviet leadership. Desperate to lower tensions and gain recognition from the outside world, the new Soviet leaders at the time had been in a hurry to secure their external borders, and later claimed that their vulnerability had impeded a mutually acceptable settlement with the Finns. In mid-April 1938, a Soviet attempt to rectify the blunders from Tartu began when the young Soviet diplomat Boris Yartsev made a phone call to the Finnish foreign minister, Rudolf Holsti, asking for a private meeting.[3] The message conveyed through this ostensibly junior member of the Soviet diplomatic corps would soon develop into a serious challenge to the Finnish government. Fearing a German attack through Finland, the Soviet government wanted to prevent its small western neighbour from becoming a launching pad for enemy forces. From the first contact between Yartsev and Holsti in 1938, via several Finnish attempts to appease Soviet worries through assurances of adhering to Nordic neutrality, the two countries ended up in early October 1939 at the negotiating table in Moscow.

Meanwhile that summer, Molotov and German foreign minister Joachim von Ribbentrop had signed a non-aggression pact which could be expected to take care of the Soviet defensive needs also to the northwest. As we now know, a secret protocol defined the Soviet Union's neighbours north of Lithuania, including Finland, as within the Soviet sphere of influence. The Soviets remained worried, however, and their demands on Finland were comprehensive. At the first meeting with the Finnish delegation led by Juho Kusti Paasikivi, then Finnish envoy to Sweden,[4] Josef Stalin presented a list of substantial demands for border revisions with Finland. In five points the Soviet leader listed necessary measures to ensure the security of Leningrad, including the ceding of several islands off the southern coast of Finland and the need to push the Soviet–Finnish border on the Karelian Isthmus northwards. As an unrelated but for this study interesting sixth item, he demanded a minor adjustment of the Petsamo border. Claiming that the partition of the Fisherman's Peninsula (*Rybachii Poluostrov*) at the entrance to the Petsamo fjord had been 'clumsily and artificially' drawn, Stalin demanded that Finland cede the western littoral of the peninsula.[5]

Stalin's mention of Petsamo at the time seems to have been intended merely as a reminder to the Finnish delegation that the Soviet Union would be able to take more than just a buffer zone in the south, should Finland not yield to his demands. The Soviet leader made sure the Finns realized that their territorial integrity was at stake and that parts of their northern territory were also in danger of being annexed.[6] There is little to indicate that the Soviet Union at the time had serious designs on the northern areas that had been ceded at the Tartu negotiations nineteen years earlier. Be that as it may, the negotiations were not successful. As a result, the Winter War broke out on the last day of November 1939, making Petsamo the northern section of a long front line.

Since the outbreak of the Second World War following the German attack on Poland on 1 September that same year, the situation at the Petsamo plant had been a source of anxiety for INCO. How should the company deal with the imminent threat of its property being taken over by the Soviet Union or – as was also becoming increasingly likely – by Germany? As Finland was not a belligerent party prior to the Soviet attack in November, the wartime clause in INCO's concession agreement with the Finnish government, effectively giving ownership over the mines to Finland in time of war, had not yet come into play. Nevertheless, the tense situation did bring up a question that needed an answer: How to keep the Petsamo mines out of the hands of warring and nickel-thirsty powers?

In this situation, it seemed unwise to maintain the development work for a speedy production start. INCO and Mond Nickel, both companies that in times of war were used to collaborating with their home governments and with the political authorities of the countries where they were working,[7] readily suggested to the British Foreign Office that operations at the Petsamo mines be curtailed, and even proposed a strategy 'amounting if necessary to mild sabotage'. Neither British nor Finnish authorities were convinced that such measures were necessary. The Finnish government did not see a German or Soviet threat to Petsamo as imminent and was not about to condone actions that would serve to increase domestic unemployment rates. The British Foreign Office suggested following the Finnish advice, albeit under the condition that Finland would commit to withstand German attempts to acquire output from Petsamo.

In a scheme accepted by the British Foreign Office, INCO, Mond and Petsamon Nikkeli OY developed a compromise programme that would satisfy the Finnish government while also lessening the industrial attraction of the site. In effect, this meant reduced construction activity in the mines and the suspension of further development work for the time being. The whole programme, it was said, was aimed towards 'keeping our [INCO's] property less attractive to Germany [and] Russia and helping Finnish government to resist overtures by Germany'. These measures were soon accepted by the Finnish government as necessary and in compliance with national interests. INCO was reassured by Väinö Voionmaa, Finnish minister of trade and industry, that Petsamon Nikkeli OY would not find itself in a situation where the company was obliged to provide nickel to 'any interests strange to its head company [INCO]' – in other words, Germany or the Soviet Union.[8]

As events unfolded, this particular promise would not be within the Finnish minister's power to keep. Soon after Soviet bombers broke the peace on the morning of 30 November, it became clear that Finland would concentrate its defences in the south, leaving Petsamo and Kolosjoki open to attack from the east. The Fourteenth Army, as one of the very few unopposed Soviet units engaged in the attack on Finland, took control over Petsamo a mere two weeks later. From then till the end of the war in March the following year, the newly formed Red Army unit 'Petsamo' exercised complete authority over strategic points of interest, such as the *Rybachii* and *Srednii* peninsulas, the port of Liinahamari and the Luostari airfield.[9]

Construction of the Petsamo mine's hydropower plant on the Jäniskoski waterfall was at that time already at a standstill, and the little ongoing activity in the mines and the smelter was aborted. For Petsamon Nikkeli's Canadian manager, I. J. Simcox, it had been important to bring his compatriots to safety. With prearranged visas and travel documents, the Canadians were transported to the North Norwegian port of Kirkenes in early December,[10] from where they could travel to Bergen in Western Norway and connect with transatlantic sea routes. Simcox himself remained right across the Norwegian border in Svanvik (see Map 1), until the Soviet forces reached Kolosjoki on 14 December. He then moved to Helsinki, where he stayed till the end of the Winter War to safeguard INCO's interests.[11] In these dramatic days, INCO again raised the question of a company-organized sabotage of the Kolosjoki mine and its adjacent industrial complex. The head of the Scandinavian desk in the British Foreign Office, Sir Lawrence Collier, dismissed this course of action in December 1939.[12]

With Kolosjoki and nearby industrial facilities abandoned, INCO's Finnish property was exposed to its occupiers. For the remainder of the three-month-long Winter War, the Soviet troops had ample opportunity to study the burgeoning company town and its industrial installations. However, the invading forces were careful not to cause harm to what they perceived as 'American property'. Allegedly, Soviet pilots had been instructed to avoid bombing the industrial installations.[13] Securely in command of the area, Red Army forces closely guarded the Petsamo mines to make sure the Canadian–American concession owners could not claim damage to their installations. Historians have subsequently asserted that the Finnish army found the mines 'completely untouched' when they arrived to reclaim the Petsamo area after the conclusion of the Winter War. Reportedly, even the snow around mining installations had been left unsullied by the occupiers.[14] As we shall see in the following, Soviet sources reveal that this was far from the case.

That the Soviet forces made the Finns sign a protocol verifying the unscathed and intact nature of the mines upon the return of the Petsamo property in March 1940[15] proves just one thing: it was vitally important to the Soviet Union that the property *appeared* to be untouched. While the mines were not damaged, they were certainly no longer an unknown quantity to Soviet engineers. The archives of Glavnikelkobalt, the Soviet directorate for nickel and cobalt industries, reveal that Soviet mining specialists found the shafts and adit of PNO far too intriguing to be left unexamined while under their control. In March 1940, in the days immediately preceding the Finnish–Soviet peace agreement, a team of Soviet mining engineers from the nearby Severonikel (literally 'northern nickel') plant in Monchegorsk thoroughly inspected the mines and assessed their industrial potential.[16] Their findings would,

I contend, contribute to turning Stalin's earlier hints about reclaiming Petsamo into reality.

A section of the burgeoning Soviet nickel industry was located not far from the smelters in Kolosjoki. Much as a parallel development to what was underway in Finnish Petsamo, a so-called northern industrial centre had been established in 1937 just across the Soviet border.[17] Situated a mere 30 kilometres to the southeast of Kolosjoki, Monchegorsk offered conditions not unlike those encountered in Petsamo. Consequently, the team of Severonikel engineers who arrived in the Finnish–Canadian town sometime during March 1940, at the very end of the Soviet occupation of Petsamo, was well-qualified to assess the site. With their experience from Monchegorsk, the head of the labour camp established to build Severonikel (*Monchegorlag*) Sh. N. Rutshtein, mining engineer A. I. Petrov and materials engineer A. Frantsuzov could relate to what they saw over 'the course of several days'. And, to judge by their reports, they were deeply impressed.

First of all, they reported, the Petsamo ore deposits were vast. From translated literature and mineral sample documents they found in the administration building, the engineers could conclude that the field was well worth the efforts and money invested by INCO, both in terms of nickel content and sheer size:

> The Pechenga [Russian name for Petsamo] tundra is in every practical way a very interesting region for mining. The nickel ore (or copper-nickel ore, more precisely) found in this region contains high percentages of sulfuric nickel, and therefore does not require enrichment in the refining process. These fields are, in terms of their reserves, one of the richest bases of nickel in Europe.[18]

The Soviet engineers predicted that the field extended well into Norway and possibly further into Finland again, and recommended that Soviet reconnaissance teams verify this 'within the next two–three years'. The expected extent of the field made for interesting perspectives, also on the eastern side of the border, where the engineers recommended that one should 'continue the search for copper-nickel ore along the outer rims of the [Petsamo] field on Soviet territory'.[19]

While the ore deposits in Petsamo stirred the engineers' interest, it was the planning work and organizational efforts of the Finnish–Canadian company that really elicited superlatives from the Soviet observers. Especially mining engineer A. I. Petrov was excited by what he saw. His report gives interesting insights into a Soviet specialist's encounter with Western technology and organizational solutions. In almost panegyric terms, Petrov praises everything from the preparatory work to details in the shafts and adit. From documentation left behind he could see

> how broadly and detailed [PNO] had examined literally speaking all factors pertaining to the building of the mines and the smelter. This again allowed for correct decisions in questions like where to locate the adit, … and also accordingly define the complex location of all the workshops (that are all built in strict accordance with the technological processes included in the refinement of ore) as well as the underground equipment needed, all this while avoiding completely superfluous transportation of ore and other materials.[20]

Petrov's comments and the tone of his report seem to suggest an amount of bewildered fascination. He remarks that the comprehensive scope of the mining operations is, although costly, conducive to a wide range of options later, depending on how the extraction of ore develops. After concluding that these investments will allow for making the correct industrial decisions down the line, he goes on to a description of the work carried out inside the shafts. Highlighting details that only a true expert would be able to appreciate, he notes 'the special attention given to questions of preparatory mining construction work by the mine surveyors, especially in terms of the consistency in marking the mine units … . This is one of the factors that secures high quality of the drilling work.'[21] As an experienced miner, Petrov was able to understand and appreciate the necessity of a good ventilation system, high-quality equipment and maintenance routines for perforators and other essentials, all of which he reported finding in abundance. His overall assessment could hardly have been more positive:

> All in all, it is necessary to point out the high degree of mechanization of the underground work, with equipment working on high pressure air, i.e. transport machines, scraping winches, underground caterpillars, ventilators and other mechanisms. All these contribute significantly to the avoidance of expensive spending on power lines and corresponding electrical equipment, make for simplicity in the working of the mine, and diminish the hazards of the mining. … All support functions … are completely mechanized. The network of underground storage spaces is well organized, equipped with all necessary materials and their distribution prohibits all possible unproductive loss of time (waiting, delays, etc.). On each horizontal there are scaffoldings that contain full sets of fueled drills from which the workers can take whatever needed at any given time. … It seems obvious that work plans were given for a defined period, as is done in many American companies. All the above-mentioned measures have to a significant degree contributed to the tightening up of the working day and raised labor productivity. Some graphic material (sketches, drawings, etc.) that we have found show that even smaller and less important tasks are all fulfilled according to predefined plans, which has secured high-quality completion of the work. For many tasks (fortification, drilling, etc.) standardization has been broadly applied. From our inspection of the mines it is obvious that during the construction work one has avoided so-called 'provisional arrangements': The work has been completed in a thorough and solid manner.[22]

Petrov rounded off his report with a list of sixteen points for improvements in Soviet mines, all inspired by what he saw in Petsamo, and which he thought could be implemented in the Soviet Union *(izpolsovano v nashikh usloviyakh)*. Of special interest was a higher degree of mechanization of drilling and extraction work, but also more immediately practicable features like 'wide popularization of safety regulations' and the use of bright paint to mark depths and exit routes in the mines. Petrov also pointed out the advantages of the compact nature of the industrial site *(promyshlennaya ploshchadka)*, and the proximity of the smelter to the mine entrance.[23]

Evidently, Petrov and his colleagues would not have protested Soviet appropriation of PNO's industrial installations. For the time being, however, Finland remained Petsamo's sovereign at the end of the Winter War in March 1940. The Soviet engineers were obliged to conclude their scrutiny of the PNO mines as the Red Army evacuated Petsamo after the signing of the Moscow Treaty. The mines were again a potential area for industrial production. However, hostilities had cleared the area of workers and the Canadian executives were all gone.

In INCO, the news of the Soviet withdrawal was highly, if cautiously, appreciated. With reports of German interest in the ore, as well as persistent suspicions that the Soviet Union had not really left for good, a fully fledged restart of production seemed less than prudent. As the situation was fluid, INCO decided to keep running costs in Petsamo to a minimum – which meant a greatly reduced work force still active in Kolosjoki and Jäniskoski. This was accepted by the Finnish government, which understood the inevitability of moderation but was still eager to maintain some employment in the region. That there would still be some activity in Petsamo was also welcomed by the British Ministry of Economic Warfare, as this would allegedly give the British forces an opportunity to plant secret agents in the labour force in anticipation of a hostile takeover, whether by Germany or by the Soviet Union.[24]

INCO was in any case not about to give up on its Finnish property. In the spring of 1940, the head of INCO, Robert Stanley, was still sufficiently convinced of the PNO's value to want to keep it in company hands and accepted that further spending was necessary. In a telegram explaining the reasons for his decision to continue investments, the complex political nature of running a business like PNO in wartime was made apparent. Stanley listed three main objectives:

> One to show the government of Finland our desire and intent to complete and subsequently operate our project in Finland. Two to furnish maximum employment but with minimum expenditures for housing and equipment until political situation is clarified.

Three to cooperate with desires of and objectives of UK and Finland governments.[25]

INCO's apprehensions soon proved justified. The coming period would raise the strategic importance of Petsamo to unprecedented heights. This would set in motion a process which would soon make INCO's influence in northern Finland a thing of the past.

The Moscow parenthesis: Petsamo in the spotlight[26]

Despite bleak prospects at the end of the Winter War, Finland would before long, paradoxically enough, find itself in a position that provided some room for manoeuvre. Much of this was related to the continuing, and somewhat surprising, Finnish sovereignty over Petsamo, which provided an important bargaining chip in Finland's efforts to optimize its position in anticipation of the upcoming Great-Power battle. Petsamo was economically and strategically important to Finland in and of itself. But its real significance in the interim peace between the Winter War and the Continuation War derived from the rivalry that developed between Germany, the Soviet Union, and to a certain extent Great Britain for influence in the area.[27] Throughout the so-called Moscow parenthesis (March 1940–June 1941), Helsinki balanced Great-Power interests in Petsamo against each other with a view to maximizing Finnish security. The Great-Power attention was strategically motivated, in both a geographic and an economic sense, although to varying degrees for the different states involved.

While Great Britain did have a vested interest in PNO through Mond Nickel's partnership in the venture, it was likely the military strategic element that was at the forefront of British thinking about Petsamo: To the British government it was the ports in the Petsamo fjord as potential loopholes in the Royal Navy's control of the Atlantic traffic that first and foremost constituted a problem. That said, the British claim stemmed from Mond Nickel's (and INCO's) stake in PNO, and it was the question of the nickel concession rights that provided London with an opportunity to influence proceedings. Opting to counteract German interests rather than directly promoting their own, British officials restricted their involvement to encouraging Moscow to press for the Petsamo ore, albeit with some provisos: they would raise no objections to Moscow's claims provided that INCO's ownership was restored after the war and that no nickel output from Petsamo be sold to Germany. The British approach thus was to try to exploit the increasing divergence between Germany and the Soviet Union to achieve the end target: avoiding Nazi control of the Liinahamari port and curtailing German consumption of nickel as much as possible.[28]

The German interest in Petsamo seems to have been a 50–50 case, where geographical realities and economic significance weighed in equally. On the one hand, Germany was in dire need of regular shipments of nickel matte to feed its frantic armaments industry. On the other hand, as Nazi control extended towards the north of Norway and the Barbarossa plan for the invasion of the Soviet Union grew closer, getting a foothold in the Petsamo territory represented a logical extension of German war plans.[29] We shall trace the ever-deepening German involvement in Petsamo in more detail below.

The Soviet position in the Petsamo matter was less straightforward. As we have seen, Soviet forces had comfortably controlled Petsamo throughout the Winter War but had handed it back to Finland – allegedly against the expressed wishes of Red Army officers who wanted to keep the area in Soviet hands.[30] Indeed, Moscow had seemed utterly disinterested in regaining Petsamo ever since giving it up in 1920, an impression reinforced by the Moscow Peace Treaty in March 1940. The Soviet position changed dramatically, however, just three months after signatures were put to the March treaty: On 23 June 1940, Finnish envoy to the Soviet Union Juho Kusti Paasikivi was summoned to Vyacheslav Molotov's offices. The foreign minister presented Paasikivi with a request that took his visitor aback: The Soviet Union would very much like to take over the mining concession. Alternatively, Molotov stated, a Soviet–Finnish mining company could be established, if

Finland so preferred. He motivated his demand simply by stating that his government's interest in the local mining operation had been piqued (*Sovetskoe pravitelstvo v etikh rudnikakh zainteresovano*), while not mentioning specifically by what. In closing, Molotov made it clear that 'the Soviet government hopes for and insists on a positive response'.[31]

Faced with Molotov's aggressive overtures, the Finnish government would show itself to be quite resistant to its covetous neighbour. Paasikivi explained to Molotov that the existing concession agreement with INCO barred Finland from conducting negotiations with other interested parties. Molotov brushed Paasikivi's arguments aside as legalistic irrelevances, retorting that Finland was at liberty to annul INCO's concession before handing it over to a Soviet – alternatively Finnish–Soviet – company. He also made it clear that the Soviet Union was interested not only in the nickel, but in the area as such (*ne tolko sam nikel, no glavnym obrazom etot raion*). It was important, he stated, that Petsamo was accessible only to the Soviet Union and Finland: 'We do not want the British, who are doing their utmost to stand in our way, to be there.'[32]

The Petsamo question was not to be solved by way of negotiations. Despite Molotov's growing impatience and, in later exchanges, increasingly threatening language from his deputy Andrei Vyshinskii, the Finnish government was able to withstand the accumulating Soviet pressure throughout the following twelve months, before finally entering the war as Germany's co-belligerent. Finland remained the sovereign of Petsamo until Helsinki was finally forced to cede it to the Soviet victor in 1944.

Why would Paasikivi be so surprised by Molotov's demands for the Petsamo concession when it was made in June 1940? With Europe already at war and the Soviet Union at pains to secure its borders against Western aggression, any attempt from Moscow to bring neighbouring areas under stricter control – politically, militarily or economically – was only to be expected.[33] Paasikivi was, as any Finnish citizen at the time, acutely aware of his country's perilous geopolitical position.

But Petsamo had seemed not to figure among Soviet strategists' priorities: A permanent Soviet annexation of Petsamo would have been, in terms of military realities on the ground, utterly unproblematic as the Winter War drew to a close. Nonetheless, as part of the armistice concluded between Finland and the Soviet Union on 12 March 1940, the Red Army withdrew its forces.[34] Apparently, the Soviet Union 'put no value on Petsamo', as German envoy to Helsinki Wipert von Blücher commented upon learning the details of the Moscow treaty.[35] His words rang true: Neither the Petsamo territory, nor the local nickel ore had raised significant interest in Moscow in March 1940, less than four months before Molotov forcefully presented Paasikivi with Soviet claims to the very same nickel.

As the foremost German diplomat in Helsinki, Blücher was well acquainted with Petsamo, as it was one of the very few sources of nickel that Berlin hoped would become available to German armaments industries after the outbreak of the Second World War.[36] His comment was presumably meant to express astonishment at the lack of Soviet interest in this strategically important resource. That Moscow was disinterested in or, more likely, unaware of Petsamo's industrial significance at the time, is supported by accounts of the Winter War. Soviet military planning for the northern offensive in 1939 was exclusively preoccupied with the defence of the Leningrad-Murmansk railway line and the naval bases located on the Kola fjord.[37] In his memoirs, Red Army Marshall Aleksandr M. Vasilevskii opines that all Soviet objectives in the Winter War were reached: 'The Soviet Union was able to improve its strategic position in the North and North-West. The security issues regarding Leningrad, Murmansk and the Murmansk-Leningrad railway were solved.'[38] No mention of the nickel resource or PNO's industrial installations is to be found.

Again, that all changed on 23 June the same year, when Paasikivi entered Molotov's offices. What had caused the Soviet turnaround? Which developments had taken place between the signing of the Moscow Peace Treaty on 12 March and Paasikivi's visit to Molotov that so dramatically changed the Soviet assessment of Petsamo? We will return to these questions in the concluding sections of the present chapter.

German industry had, as we have seen in Chapter 1, long been interested in obtaining nickel wherever possible, also in Finland. One of Germany's foremost industrial companies, IG Farben, had the refinement technology, but lacked the raw material. Germany's appetite for nickel grew throughout the 1930s. In this period, IG Farben became centrally positioned in the German military-industrial complex, which was preparing the Nazi state for future clashes with the enemy.[39] With the outbreak of war in September 1939 (Canada declared war on Germany on 10 September 1939), IG Farben's agreement with INCO for the delivery of 10 per cent of the latter's non-American sales (see Chapter 1) was effectively annulled.[40] Consequently, Germany and IG Farben had to look elsewhere for ore, and a Finland in need of the friendship of any great power willing to defend them against the Soviet Union must have seemed a promising prospect. Throughout the fall of 1939, German interests had made overtures to buy output from or even completely take over the Petsamo mining concession.[41] At the time, however, the Nazi war plans required adherence to the Molotov–Ribbentrop pact, including its secret protocol that defined Finland as within the Soviet sphere of interest. Hitler found it best not to intervene, at least not yet.

After the Winter War, a German takeover in Petsamo, or even a Finnish–German agreement on nickel deliveries, was no trifling matter. Firstly, Germany was among the countries that in Finnish popular opinion, and in the minds of many leading politicians, had let the struggling Finnish people down when it was faced with an overpowering Bolshevik enemy. Why should the Finns be accommodating to them? Secondly, there was the obstacle of the Anglo-Canadian concession rights. INCO and Mond had, through their stake in Petsamon Nikkeli OY, full rights to all production of nickel in Petsamo for the coming forty years. In the case of Germany, this was of significance, since Petsamon Nikkeli OY was a British concern by virtue of Mond Nickel's role as holding company. It was also a matter for the Canadian government, through INCO's ownership. Both governments were at war with the Nazi state and were intent on eliminating Germany's influence, and at the very least keeping the Petsamo nickel completely out of reach of the German war industry. The opening for Berlin was that Finland still owned the land, and, if sufficiently persuaded, might opt to expropriate the Petsamo mining complex. Consequently, the Germans would have to proceed prudently if they were to have any hope of quenching their nickel thirst with Petsamo ore. Careful not to complicate matters further by openly claiming ore output and thereby raising Soviet interest in Petsamo, the Germans conducted silent negotiations with the Finns in the spring of 1940. Obtaining nickel ore from Petsamo was so important from the German point of view, that the matter of Petsamo was given the highest priority in their trade talks with Finland late spring and summer 1940.[42]

The tide was moving in favour of the Third Reich. The *Wehrmacht*'s capture of Denmark and Norway in April/May and the Nazi tour de force in the Benelux countries and France from May onwards cemented Germany's position as the dominant power in Europe. This had a profound effect on the Finnish leadership and prompted a re-orientation of the country's foreign trade policy which would in time put Finland within the German orbit.[43] In bilateral trade talks in May and June 1940, Germany and Finland discussed the possibility of southward nickel exports. The Finns knew from the start that a German–Finnish agreement on Petsamo nickel would have far-reaching political implications.[44] Nevertheless, given the geopolitical realities of the time, Finland's precarious position was worrying the country's political elite. The future existence of independent Finland could be on the line, and the country was looking for protection. Reconsidering their earlier reluctance to sell Petsamo nickel to Germany would therefore appear to be a logical path for the Finnish negotiators to follow. In the first half of June 1940, during trade talks in the German capital, the Finns were increasingly accommodating to German requests, and Petsamo nickel seemed to be on its way to IG Farben's refineries.[45]

These developments in Berlin soon evoked reactions in London. Through Finnish associates in Petsamon Nikkeli OY, Mond and INCO were privy to first-hand information about the ongoing Finnish–German negotiations. This, in effect, also meant that the British government was fully informed due to its close association with Mond. On 17 June, Dr Johan Söderhjelm, former managing director of Petsamon Nikkeli OY and then minister of justice in Finland, spelt out the consequences of the German interest to INCO and Mond. The harsh reality was that INCO would have to agree to sell the output to Germany or forfeit the concession. This prompted a spate of hectic discussions in London and Ottawa, involving various parties. Unsurprisingly, the Finnish authorities and Petsamon Nikkeli OY were in favour of keeping the concession in INCO's hands, even if that meant giving up nickel to Germany. The Ministry of Economic Warfare in London also agreed that exporting the nickel to Germany was the best, or the least bad, option. The Ministry's rationale was that retaining the Petsamo nickel under Canadian–British control would provide the opportunity to keep production at the lowest possible level, an opportunity that would be lost if the Germans actually took over. Furthermore, with reliable Canadian employees at the nickel plant, British intelligence could make sure that any significant ore transport to Germany from the ports of Petsamo could be intercepted by the British Navy. INCO president Robert Stanley accepted this solution and was willing to go along with it as long as it gained the concurrence of the Canadian government,[46] thus bringing in a new and so far, uninitiated player.

The new player, Canadian prime minister Mackenzie King put a stop to the scheme. He was opposed to anything that smacked of a Canadian breach of the Trading with the Enemy Act, and harboured deep worries about popular reactions in Canada should it become public knowledge that a Canadian company, with his blessing, provided Germany with nickel essential to the Nazi war effort. He expressed this in a 29 June telegram to the Canadian High Commission in London: '[The] political and psychological effects of concurrence in arrangement … still seem to us to be very serious and to outweigh economic and military importance of limiting supply of nickel available to Germany.'[47] With the official Canadian refusal to condone the scheme, INCO's active engagement in Petsamo affairs had effectively come to an end, although the mining concession formally remained in the possession of the company. This formality was to prove more important to Finland than to INCO.

As mentioned, Paasikivi's response to Molotov's demand shows that the Anglo-Canadian concession, still formally in existence, would be an important element in Finland's defence against Soviet attempts to gain control over Petsamo. Molotov was of course correct in assuming that Finland, still a sovereign state controlling the Petsamo territory, could have expropriated the nickel mines. The real obstacle was that the Finnish government did not see it in its best interest to invite into their homeland the one power from which it sought protection. The Finns would henceforth play a double game. They would persist in referring to the legal obstacles set by the British–Canadian concession, infuriating their Soviet counterparts in the process.[48] At the same time, they continued negotiations with Germany that entailed a breach of the very same concession.

Germany's position demanded a balancing act. On the one hand, they had to consider their non-aggression commitments to the Soviet Union which also defined Finland as within the Soviet sphere of interest. On the other hand, they would try to exploit Finnish fears of the Red Army. In hindsight, it seems obvious that the Nazi apparatus never intended to give up on Petsamo. However, there was little room for declarations of support for Finland if Berlin needed to keep Moscow calm through at least nominal adherence to the Molotov–Ribbentrop Pact.

Germany would limit its engagement to push for a substantial share of the output from the Petsamo mines, irrespective of how the concession question was solved, while not openly challenging Soviet pre-eminence in the area.[49] Simultaneously, Germany encouraged Finland to stall on all Soviet demands. In the end, Finland had to wait till March 1941 to receive unambiguous reassurances from Berlin that any aggression from the east would be met with German retaliation.[50] By then, developments in the European war had put the Petsamo question firmly in the background. Nazi German expansion in the Balkans was already challenging the Soviet–German pact, and a clash between Europe's two foremost dictators seemed inevitable. At this point, Finnish officials did not even have to pretend to listen to Soviet demands for Petsamo.[51]

Before receipt of unequivocal German support, however, the Finns had been hard-pressed to reject Soviet overtures completely. In fact, from Christmas 1940 till the end of February 1941, a Finnish–Soviet commission worked on how to solve the Petsamo issue to the satisfaction of both states. It is hard, however, to see Finland's participation in this commission as anything but a smokescreen. Actively encouraged by the Germans to keep the talks alive, the Finns staunchly rejected demands for the creation of a joint mining operation in Petsamo under Soviet leadership.[52] Germany held parallel talks with the Soviet Union about how much of the nickel output could be sold to Germany, should a Finnish–Soviet operation be realized.[53]

Gradually, the Finnish refusal to allow Soviet control over the Kolosjoki mines and the stubborn insistence on legalistic principles relating to the Canadian–British concession owners came to infuriate Molotov and his deputy Andrei Vyshinskii to the extent that they repeatedly threatened alternative solutions – which could not be construed as meaning anything but Soviet military annexation of the Petsamo area.[54] With German–Soviet relations steadily deteriorating, these threats likely seemed less and less intimidating to the Finnish leaders, who must have felt increasingly confident of their place within German war plans.[55]

As we see, in the interim peace period between March 1940 and June 1941, Petsamo, with its industrial importance, became the centrepiece in a high-stakes game for strategic advantages in the build-up to the upcoming battle that would soon involve all the great powers. With Petsamo nickel in its possession, Finland was no longer just a Soviet concern, but attracted the interest of Germany and Great Britain as well. While being the object of such smothering attention was likely not an enviable position, at least Finland could use its nickel resources for what they were worth to achieve a modicum of security. By means of deft negotiating technique, Helsinki had kept the Soviet Union at bay long enough to feel assured of German protection in the event of Soviet aggression. Finland elected to become co-belligerent of the *Wehrmacht*, thereby winning a temporary respite from its Soviet nemesis.

Petsamo in German war industry 1941–4

Finland was formally a neutral state until it declared war against the Soviet Union on 25 June 1941, three days after the German army had put its Barbarossa plan into effect. War was declared, according to former prime minister and then president of Finland Risto Ryti, as a direct result of Soviet air raids the same morning.[56] Ryti's attempt to ascribe the commencement of the Continuation War solely to Soviet aggression must be characterized as an act of deception. The Finnish forces were well prepared for an attack on the Soviet Union and had been so for a while. The number of German troops had been rapidly increasing in northern Finland from early June, and the Finnish army had been mobilizing accordingly from 10 to 17 June. These preparations were sanctioned by Finnish military leaders as a result of their talks with German colleagues in late May and early June – talks that never explicitly touched on the Barbarossa plan or a German occupation of Petsamo (*Operation Renntier*) but nevertheless implied tacit Finnish concurrence to contributing to the German plans to attack the Soviet Union. In his book on the Petsamo dispute, H. Peter Krosby makes a convincing evidence-based case to show that Finland's destiny as Germany's co-belligerent had been sealed, and even accepted by Finnish military and political authorities, well in advance of 25 June.[57] Krosby's conclusions are supported also in more recent literature.[58]

At 2:30 in the morning of 22 June 1941, General Eduard Dietl ordered his troops to commence preparatory manoeuvres for *Operation Renntier*. The soldiers were invited into Petsamo by Finnish border guards at the Norwegian–Finnish crossing point, and before noon the same day General Dietl could conclude that the manoeuvre had been successfully completed. German control over Petsamo was, as expected and planned, imposed without a single casualty.[59] As Finland was neutral for another three days, the operation was formally an occupation of Petsamo. The Germans expelled all unwanted individuals from the territory, including Soviet consular personnel. The British consul and his staff had been warned to leave the area and had done so on the eve of the German invasion.[60] With Petsamo under control, all the German forces had to do was to keep the Red Army at bay and restart work at the plant to keep up nickel deliveries to the industry at home. As it turned out, the first would prove easier than the last.

On 5 August 1941, Finland expropriated the mines in Kolosjoki. The legality of this action was provided by the wartime article of the 1934 concession agreement, which also stated that the property should be returned to INCO once Finland was no longer engaged in war. Although Petsamo ore had already been shipped to Germany throughout the summer, this was more than just a formality to IG Farben. With the Anglo-Canadian owners out of the picture, at least temporarily, the German company saw an opportunity to secure supplies for its nickel division not only for the duration of the war, but also afterwards, which would increase its ability to compete with INCO in a post-war future. The directors of IG Farben, who had been limited to INCO deliveries of nickel matte throughout the 1930s, wanted to seize this chance to acquire independence from the Canadian monopolist. They proposed that the Petsamo concession be transferred to a new company under IG Farben's control. The Finns' response to IG Farben's proposal illustrates their reluctance at becoming more closely associated with Germany than they already were. Staunchly opposed to any arrangement that would deprive INCO of the right to reclaim the Petsamo property after the war, the Finns applied the dilatory tactics that they had grown accustomed to employing against Soviet negotiators:

> Neither the company's [IG Farben's] own representatives nor the German Foreign Ministry could break down the passive resistance of the Finns in the concession matter. It seemed as if the Germans

were falling victims to the very strategy of procrastination which they had prescribed for the Finns when the Russians were pressing their demands in 1940-41.[61]

This tactic proved efficient. German authorities, to the dismay of IG Farben, chose not to press Helsinki further on the matter.

This was not the only problem the Germans faced in Petsamo. The smelter furnaces had been projected to produce nickel matte by the end of 1941. In fact, this did not happen till February 1943, and then only at half capacity. There were several reasons for the initial low productivity. Firstly, almost all the Finnish workers in Petsamo had been drafted during the mobilization in the build-up to war. This meant that there was no manpower at the unfinished Jäniskoski power plant, which again meant that the energy-intensive smelters would stay idle for one year longer than projected. When one of the furnaces in Kolosjoki finally started heating up in July 1942, it soon malfunctioned, and smelting was further delayed until December that year.

Then there was the problem of transportation. The choice stood between Kirkenes (in northern Norway) and Rovaniemi (in northern Finland). Trucking the ore and matte to the ice-free Kirkenes harbour was much shorter than to Rovaniemi (see Map 2). Also, Rovaniemi is inland, so that option presupposed further train freight to the Baltic Sea (Bottenviken), which is frozen for parts of the winter. On the other hand, onward shipping from Kirkenes was far riskier. The danger of being torpedoed off the coast of occupied Norway was very high, with the British Navy patrolling the Northern Atlantic. Nonetheless, the Germans decided that Kirkenes was the better option, due to much lower costs and less time lost. Kirkenes, however, soon proved to be a bottleneck, as the massive bulk of raw ore and nickel matte overwhelmed the relatively small harbour. There was simply not enough loading capacity to meet the German demands.[62]

Despite all these problems, Petsamo turned out to be well worth the trouble for Germany. Raw ore and matte shipped from Kolosjoki made up four-fifths of the country's nickel supplies in 1943 and 1944. It is therefore no exaggeration to say that Petsamo was indispensable to the

German war effort, a point reflected in Hitler's assessment of it. On several occasions, the dictator made it clear that Germany would have to protect Petsamo at any cost and expressed concern that Germany could not win the war without control of the nickel resources in northern Finland.[63]

When the German war machine experienced a string of defeats against its Soviet opponents from early 1943, most prominently in the battles of Stalingrad and Kursk, it became clear to the Finnish government that the time had come to break free of the increasingly uncomfortable association with the Nazi leadership. In February and April 1944, Finland held preliminary peace talks with Moscow.

The Germans, for their part, were set on continuing production at the Kolosjoki mines to the very end. Even when the Finnish government evacuated the work force and the remaining women and children from Kolosjoki on 10 and 11 September 1944,[64] Berlin immediately developed plans for replacing them. Only over a month later, more than two weeks after Finland and the Soviet Union had signed a separate armistice agreement, did Berlin abandon these plans. The Germans faced a fait accompli with the Red Army's successful offensive on the Murmansk front that had started on 7 October. Three days later, Soviet forces were breaking through the German defences east of Kolosjoki, and the officers were now left with the final option. On 10 October, true to their accustomed mode of taking unauthorized initiatives, the officers in command of the German armies in northern Finland ordered the destruction of the company town Kolosjoki and the adjacent industrial installations.[65] The demolition went on for some time before the decisive battle for Kolosjoki took place.

Already at that point the Finns had been considered unreliable by their German partners for a while. In the summer and fall of 1943, the Germans had started developing plans for their retreat from Finnish soil, while at the same time working on how to protect the nickel mines. The Soviet Union, however, was set on not only expelling the Germans from northern Finland – it wanted Petsamo for itself. This was made abundantly clear to Paasikivi when he visited Molotov in Moscow on

26 April 1944.[66] Finnish peace feelers continued as the war continued, Nazi weaknesses became clearer, and the Finnish position became less tenable by the day. When President Ryti resigned and was succeeded by Gustav Mannerheim on the last day of July, it was clear that Finland was moving in only one direction – away from the Germans and towards the negotiation table in Moscow.[67] Mannerheim requested Soviet peace terms in late August, and Moscow accepted that negotiations could start on the condition that the Finns expelled their former German brothers-in-arms from their territory.[68] Thus the Lapland War started, and lasted well into 1945. German–Finnish hostilities would be confined to areas south and predominantly west of Petsamo.[69] The nickel-rich region to the north and east was a matter for the Soviet forces to deal with.

Petsamo becomes Pechenga

The Soviet forces entered Kolosjoki on 22 October 1944[70] – and this time they arrived to stay. The armistice agreement with Finland of 19 September stated that Petsamo would be transferred to the Soviet Union. Soviet negotiators could safely make this demand against Finland: Stalin had already in a conversation with the British minister of foreign affairs Anthony Eden on 16 December 1941 insisted that Petsamo, which he described as 'a gift given to Finland in 1940', be returned to the Soviet Union after the war. The Soviet claim on Petsamo was repeated and accepted in late September 1943 during Stalin's Teheran conference with Churchill and Roosevelt.[71] Clearly, the Soviet leader was at an early stage of the war intent on finally securing the troublesome, but valuable, piece of land for the socialist state.

This brings us back to this chapter's main query: Why did the Soviet Union return Petsamo to the Finns in March 1940, only to insist on the creation of a Soviet–Finnish company to replace PNO a mere three months later? To explain the somewhat surprising Soviet decision to let Finland reclaim Petsamo after a full victory in the Winter War, H. Peter Krosby makes note of, as did Gustaf Mannerheim at the time, the supposed Soviet sensitivity to British–Canadian interests in the nickel production there. Analysing the Finnish–Soviet peace talks in March, both Krosby and fellow historian Matt Bray conclude that the Soviet leadership did not want to risk estranging Great Britain and the United States by annexing the property of a partly British–American owned company whose production figured in the wartime planning of Western countries.[72] But why should this alleged sensitivity disappear in the course of three months in 1940? When Molotov presented the new Soviet demands on the nickel concession, INCO and Mond were still the legal owners of PNO. Anglo-Canadian industry, so important for the Soviet Union not to offend in March, was still a factor. Logically, then, something must have happened to change the Soviet opinion and render the Anglo-Canadian company's concession rights less relevant.

To account for this change, Krosby has pointed to geopolitical factors. In March, the North Atlantic was still not an arena in the war and the Germans had yet to invade Scandinavia.[73] This situation changed during the spring of 1940, with Nazi Germany's advance northwards through Norway. Similarly, Finnish historian Arvi Korhonen puts great emphasis on the increasing geostrategic significance of Petsamo that spring: 'Such as the situation was developing in the year 1940, the question of control over the [Petsamo] area should have appeared on the agenda even if there was nothing there but reindeer lichen.'[74] Historian Anthony F. Upton emphasizes the same geopolitical factors in his explanation. As the Nazi forces advanced towards Kirkenes, right across the border from Kolosjoki, Petsamo became a potential launching pad for a future German attack on the Soviet Union. Upton does raise the possibility of a Soviet economic interest in challenging the world's leading nickel producers but dismisses this as less probable as a motivating factor than the sheer military-defensive and intelligence-related advantages of having a foothold in Petsamo.[75]

Russian historian N. I. Baryshnikov goes further in both forcefully and explicitly rejecting any notion that Soviet claims to Petsamo from June 1940 were economically motivated. The fact that Petsamo with its abundant nickel ore was handed back to Finland in March 1940 is, he argues, ample evidence that economic factors did not play a part in Moscow's decision making. Soviet leaders wished to counter contemporary allegations that the Winter War was waged with expansionist ambitions.[76] They hoped, according to Baryshnikov, that the restoration of Petsamo to Finland would convince other states (Great Britain, Sweden and Norway are mentioned) that their objectives were purely defensive. While Moscow's primary goal was to annex a buffer zone on the Karelian Isthmus in the south, their awareness of Petsamo's nickel was piqued only when Germany displayed a thirst for the same resource, Baryshnikov argues.[77]

Certainly, there is much to suggest that Moscow's initial approach to Petsamo was indeed defined by defensive needs. As shown by Norwegian historian Sven G. Holtsmark, the area was becoming more important to Soviet authorities as the Winter War progressed. In Holtsmark's reading, Moscow became progressively preoccupied with defending Soviet naval bases on the Kola fjord and the railway line between Murmansk and Leningrad and was seeking to maximize the distance between these objects and the western border. As Holtsmark points out, however, these concerns were in March 1940 (as they had been in the Tartu Treaty of 1920) deemed subordinate to the need for the protection of the city of Petrograd/Leningrad. In both cases, control of Petsamo was ceded to Finland while buffer zones were established on the Karelian Isthmus.[78]

Both Baryshnikov and Holtsmark base their interpretations mainly on extensive readings of protocols from Molotov's meetings with various actors, predominately Finnish officials, that are also reflected in this study. While these sources support the notion that Soviet authorities gradually devoted more attention to the defensive needs of military and civilian infrastructure on the Kola Peninsula, they provide no satisfactory explanation of why Soviet authorities changed their minds about Petsamo between March and June 1940. While Baryshnikov, as mentioned, ascribes the Soviet turnaround to the rise of German demands on the Petsamo nickel, Holtsmark does not directly address this question.[79]

One of the central players, Paasikivi, doubted that the geopolitical dimension provided a full explanation for the Soviet *démarche*, although his conclusion is that the underlying motivation was a pure case of power politics. The Soviet Union, in his mind, simply did not want other powers present in an area that Moscow considered to be within the Soviet sphere of influence.[80] But this explanation, as Paasikivi himself points out, does not solve the enigma of the Soviets' returning Petsamo to Finland in March, when they could have retained possession with a minimum of fuss as victors in the Winter War.

That the geopolitical significance of Petsamo had increased during the spring of 1940 is true but does not provide the full explanation. Petsamo had been strategically important also in March 1940, when Moscow returned the area to Finland. It is therefore hard to see Germany's latest military moves as dramatically changing the game. True, the German *Wehrmacht* must have been expected to pose a threat to Soviet territory from the northern Norwegian county of Finnmark, once they had progressed that far north.[81] It seems doubtful, however, that the German expansion constituted anything essentially new to Soviet decision makers. After all, the Winter War itself had been a result of Soviet defensive needs against a perceived threat, from Germany or elsewhere. Thus, although it may have been a contributing factor, the approaching German forces cannot fully account for the sudden Soviet demands on Petsamo.[82] This was also the case when it came to German interest in Petsamo's nickel resource. Berlin had long signalled their desire to consume as much nickel from Petsamo as possible, a fact that was abundantly clear to Moscow well prior to March 1940.

As is argued here, Soviet sources would indicate that the availability of new information about the *economic* value of the Petsamo area played a role in Molotov's sharp about-turn on 23 June 1940. To provide a satisfactory explanation of the Soviet reversal, we must trace the path of the reconnaissance reports made by the three engineers from Monchegorsk in the final days of the Winter War. As we have seen, Sh. N. Rutshtein, A. I. Petrov, and A. Frantsuzov reported an enormously rich nickel ore as well as mining techniques and technology that could, in their expert opinion, enhance the growing Soviet nickel industry. Molotov's sensitivity towards the Anglo-Canadian trust owners and their associated governments in March 1940 might well have been dampened, had he seen the findings of his Severonikel engineers. However, since the fact-finding mission and the peace negotiations in March 1940 took place at the same time, the engineers' findings were not to be known in Moscow before Petsamo was again in Finnish hands. That the Soviets suddenly showed a renewed and keen interest in Petsamo a mere three months later is thus very possibly connected to the engineers' reports about the value of the Petsamo property.

Those reports were to play a role some years later, a role which also attests to the impact that they probably had made when they reached Moscow sometime after March 1940. Only months prior to the Soviet Union's annexation of Petsamo in September 1944, the central authorities in Moscow requested the reports again. Glavnikelkobalt, the Soviet directorate for nickel and cobalt industries, instituted a search for the reports after having lost track of them during the chaotic war years. These circumstances are evident in a dispatch note of 17 July 1944, from engineer Sh. N. Rutshtein to his superiors in Moscow:

> In connection with the query from Glavnikelkobalt … as to the whereabouts of the documents stemming from our examination and the difficulties locating them, caused by the evacuation and re-evacuation of the institutions in which the originals and copies were placed, I have decided to try to again give some information about the nickel ore in Petsamo.[83]

It is difficult to ascertain from this quote whether the reports had gone astray locally or in Moscow – possibly both. Clearly, though, they were very much in demand as the Second World War was drawing to a close and the post-war spheres of influence had been shared out between the victorious powers. Soviet demands for Petsamo from June 1940 onwards and the eventual Soviet annexation of the area in 1944 certainly support this interpretation. It also indicates that the role of *economic* concerns in shaping the Soviet position on Petsamo in the war years needs to be revisited and accorded greater emphasis.

To fully appreciate the Soviet economic interest in Petsamo, we need to consider the development of the country's domestic nickel industry. According to Upton, 'as far as is known, the Soviet Union produced all the nickel she needed at the time.'[84] That is not completely accurate. True, the Soviet Union had a growing nickel industry of its own. But this industry was still in its infancy, and not able to completely satisfy the current or future needs of the armed forces. In 1939, building up to the Winter War, and later in 1942/43, the Soviet Union imported much-needed Canadian nickel matte for its armaments industries.[85] With this nickel deficit in mind, we should not be surprised that the Soviet leadership viewed Petsamo in a new way once informed by Soviet engineers about the unusually rich nickel deposits and well-organized industrial complex there. Soviet control of the ore could provide not only access to more of the strategically important metal, but also valuable insights into Western methods of production and of organizing mining operations.

Petsamo fitted well into Moscow's long-term goals of achieving resource autarchy and the industrialization of northern natural resources, epitomized in the 1930s and 1940s Soviet rhetoric about 'settling the North' (*osvoenie severa*).[86] With a great sense of urgency, mineral resources of the Soviet North were surveyed, extracted and refined. The Arctic and High North areas were in this period to be included in the realm of the socialist homeland, the faster the better.[87] One expression of this is the statement of Leningrad party leader Sergei Kirov in a meeting with the Karelia-Murmansk party organization in 1932:

> Concerning money – you are saying seven or eight million – I can with all my weight assure you that the cause [geological surveying and building of industry on the Kola Peninsula] is not going to be stopped by lack of funding. What you need is what you are going to get.[88]

Kirov went on to say that 'only when the Soviets came to power were the riches of Kola extracted, and in the years of the five-year plans the peninsula was transformed into a powerful outpost of socialism in the high north of our fatherland'.[89] Kirov's enthusiastic progressivism, which was also conveyed from other parts of the top echelons of the Soviet state, must have had its effect on lower-level actors.[90] Engineer A. I. Petrov, in Soviet terminology a representative of the educated vanguard of the working class, displayed through his report a reflection of the industrialization spirit. Interestingly, this spirit also allowed for praise of non-Soviet industrial ventures, like the Petsamo mines. Petrov's approach was to apply the good production and organizational techniques seen in Petsamo to Soviet industry. Moscow went in 1944 even further, not only admiring the industrial site, but eventually acquiring it.

* * *

To sum up this discussion, the reasons behind the Soviet about-face in June 1940 were complex. Firstly, developing geopolitical factors must have directed the Soviet leadership's attention to the North. There is little doubt that the imminent, though in June still not commenced German fortification of the Norwegian county of Finnmark provoked alarm in the Kremlin. Also, the mere fact that Petsamo was part of Finland, a country that by Molotov and Ribbentrop had been placed within the Soviet sphere of influence, made both British and German presence almost intolerable to Moscow. However, none of these factors were new to Moscow between March and April 1940. Of course, they became more important as the war progressed, but both the threat from Germany and the Anglo-Canadian concession ownership had been in the picture well in advance of the Finnish–Soviet peace negotiations in March 1940.

There was to our knowledge only one genuinely new factor that was added to this picture in the spring and early summer of 1940: the reports from Soviet specialists' inspections of the Petsamo mines. It seems reasonable to assume that Moscow's receipt of new information about the Kolosjoki industrial complex spurred an intense Soviet interest in Petsamo, which manifested itself first in June 1940 and was sustained throughout the various phases of the Second World War.

Though this study does not offer a direct linkage between the Severonikel reconnaissance reports and the Kremlin's decision making prior to 23 June 1940, it does document that Soviet awareness of Petsamo's immense resource base and industrial potential was indeed heightened early in the interim peace period after the Winter War. It is therefore argued, that future research could benefit from a stronger emphasis on economic factors and incentives when attempting to dismantle the full motivational complex behind the sudden Soviet interest in Petsamo, so forcefully presented to Paasikivi by Molotov. This, of course, is not to say that earlier interpretations emphasizing geopolitical factors are irrelevant. However, as stated above, they alone do not provide a fully satisfying answer to the riddle.

More broadly, the Petsamo case illustrates the necessity to fully appreciate the Soviet emphasis on economic factors that underpinned the Union's overall strategies in the High North. Soviet intentions regarding Petsamo must have been shaped also by perspectives that outweighed the shorter-term geopolitical concerns of the war years. Considering the technical information provided by the Monchegorsk engineers to the Kremlin, and the wider context of Soviet industrial ambitions for fully exploiting the natural resources of the North, it would have been surprising if Moscow failed to grasp Petsamo's potential as a future centre of its nickel industry. In the ensuing years, Petsamo (or Pechenga, as the region would be called by its new sovereigns) was to play a central role among Soviet nickel producers, helping the socialist state become the world's foremost supplier of this strategic metal.

4

Sovietization[1]

Rebuilding a company town

On the morning of 18 October 1944, Soviet soldiers of the 14th Army set out from Pilgujärvi, some 50 kilometres east of Kolosjoki, on a long march over the frozen Petsamo tundra. Their mission was to deal the final blow to German resistance in the mining town. It took them two days to reach their target, apparently unopposed. While rummaging around in German storehouses containing much-coveted foodstuffs, the 3rd battalion of the 69th brigade attracted enemy fire. Surprised and disappointed, the hungry soldiers had to flee back up the mountainside to take refuge there, while witnessing the stored food being consumed by flames. The ensuing battle lasted for two days, until the Soviet forces rallied for a night-time attack. Cloaked in darkness, they came upon an enemy about to finish its destructive business:

> As we stormed towards the outskirts of the village, we could see the silhouettes of German 'torch bearers' scurry between the houses. Our nocturnal attack interfered with the enemy's attempt to blow up or set fire to the remaining buildings. The battle lasted until morning. Isolated groups of Germans in various houses and behind defensive points were obliterated. The smoke from the ruins rose around us, broken glass crunched under our feet and the wind whirled with dust and remnants of burnt documents. Here and there lay bodies of [German] Jägers.[2]

Thus, on 22 October 1944, the town of Kolosjoki was captured by its new owner, all in accordance with the armistice agreement of 19 September 1944 between Finland on the one side and the Soviet Union and Great Britain on the other.[3] The transfer of ownership was not merely a result

Figure 3 The sight that met advancing Soviet troops. The Kolosjoki nickel plant was demolished by retreating German soldiers in October 1944. Photo: Archive Rune Rautio.

Figure 4 German soldiers atop the river bank shortly before dam in Niskakoski is destroyed, October 1944. Photo: Archive Rune Rautio.

of Soviet forces gaining the upper hand in the northern war theatre, but had been prepared for through a set of negotiations between the Allied powers the preceding year.

When the tide of war turned in 1943 and Germany looked more and more like the losing side, Stalin had reiterated to his allies that the Petsamo area was of great interest to the Soviet Union. However, the matter of the Anglo-Canadian concession remained to be settled. With the end of war and return of the rule of law in sight, INCO would not relinquish a fully equipped mining operation and a promising ore deposit without compensation. While the war was still being fought, though, these questions were a matter for governments, not private companies, to decide. After Stalin's unopposed request for a Soviet takeover of Petsamo at the Teheran summit in September 1943, the British government left the Petsamo question to be dealt with by its newly established Post-Hostilities Planning Committee.

From November that year, lengthy discussions took place between the Allied governments, and the British committee concluded that a Soviet takeover of Petsamo was acceptable, provided the private owners were compensated. The Canadian government concurred.[4] INCO was presented with a fait accompli, very late in the game. A mere four days before the signing of the Finnish–Soviet armistice, on 15 September 1944, the lawful holders of the Kolosjoki concession were consulted. The secretary of INCO, Henry S. Wingate, was telephoned and given two hours to come up with a compensation fee that would satisfy his company. Wingate could not reach INCO president Robert Stanley and had to make a qualified guess. He suggested USD 50 million.[5] What Wingate did not know was that Molotov had already put a price on Petsamo. In a confidential conversation with the British ambassador in Moscow he had mentioned a sum that was very close to what Finland had estimated in the sham Finnish–Soviet concession negotiations in February 1941, namely USD 20 million.[6]

Moscow did not budge, and the price was set at USD 20 million. That Moscow was willing to pay compensation to INCO at all came as a surprise to the British government. Whether it was out of loyalty to the Allied powers or even to INCO, which had provided much-needed nickel matte to the Soviet Union during earlier war years, or for some other reason, is unknown,[7] but it is clear that Moscow saw the whole deal as part and parcel of their post-war settlement with Finland. Moscow stubbornly tried to link payment of the compensation with Finland's war reparations to the Soviet Union. The Soviet negotiators even suggested that Finland should pay the compensation directly, thus attempting to exempt Moscow from pecuniary obligations to INCO. Both INCO and the Canadian government protested vehemently, and Moscow was left with the bill. Nevertheless, Moscow negotiated a plan of payments to INCO that corresponded nearly precisely with scheduled Soviet receipt of war reparations from Finland. The last payment from Moscow reached INCO's account in November 1953, over nine years after the Soviet annexation of Petsamo, and over three years after what had been stipulated in the Soviet–Canadian compensation agreement.[8]

For all practical intents and purposes, however, the property had been in Soviet hands ever since 22 October 1944, when the 14th Army took possession of Kolosjoki. How, then, did the new Soviet owners make use of Petsamo after having acquired it? This chapter looks more closely at activities in Petsamo in its first period as a Soviet property and thereby gives a sense of how the new acquisition became, by 1947, an integral part of the Soviet production regime. Three periods of this process – damage assessment, resurrection and finally achieving a place in the Soviet industrial complex – are addressed in turn. This development sheds light on the interests and forces that drove the property into Soviet hands in the first place, and on some of the challenges, related to labour and infrastructure, that faced the new community and industry in Petsamo. The major obstacle to industrial expansion was the lack of sufficient power supply, which proved to be a challenge that could be tackled only through international cooperation. Thus, the predominantly domestic Soviet story documented in this chapter provides the necessary background for understanding the ensuing period, where international relations come once again to the forefront.

Damage assessment

The destructive power of the Nazi scorched earth tactics was acutely felt in Petsamo. Using military communication lines, Yevgenii Shchelkunov and Aleksandr Gribin, respectively the newly appointed director and head engineer of the Soviet nickel plant, reported to the leader of the People's Commissariat for non-ferrous metallurgy, Petr F. Lomako, in Moscow about the situation in late November 1944.[9] In this communication, in addition to Petsamo's Russian name *Pechenga*, the new names of both the company town and the Soviet venture that would operate the mines were used. Kolosjoki became *Nikel* (simply Russian for nickel) and Petsamon Nikkeli OY was replaced by *Gornometallurgicheskii kombinat Pechenganikel* (the Pechenganikel Mining Combine – hereafter Pechenganikel for short).[10] These Soviet names will, from this point forward, be used in our narrative as well.

While acquainting themselves with the industrial and municipal infrastructure of the company town and its surroundings (see Map 3), Shchelkunov and Gribin observed that there was much to be done before production could resume. The smelting factory was almost completely destroyed, with only the metal parts of the building left standing. The smokestack, rising 150 metres above ground, had been blown to pieces, contributing to the destruction of the factory building when the remnants fell over it. To the south, the Jäniskoski power plant had suffered a similar fate. The turbine hall was in shambles, and the dam had been torn up by explosives in three places. Further upstream, the dam that regulated water flow to the power plant had also been blown up. However, the underwater parts of both dams seemed intact, and the high-voltage power line from Jäniskoski to Nikel was still standing.[11] Also the mines had suffered, albeit mostly surface damage. The nickel ore was still accessible in the relatively undamaged shafts. The problem was how to get the ore out of the mines. The shaft towers and heaving mechanisms had been severely damaged (one of them completely demolished), and it would take time to replace them.

Map 3 Industrial network in Pechenga 1944.

There was no output left over from earlier production on the site, as all nickel ore and nickel matte had been shipped away by the Germans, both from Nikel (Kolosjoki) and from Kirkenes port. Of the two supporting factories in the area – the brick factory (*Kirpichnyi zavod*) and the sawmill – Shchelkunov and Gribin had been able to inspect only the latter. They reported that it was burnt to the ground.[12] The industrial prospects looked bleak indeed.

But things could have been worse. Although the bridges between Nikel and the port of Liinahamari needed repair, the stretch of road connecting them was in good shape. In Nikel itself, both the water pipes and the central heating furnace were unscathed by explosives, albeit not in working condition. Fuel for the furnace was the main problem, as the Germans had set fire to 3,000 tons of coal. That fire was extinguished, and the new Soviet inhabitants hoped to save a third of the coal. By November, about 550 people – 400 soldiers that were kept in service for the purpose of initial rebuilding and 150 civilians – were working in and around Nikel.[13] They had recovered 3,500 square metres of housing (*zhilaya ploshchad*).[14] The risks involved in the clearing of housing and roadsides were palpable, and several soldiers lost their lives in removing German mines.[15] But, at least, the Finnish housing complexes provided better shelter from the approaching Northern winter than military tents or dugouts.

The task of building Nikel on the rubble of demolished Kolosjoki must have seemed overwhelming. There was no electricity, very little fuel of any sort, debris everywhere and the ever-present danger of being blown up by mines. And it was November. Daylight was already gone from the region, and the initial restructuring of the company town had to be conducted in the three-month-long polar night. Nonetheless, Shchelkunov and Gribin's messages to headquarters in Moscow reflect a strong will to emphasize possibilities rather than the seemingly insurmountable obstacles.

The first problem to tackle was the lack of manpower. The amount of work that lay ahead required many more than the 550 soldiers and civilians already in Pechenga. There was, however, a potential source of fresh hands nearby. Gribin had visited Kirkenes, about 50 kilometres to the northwest, and discovered 570 Soviet citizens in a deserted German camp. Apparently, the civilians had been transported by their German captors from Leningrad and Orel, the latter some 160 kilometres southwest of Moscow, and interned in Kirkenes. He immediately saw the potential in the able-bodied among them – 87 men and 234 women by his assessment – and asked that their assignment to Pechenganikel be arranged. Gribin also located captured soldiers. He proposed that 500 Soviet prisoners of war, also left in Kirkenes by the Germans, be transferred to Pechenganikel, in a tone that reveals the instrumental

Soviet approach to labour force: 'There are around 800 Russian [sic] former prisoners of war in Kirkenes. Out of these, 500 are exploitable for work, 150 are emaciated and in need of care and the rest are not able to work.'[16] He wanted Minister Lomako in Moscow to cut through the red tape, so he could employ the able-bodied among them as soon as possible. These misplaced persons were the responsibility of the all-powerful State Defense Committee (*GKO*)[17] and its division for repatriation. Gribin feared that this committee would allow them to go home. Lomako did intervene. In a cable to Anastas Mikoyan, the deputy prime minister (deputy chairman of the Council of People's Commissars) of the Soviet Union, he emphasized the need for a quick decision in the case of the civilian detainees: 'If we do not obtain permission [to include them in Pechenganikel's workforce] in time, they will be returned to their previous places of residence.'[18] It is unclear from the sources whether Gribin and Lomako's requests met with approval,[19] but we may assume that these prisoners, like other Soviet citizens – soldiers and civilians – who had spent time in German war camps were subjected to intense interrogations and sometimes severe punishment for 'treason' upon their homecoming.[20] In any case, this incident illustrates a problem that would haunt Pechenganikel for many years: insufficient labour recruitment.

It was not only unskilled labour that was in demand. Lomako pleaded with Mikoyan to confirm that several ITRs *(inzhenerno-tekhnicheskie rabotniki:* engineers and technicians) be posted for duty in Nikel. He presented the deputy prime minister with a list of named specialists. Interestingly, among them were two of the Severonikel engineers who had examined the Petsamon Nikkeli OY mines almost five years earlier, Petrov and Frantsuzov. The two were already on location but needed confirmation from the top that their positions at Pechenganikel would be permanent. Lomako called for a range of qualified labourers to be sent to Nikel, such as geologists, mining surveyors, mining engineers, workshop leaders and construction leaders. Many of these would come from factories that were under the command of his ministry already. In addition, to ensure that the political aspect was taken care of the new

Soviet company town would have to have its own party committee. To organize and head this, Lomako nominated Aleksandr Smirnov from the Murmansk *oblast* committee. Smirnov had, according to Lomako, already accepted the task.[21] Thus we see that a number of highly specialized people were required to make up a Soviet local community, and the specific personnel that would live and work in Nikel were selected and approved at a very high level.

In general, a sense of great haste is evident in the first dispatches from Nikel. There is little doubt that it was important to both Moscow and the local engineers that the nickel mines should restart production as soon as possible. However, a more prosaic reality called for expediency, as Gribin explained in one of his messages: 'In the winter there are usually big snowdrifts in the area. Therefore, we need to make use of the coming 1.5 to 2 months for moving goods. Later all transport will be impossible.'[22] Well aware that Nikel would become almost isolated under the heavy snow, Shchelkunov and Gribin wanted to ensure that their stocks were as full as possible before winter rendered any substantial transfer of supplies impracticable.

From Mintsvetmet's dispatches we can get an idea of which items were direly needed in Nikel. For transport, fifty Studebaker trucks,[23] four passenger vehicles, ten tractors and ten horses were required. The horses had to come fully equipped with harnesses and accompanied by fodder. The fuel situation was not good, and 400 tons of diesel, 200 tons of gasoline and 45 tons of motor oil was provided. Sawmill equipment, excavators, caterpillars and even two airplanes were requested. Warm clothes and footgear, protective clothing for work, bedding for 500 people and cutlery and crockery would reach Pechenganikel from the Red Army, Leningrad and Severonikel. Most importantly, however, food for six months to keep the isolated place afloat through the winter was needed.[24] These were just a few of the supplies that were partly requested and received, and partly only requested. Of course, a lot more was necessary to make up a well-functioning community, but for the time being the residents of Nikel would have to get by on whatever was available. Interestingly, and somewhat predictably, Gribin requested to have a supply of vodka sent. He had agreed with the military officers in Nikel that a daily ration of 100 grams of the comforting drops be given to the soldiers.[25]

For Shchelkunov, Gribin and their workers there was no time to lose. The nickel mines should yield metal as soon as possible. After all, the precious nickel was still very much in demand, as the Red Army continued to be engaged in a war with Germany. Now, there was no possibility of refining the ore in Nikel, but it could be transported to the Severonikel plant in Monchegorsk. The planned nickel smelting plant in Nikel was eagerly awaited by Moscow, as this would make it possible to reduce the ore to nickel matte, a product that was much easier and less expensive to transport for further refining. All these developmental demands were put to Pechenganikel's management, and there was no doubt about Nikel's significance – for the short-term war effort, but even more so in the long run. Nikel was an integral part of the future Soviet rise to the pinnacle of the world nickel industry.

Phase one: The resurrection of Nikel

Transforming Kolosjoki the war theatre into Nikel the productive company town happened remarkably fast. This process involved linking three locations – the nickel plant and mines, the Liinahamari port and the company town – together into a functioning network. The challenges faced were also threefold. Enough workers had to be not only attracted, but also retained and shaped into a productive work collective. Then, supplies needed for both industrial development and for human consumption had to be secured. This was at the outset difficult in a country reeling from the damaging effects of war. Finally, it was of utmost importance to develop a satisfactory system of infrastructure, in terms of transport routes, industrial installations and housing.

In a manner typical of the highly encouraged and undoubtedly superimposed Soviet popular enthusiasm, the new workers of Nikel fought their way through the winter of 1946 and made progress. It is said about this period in Nikel that '[i]t was a time of mass enthusiasm and brave and creative decision-making'. The same, clearly patriotic author describes the tempo of work in the company town as 'bordering on the humanly possible', noting how the workers, 'after having finished one shift, went straight on with the second clearing off debris in the polar night lit up only by campfires'.[26] There is something to be said for such a description, the somewhat romantically uncritical approach to the Soviet system notwithstanding. The superimposed production targets that reigned in the Soviet command economy might not have been sustainable over time, but the planned economy did at certain times yield impressive short-term results. This was probably never truer than in the last years of the Second World War and the first period after the war. It was a time of crisis and rebuilding, and the collective spirit in the victorious Soviet Union, and in Nikel, seemed to thrive despite the hardships to which the workers were subjected.

The workers' efforts were of course directed and controlled in a detailed fashion from the top echelons of the Soviet state. In the spring of 1945, the Leningrad-based Soyuznikelolovoproekt, a so-called scientific research institute (NII),[27] was given the task of developing complete plans for restarting the nickel industry in Pechenga. A group of forty-five specialists set up and manned a local branch of Soyuznikelolovoproekt in the company town,[28] and throughout the spring and early summer formed a plan for the rebuilding and development of Nikel. Their results were discussed in a meeting in Moscow between the specialists, Mintsvetmet and Glavnikelkobalt, on 27 July 1945. The first phase *(pervaya ochered)* of Soyuznikelolovoproekt's plan was geared to achieve pre-war capacity at the nickel plant by the end of 1946, employing two electric furnaces and two convertors (vessels for chemical reaction).[29] This would enable Pechenganikel to produce 6,000 tons of nickel matte a year, and annually extract 210,000 tons of ore.[30] Compared to the result during the one full war year when Petsamon Nikkeli OY was under German control, the Soviet ambitions were a bit lower. In 1943, just in excess of 222,000 tons of ore and slightly less than 8,000 tons of matte came out of Petsamo.³¹ However, as we shall see, Soviet plans for the near future were far more ambitious.

One of the basic Soviet premises for the development of Nikel was that it should strive to preserve the technological solutions already in place and make use of any equipment left by its previous owners.³² As we saw in Chapter 2, the industrial site of Kolosjoki was indeed state-of-the-art when it was first built up. This was something that the Severonikel engineers had witnessed and reported on at the tail end of the Winter War (see Chapter 3). That the Soviet authorities sought to capitalize on the access to Western technology is therefore not surprising. The technical documentation on the nickel works and test results from the ore were understandably attractive to the new owners. It seems to have been very important to Shchelkunov and Gribin to obtain Petsamon Nikkeli OY's documentation. This material was handed over in late 1944.³³ Furthermore, some German notes on Petsamo had ended up in Soviet hands, when the Nazi forces retreated on the Ukrainian front in 1945. Soviet troops had, in a formerly German-controlled nickel refinery, discovered an archive containing useful information about the Petsamo ore originating from IG Farben.³⁴ Thus, the new Pechenganikel combine could rely on comprehensive information both about the ore and the technical solutions applied at the plant. The Soviet awareness of Western technology and the emphasis on maintaining Petsamon Nikkeli OY's equipment seem to indicate that Moscow saw potential in non-Soviet production approaches. Arguably, Lomako and Mintsvetmet sought to maintain the original system of production there, perhaps for use as a model factory for the rest of the developing Soviet nickel industry.

Soyuznikelolovoproekt was not only charged with developing the industrial side of Nikel. It was also given the task of planning a complete town – with roads, airport, nurseries, schools, hospital, administration buildings, telegraph, fire station, shops and other necessities. For this, the specialists were to consult the academy of architecture, with clear instructions to make sure that there would be plenty of spaces for outdoor sports.³⁵ Also, the main transportation line had to be established. This was of particular importance, as Nikel was mostly cut off from usable roads to the east. Liinahamari port on the Pechenga Fjord was picked as the main exit. The road from Nikel to Liinahamari had to be able to take heavy transport vehicles carrying incoming supplies for the combine but also outgoing nickel matte, to be transported from Liinahamari by boat and then by train from Murmansk to Monchegorsk and Severonikel for further refining. The tasks of building Liinahamari port and dwellings for local workers and the construction and manning of public services were all assigned to the Pechenganikel combine.[36] The plans were comprehensive and added further to the combine's long list of tasks.

This first phase of work in Nikel was projected for completion by the end of 1946.[37] An average of 3,500 workers were expected to be involved in the rebuilding at any given time, some 1,500 working directly in construction itself and the rest in various support functions. In addition, 350 engineers and technical workers would be employed.[38] Again, the problem of recruitment arose. It was not easy to attract a sufficient number of workers to an isolated outpost like Nikel. Instead of 'attracting', therefore, 'mobilization' or organized recruitment (*orgnabor*) was chosen to obtain sufficient labour supply.[39] This had been done many times before in support of grand industrial projects, especially during the years of Stalin's 'revolution from above', involving the collectivization and industrialization of the Soviet state in the 1930s.[40]

However, even though subjected to massive peer pressure and pressure from normative structures such as labour unions and youth organizations, Soviet citizens were not forcibly kept at the location to which they had been ordered. Therefore, the pill had to be sweetened, to make people stick to their assignments. Applying both the stick and the carrot simultaneously, the Soviet authorities forcibly recruited people to the North, while at the same time making it financially attractive. As the most prominent executive body of the Soviet Union in wartime, the State Defense Committee had allowed for a substantial markup of the wages at Pechenganikel: workers were to receive more than a double salary. For untrained staff, the regular pay was 500 rubles, whereas in Nikel it was 1,200. For engineers and technical staff, the raise was even better: from a regular 800 to 1,700 rubles. In addition, all travel expenses for employees and their families would be covered by the state. The soldiers that were involved in rebuilding Nikel also constituted a substantial extra cost. Various expenses for equipment, uniforms and so on added up to a total of 50 rubles per soldier per month. When multiplied by the projected number of 1,000 soldiers, the annual cost amounted to 600,000 rubles.[41]

From Pechenganikel's plans for how to get all these people to Nikel, it is obvious that simply ordering them was the preferred, and probably the only possible, option:

Already in Petsamo …	870
Soldiers stationed in Pechenga waiting for demobilization	700
Transferred from other Soviet enterprises …	180
Transferred from the reserve work force	250
Transferred from Komsomol	500
By organized recruitment in the 4th quarter	1,000
Total	3,500[42]

By these methods people came to Nikel from various places, like Vologda, Arkhangelsk and Leningrad oblasts – even all the way from the Urals, mainly from the nickel works Yuzhuralnikel, in the southern Urals. In addition, many arrived from nearby Monchegorsk.

The arrival of new residents of course had the positive effect of diminishing the problem of labour shortage, but it also made an already existing shortage even more felt: housing. There was simply not enough room for everyone in the buildings that had survived the German onslaught. People were scattered in basements, barracks and some in dugouts (*zemlyanki*). As part of the Finnish war reparations to the Soviet Union, prefabricated houses were transported to Nikel, but not in time to provide shelter during the first winter.[43]

Indisputable meteorological facts of snowfall, low temperatures and wind all contributed to creating difficulties in the resurrection of Nikel.

The local unit in charge of construction work, Glavalyuminstroi's Nikel branch, wanted to make sure this was known to their superiors when they reported to headquarters in Moscow:

> The geographic location of the Pechenganikel combine and its isolation from railways and industries, the climatic conditions etc. have limited the organization and progress of rebuilding the ... combine.
>
> From the very first day of organizing the project, problems pertaining to transport, self-sufficiency in terms of building materials, electric power, recruitment of laborers and technical employees, housing and establishment of everyday-life amenities for the workers have been on the agenda, and they still are.
>
> Solving these problems has been further complicated by the fact that the project is situated in the most remote part of the European polar region, more than 200 kilometers from the nearest railroad, without normal modes of transport and communication lines, in an area where it is hundreds of kilometers to the closest settlements and where the climatic conditions of the extreme north are violently present.[44]

The head engineer and deputy director of the construction project A. E. Berdnikov, who wrote these lines, was correct in emphasizing the isolation of his new workplace. In the Soviet context, Nikel was far more remote than Kolosjoki had been when it belonged to Finland. Finnish Petsamo had been connected to the south via the Arctic Highway – a main artery through northern Finland, albeit a poor one. The Finns also had free communications to the west, over the border to Norway. With Soviet Pechenga, it was a very different story. The only possible communication links were to the east and south. To the east stretched 205 km of rough terrain – or rough seas – to Murmansk and the nearest railroad station. To the south, there was nothing but tundra and marshland interspersed with belts of taiga.

Thus, while transforming Nikel from a place of hostilities into a place of production, the first residents were left largely to their own devices. Many tasks lay ahead, both on the industrial side and in making Nikel habitable. In the late winter and spring of 1945 Pechenganikel made progress in its core activity, namely producing nickel ore. In March, the first ore was brought out of the mines, although it would take some time before any significant quantities would come regularly.[45] That summer, Pechenga and Nikel became formally incorporated in the structure of Soviet society. On 22 June 1945, Pechenganikel officially became an enterprise in the Mintsvetmet system, and a month later, on 21 July the municipal organization of the Pechenga district and the establishment of its administration centre in Nikel were decreed by the USSR Supreme Soviet.[46]

Living conditions were improving, albeit slowly. In the course of 1945, a total of 17,844 square metres of housing had been recovered or built in the area; a nursery and a school were built, and even a movie theatre with 400 seats was erected.[47] Some of the houses had central heating, and the first streets of Nikel were taking shape, their names very much the same as in all Soviet urban areas at the time: Sovetskaya, Komsomolskaya and Pionerskaya.[48]

At the same time, there was much activity in and around the smelting plant. A new smokestack had been commissioned from the same American company that had built the first one for the Finns, the Alphons Custodis Chimney Construction Company. The manner in which this impressive 152.4-metre-tall structure was raised is illustrative of the impatience that seemed to reign in Nikel's early days. Two representatives of the American firm had arrived in Nikel in fall 1945 to oversee construction of the smokestack. However, with the dark and cold season looming in December, they decided to postpone further building, claiming that they did not have the necessary experience in erecting such a structure in polar winter conditions. But the departure of the American representatives did not stop the Soviet community. Some of the local workers suggested that they should try to raise the smokestack without the Americans – and that is what happened. They worked through the winter, using mostly equipment intended for mining operations. By August 1946, the smokestack was finished. In Soviet terms, the quality of the work was highly rated *(na khorosho)*.[49]

With the official establishment of the Pechenganikel combine in June 1945, the resurrection process in Nikel was driven by a dual structure. The combine, which was part of the Glavnikelkobalt system, was paralleled by the local offices of Glavalyuminstroi, the directorate for the building of aluminium and magnesium industries.[50] Both were, however, subordinate to Mintsvetmet (until March 1946 called *Narkomtsvetmet*), and thus everything ran through the offices of the minister of non-ferrous metallurgy, Petr F. Lomako. On the other hand, the duality of the Nikel arrangement might have been a reality only on paper. For example, Yevgenii Shchelkunov is identified as the director of both the combine and the construction enterprise, and his deputy director, Berdnikov, reports on behalf of both entities in 1946.[51] Even though the people of Nikel probably saw the two enterprises as one and the same, the duality must have posed certain administrative difficulties, as they had to report to and take directions from two different directorates, with different interests.

The lack of fresh supplies of equipment and goods was one of the most serious obstacles to success in Nikel, and one that it was very hard to tackle. As indicated above, the remoteness of Nikel would have constituted a challenge to even a well-oiled transport system. In this case, the transport system was far from well-oiled, as it had to be established from scratch after the Soviet takeover. Any supplies destined for Nikel had to proceed by at least three different modes of transport: railway to Murmansk, boat to Liinahamari and then further by truck to Nikel, so the risks of cargo damage were significant. The long-distance freight and the necessity of loading and reloading also entailed that transport costs were '2–3 times as high as … in central parts of the Soviet Union'.[52] Maintenance of roads and vehicles was, according to reports, considerably below par, and the supply of spare parts for trucks and cars was erratic. The bad roads frequently resulted in flat and damaged tyres, but replacement tyres were rarely available in Pechenga due to delayed shipments.[53] Transport was caught in a vicious circle of terrible driving conditions, delayed deliveries, lack of spare parts and inadequate repair facilities.

The serious logistics problems had negative consequences for overall productivity in Nikel. One thing was that ore was not shipped out as planned, due to lack of tyres for the trucks that were to carry the load to Liinahamari;[54] more serious was the general and ever-present shortage of a wide range of necessary supplies to the various units in the nickel production line. Nevertheless, metallurgical activity moved forward steadily throughout 1946. As noted, the first nickel ore was produced already in March 1945. Regularity improved, and by 1946, the tonnage of produced ore was according to plan.[55]

If measured in content of nickel however, the figures were less encouraging. The problem of low nickel percentage in the ore was also something that could be ascribed partly to logistical problems. To mine an ore field efficiently, it is necessary to undertake continuous chemical analysis to establish which area of the deposit is the richest. The laboratory facilities in Nikel were simply not adequate to provide such important information, partly due to lack of shipments of laboratory equipment. More importantly, the combine lacked qualified personnel to do the testing, as is evident from the following quote from head engineer Berdnikov's letter to the technical department and planning department in Mintsvetmet and Glavnikelkobalt:

> We have already for a full year asked the directorate [Glavnikelkobalt] to send an experienced chemist who can head our laboratory. Now, after the opening of the metallurgical workshop, the situation has become intolerable. The analyses we get are systematically wrong and come with enormous delays of 5–7 days, by which time they are already useless to us. Severonikel's analyses of the nickel matte we sent there in December, showed a nickel content that was on average 2% higher and a copper content that was 1% lower than our own samples. … Clearly, we cannot work like this any longer. … Please send, without delay, if only one experienced chemist in a permanent position.[56]

Obviously, it was not easy to get highly qualified personnel, especially to an outpost such as Nikel.

The combine did, through its Department for Rationalization and Innovation (BRIZ), attempt to ameliorate the efficiency problems. The management was eager for any suggestions from the employees that could help increase efficiency and was pleased to report that several measures had been enacted, with good results.⁵⁷ In November 1946, the combine made a breakthrough in its metallurgical process. The smelting plant – or metallurgical workshop (*metallurgicheskii tsekh*) as it was called – was put into production after an intense effort by the workers, who reportedly 'forgot about sleep and rest' in the days leading up to the opening.⁵⁸ The first smoke rose from the industrial chimney: the Pechenganikel combine had started to produce nickel matte. The hard work that lay behind this development was reported to Moscow, with unrestrained pride:

> even under these [polar] conditions … the metallurgical workshop ran evenly and without the hopeless practices and adjustments seen in many other enterprises. This big achievement is one of the metallurgical workers and the combine as a whole, who have approached the task with their full conscientiousness and thoroughness.⁵⁹

In the evening of 6 November 1946, the first half-ladle of a melted mixture of iron, nickel and copper sulfides came out of the electrical furnace, and 13 days later the first five tons of converted nickel matte were produced.⁶⁰ This marked the completion of the resurrection of the nickel production in Nikel. Pechenganikel was now a full member of the Soviet economic system.

An important part of the efforts to raise productivity in Nikel involved improving the formal competence of the workers. This was done both on site in the various workshops of the plant, where they would receive basic training *(tekhminimum)*, but also through funding of employees' education in technical colleges *(tekhnikum)* out of town. The most expedient way of raising the combine's level of competence was of course to try to recruit people who already had degrees or other formal qualifications. However, it proved very difficult to reach the number of 139 fully qualified engineers that was deemed necessary. By 1 January 1947, the combine had only eighty-three people in positions as engineers, although this did not mean that it actually employed eighty-three trained engineers. Only eleven had completed an engineering degree, sixteen had vocational degrees and the remaining fifty-six had no formal technical education whatsoever.⁶¹

Things were not made better by the very high turnover rate in the workforce. In the course of 1946, a total of 1,290 workers left the construction company in charge of the rebuilding of Nikel, to be replaced by only 910 individuals. In a workforce numbering a total of 1,768 individuals by 1 January 1947, the turnover was worrying.[62] The situation at the Pechenganikel combine itself was better. From 274 persons at the start of 1946, the number of industrial workers had risen to 811 by 31 December. However, a total of 255 individuals had left, for reasons such as death, illness, disability, arrest or simply failure to return after vacation.[63] Due to the turnover and the many new arrivals, productivity was lower than what the combine's management had hoped for. The need for introductory training was substantial in all modern industries, and even more so in Pechenganikel, a combine that was different from comparable enterprises because of its extensive usage of Western equipment. In the metallurgical workshop, the challenges of mastering techniques specific to the Pechenganikel equipment temporarily weakened the productivity and quality of work.[64]

The Soviet economic system had, since the introduction of the first five-year plan in 1928–32, been based on the central premise that almost every factor in the production cycle was quantifiable. To be able to plan the economy, the State Planning Commission (Gosplan) would establish numerical expressions for every input that went into a production process and any output that process might generate. One of the central inputs in Soviet industry was of course human labour. Goals for labour productivity on the central aggregate level in the documents of Gosplan were broken down as one moved closer to the actual production site. For grassroots enterprises like Pechenganikel, the workload was expressed in productivity goals, or norms that each individual worker was expected to fulfil. These norms were not only tools for planning but also actively used to increase individual productivity. Workers would be rated according to their ability to reach the set production targets, and could, depending on the degree of success, be awarded the title of either 'shock worker' *(udarnik)* or stakhanovite *(stakhanovets)*. The norms did not represent upper limits to production. Far from it, overfulfilling the plan *(perevypolnyat plan)* was the goal and was required if a worker wanted to be considered either an *udarnik* or a *stakhanovets*. At the Pechenganikel combine, as in all Soviet workplaces, this system of internal 'socialist competition' between workers was applied to boost labour efficiency.[65]

In the mines, measuring individual output was a matter of weighing the amount of ore each person, or work-team, managed to bring out. Since the start of production in 1945, the Pechenganikel miners had learned to tackle their equipment and the conditions in the mines and had therefore become far more efficient by the end of the year. This change was reflected in drastically increased production norms for the mines in the planning for 1946, in one sector by as much as 75 per cent. Nevertheless, fulfilling the norm was achievable for most of the miners, if we judge by the percentage who managed to do so. In 1946, 96 per cent of them reached the set target.[66]

From the Pechenganikel annual report to Glavnikelkobalt, it becomes clear that the management of Pechenganikel saw 'socialist competition' as an important means of fulfilling not only one-year plans, but also the current five-year plan. Using the experience of the most productive workers to better their peers, and publicizing production results in the 'book of honour' and on the 'honour board', they hoped to stimulate further heightening of norms:

> Of all the employees at the combine, 18 people have made a personal commitment to fulfilling the five-year plan on time, and 102 people fulfilled their annual norms on time. Comrade PERSHUKOV has transferred his experience in multiperforation drilling techniques, which is now being applied by all the other drillers. In the mechanical repair-workshop, carpenters TSVETKOV and SHOKIN have moved on to operating several machines simultaneously and teach the others to do the same through visual demonstration and conversation. Blacksmith SHESTAKOV started working with two assistants, welding material over constant heat in several forges simultaneously, by this increasing his monthly production to 200–250 percent [of the norm]. His know-how is now used by all the other blacksmiths in the workshop.

For productive successes in 1946 we have introduced:

    To the honour board 15 individuals
    Into the book of honour 13 individuals

The increasing number of competitors and the growth of the stakhanovite movement, the strengthening and multiplication of the productive achievements of the competition's frontrunners in their struggle to fulfill Stalin's post-war five-year plan on time constitute a genuine foundation for the completion of the plan for 1947.[67]

This 'socialist competition' was further augmented by piecework (*sdelshchina*), whereby workers were paid according to what they produced. As the resurrection of Pechenganikel got underway, the management planned to introduce more workers to this wage system. Although piecework would lead to higher wage costs, it was assumed that the cost per produced unit of nickel matte would go down or at least remain constant.[68]

The wide use of piecework must be seen in relation to the general push in post-war Soviet industry. The fourth five-year plan (1946–50) had many of the same qualities as the mass mobilization seen during the first five-year plan in the early 1930s. The Second World War had wreaked havoc on the Soviet economy, and the drive to re-establish the production base was intense. Again, as in the 1930s, the emphasis was on higher output from the heavy industrial complex.[69] However, 'socialist competition' did not always create 'superworkers': it could also push people beyond the limits of endurance. Norms were sometimes inflated to unattainable levels, and the pressure for efficiency created tensions between managers and their subordinates.[70]

In Nikel, the high demands on the workers were combined with very difficult living conditions. As each worker had an average private living area of 2.45 square metres,[71] it is rather unlikely they were able to get enough rest between shifts. As could be expected, the statistics reflect a degree of faltering morale. In the construction enterprise, 523 workers had been put down for disciplinary breaches. Of them, 280 had been shirking, 34 had left work without permission, 4 soldiers had deserted and 27 had simply refused to work. For these offences, 251 had been ordered to correctional work, 17 had been imprisoned and 143 had been 'subjected to administrative punishment'.[72] On the other hand, when reporting to central authorities in Moscow, the combine management did find that the reasons for disciplinary breaches were more complex than a plain case of poor work ethics:

> In addition to the well-known factor of personal lack of discipline, the harsh living conditions at the combine play a role. The village [*poselka*], having twice been a region of bitter battles and subjected to additional and malicious destruction at the hands of fleeing Germans, was completely demolished at the beginning of 1945. Through rebuilding of the living quarters that remained relatively undamaged and construction of new prefabricated housing, the overall building mass has been expanded to 21.5 thousand square meters at the end of 1946. Of this, 2.8 thousand square meters are in temporary barracks. In addition, 1.8 thousand square meters that are not defined as living space [*nezhilaya ploshchad* – dugouts, tents etc.] are used for housing purposes. This is of course far from sufficient, all the more so because 2.5 thousand square meters of the overall surface is used by regional institutions and organizations. The average living area per inhabitant is 2.45 square meters. These harsh living conditions are compounded by the high level of prices on municipal services, and on central heating in particular. … [I]t is completely clear that alongside the harshness of living conditions described above, the high living costs by no means encourage a consolidation of the workforce.[73]

As we see, Pechenga was at the end of 1946 still a very difficult place to live. Housing was crowded if not downright awful, transport was terrible at best, and consumer goods overpriced if at all available.

Despite all these problems related to labour, housing and supplies, the construction enterprise in charge of rebuilding Nikel had accomplished a long list of projects in the course of 1946. A power unit providing electricity to the smelter was in place, an ore crusher had been set up and a storage building for crushed ore had been built; the smelter was working, the smokestack was up, cranes at the two shaft towers were working, a water tower was in place, and ventilation was provided in the factory. So, although there was much room for improvement, especially in living conditions, the combine concluded that it was prepared to take on the challenges of the following year. According to the annual report, 'the preparatory work in the mines and the start-up of the metallurgical workshop in 1946 constitute necessary conditions for the successful fulfillment of the plan in 1947.'[74] Pechenganikel was, at least in the minds of its managers, no longer a construction project: it was ready for the next phase in its life as a Soviet combine.

Phase two: Becoming a Soviet enterprise

By the end of 1946, the reconstruction of Nikel had reached the point where full industrial production could commence. In a decree dated 9 October 1946, Minister of Non-ferrous Metallurgy Petr F. Lomako ordered a commission of engineers and bureaucrats to travel to Nikel. Their task was, through thorough examination, to make sure the Pechenganikel combine was ready to stand on its own feet. The minister wanted frequent updates on their findings, and a detailed report containing recommendations as to which measures, if any, still remained to be taken to ensure a speedy start to full production.[75] Under the leadership of Severonikel director V. I. Nosal, the group of engineers reported: 'From the moment of the first production of nickel matte, on 19 November 1946, the commission considers the first phase of the "Pechenganikel" rebuilding project completed, and that [the combine] is now in production.'[76]

In February 1947, Lomako ordered the closure of Glavalyuminstroi's construction branch in Nikel and the transfer of all its workers, ITRs and executives to Glavnikelkobalt and the Pechenganikel combine. All equipment, workshops, means of transport and building material were to go the same way.[77] By this decree, Pechenganikel was counted among the nine enterprises in the Soviet metallurgical industry that contributed to providing the socialist state with nickel.[78] This is not to say that the housing and logistics problems described above had been solved. Quite the contrary, Pechenga was a place of hardship for many years to come,[79] but at least industrial production was underway, providing the area with its raison d'être.

With industrial progress came higher expectations from central authorities. Pechenganikel, like all other Soviet enterprises, faced heavy demands on productivity in the annual plans, and had to find ways to increase its output. A restrictive element in these efforts was the limited supply of energy. The nickel refining process, involving convertors and electrical smelting furnaces, was extremely power-intensive, but electricity was scarce in Nikel after the German demolition of the Jäniskoski power plant. A high-voltage power line had been set up in the summer of 1946, stretching all the way to the Tuloma hydroelectric power plant 154 km to the southeast,[80] but this did not supply sufficient energy for any substantial increases in production. In 1947, Pechenganikel did not manage to reach the target amount for smelted nickel ore envisioned in the annual plan.[81] Power shortages were experienced by the whole of Murmansk *oblast* after the war, caused primarily by the growing industrial consumption in Nikel and Monchegorsk and at the aluminium works in Kandalaksha. We will have a closer look at the long-term solution to Nikel's power deficit problems, which involved the active participation of both Finland and Norway, in the next chapter.

One of the actors that tried to ameliorate the energy deficiency problem may be described as a virtually new player in Nikel. Although the local Communist Party organization had been present since 1945, it took some time before it developed into a force to be reckoned with. Alongside the rest of the new Soviet settlement, the Pechenga regional committee of the Communist Party struggled to get on its feet for the first few years. As of 1946, the committee had no furniture or party office, although it did have access to a small house in Nikel.[82] It would not be long, however, before this changed. With an organization paralleling the state structure, the Communist Party was present on all levels in Soviet life and was becoming increasingly active in Nikel as well. The Party

Figure 5 The dam in Jäniskoski destroyed by retreating German troops, October 1944. Cascades of water push through the breaches. Photo: Archive Rune Rautio.

Figure 6 The power plant and dam in Jäniskoski before demolition, 1944. Photo: Archive Rune Rautio.

had the right to meddle in matters of industrial production and did so with few constraints. In workshops and offices in Nikel, there were party agitators responsible for spreading proletarian consciousness among staff, whether they were Party members or not. Communist agitation at the workplace was a very palpable part of Soviet industrial life and was meant to give the employees a broader perspective on their work efforts. Individual productivity was described as the worker's own contribution to the Soviet Union's ascendancy on the world political stage. To the extent that this message was accepted, the Communist Party provided the workers with a deeper, albeit markedly propagandized, motivation for participating in the ever-present campaigns for higher productivity.[83]

The ability of the local party organization to remedy problems in production was mostly limited to initializing various drives to boost productivity. In the case of energy deficiency in Murmansk *oblast*, the Party organized a competition for energy economization involving all the enterprises in the region, and also exerted pressure to speed up the construction of the Niva hydropower plant near Kandalaksha.[84]

The Party was also a channel through which other questions, less weighty than those relating to the place of the Soviet Union in international politics, could be raised. The following complaint at a plenary session in the *oblast* committee in Murmansk was probably meant to make alarm bells go off in the concerned enterprises:

> The chairman of the Pechenga regional committee harshly criticized the work of Murmansk shipping company for its unsatisfactory service to passengers. The passenger terminal is dirty and has no hot water, on the passenger boats the most basic amenities are missing, the ships sail very irregularly, and passengers are forced to wait for weeks for a voyage. Newspapers and journals are very delayed coming to Pechenga. The oblast education office, health services and others are not supporting the newly established region.[85]

By bringing such problems to the attention of the party structure, one could hope that pressure would be exerted to solve them. However, for Pechenga, the main problem was one that could not be readily solved: the remoteness of the place. It remained difficult to get there. A Party report on the sea transport problems two years later shows that little or nothing had been achieved in bettering the situation. The Party was still pressing the ministry to guarantee a minimum of regularity in ship services, and that passengers should be provided with a 'civilized voyage' (*kulturnaya perevozka*).[86] Transport was to remain a problematic sector for Pechenganikel for as long as it had to rely on boats to carry supplies and people for the better part of the journey along the Murmansk coast (see Map 4).

In the face of unsolvable problems, the Communist Party and the combine concentrated on what could be done. As usual, intensifying the productivity of already strained workers was a popular choice among Party officials and managers, if not so much among the employees themselves. Nevertheless, there were reports of workers who excelled far beyond what could be expected and effectively rendered the planning figures obsolete.

An example from Pechenganikel was the stakhanovite driller Shershukov, who on 9 June 1946, allegedly drilled a total of 200 metres of explosion holes in hard rock. He thereby overfulfilled his daily norm by 1,038 per cent,[87] a number that in and of itself raises several

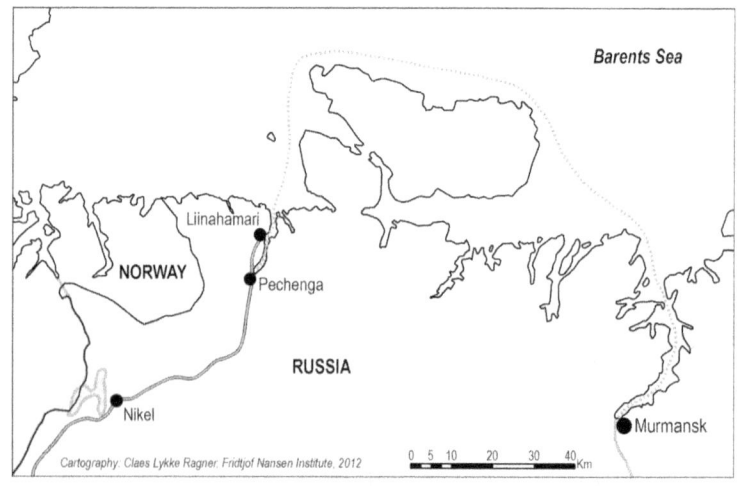

Map 4 Sea voyage Murmansk–Pechenga.

questions about the accuracy of norm-setting. In any case, both the combine and individual employees did well in socialist competitions. In 1947, Pechenganikel achieved second place in the all-Soviet Union competition between enterprises within non-ferrous metals, received eight prizes in the all-Union competition between mining brigades, and obtained the travelling trophy banner *(perekhodyashchee znamya)* from the Murmansk Communist Party committee for energy economization.

The government gave prizes to sixty-six individuals at the combine and 155 received medals from Mintsvetmet. A total of twenty workers were inscribed in the book of honour and thirty-four on the honour board.[88] Judging by the sources, both from the industrial realm and the party orbit, socialist competitions were considered the single most important non-industrial input in production.[89] However, a problem associated with overfulfilment and the 'storming' *(shturmovshchina)* efforts to achieve set targets in production plans was that they often simply moved a problem from one sector of the economy to another. The feverish productivity tended to create bottlenecks through irregular delivery of supply, low-quality output and mismanagement of labour and the means of production.[90]

The measure to beat was always the plan, and therefore the most important adversary in any competition was the norm. There could be no victory without overfulfilling the production target. Socialist competition went further than merely boosting productivity. Earning the title of 'shock-worker' meant being recognized as a successful Soviet citizen in many ways. Stakhanovites or shock-workers not only received higher incomes enabling better material lives for themselves and their families. As labour was equated with heroism and high morale, stakhanovites were also considered morally superior to lesser workers. The implications of socialist competition, as expressed in a tight industrial town, thus went much further than just the professional status of the employees. It permeated the lives of the workers, also at home.[91] Any member of the production collective was measured against the ideal of stakhanovites. A typical expression of the juxtaposition between 'good' and 'bad' workers is found in the Pechenganikel annual report from 1947. After a thorough overview of offences perpetrated by various employees at the combine, the management quantifies – without pause – the opposite behaviour, reporting a total number of 1,142 premiums given to 'good, honest workers with high production figures'.[92] In other words, producing high volumes was associated with the virtue of honesty – whereas the less productive workers would be seen as dishonest shirkers.

Irrespective of the workers' productivity, and despite logistical and other problems, the industrial future of Pechenganikel seemed very promising. During 1947, the permanent geological surveying team working in the Pechenga area had certainly overfulfilled their plans. Substantial new and thus far unexplored nickel resources had been located, increasing the projected ore occurrence in Pechenga by a staggering 641 per cent.[93] The expansion of Pechenganikel would in the following years be a formative activity for the combine. As new and more promising ore deposits were discovered and exploited, it became increasingly evident that the Soviet Union had struck gold, or at the very least a lot of nickel, when acquiring Petsamo at the end of the Second World War.

Making haste

As we see from the previous sections, the Soviet approach to its new property was one of great impatience. Nikel was to be rebuilt as soon as possible, and little time was wasted on meticulous planning and preparation. Kolosjoki had barely ceased to be a war zone when the first civilian mining specialists, Shchelkunov and Gribin, were on site to assess damages and make plans for a speedy recovery of industrial production. Before the end of 1944, soldiers and prisoners of war were already clearing off debris in the demolished company town.

Allegedly, contemporary Western experts estimated that the rebuilding of the factory would require at least ten years.[94] However, by the end of 1946, only two years after the final battle for Kolosjoki, the complex and power-intensive metallurgical processes of smelting and converting nickel ore were underway in the renamed, if not completely revived, town of Nikel. In 1949, a second electric smelter furnace and a second convertor were both installed, marking the end of what Soyuznikelolovoproekt in 1945 had referred to as the first phase of the rebuilding project.[95] This meant that the plant had returned to pre-war capacity in a mere four years. By any measures, the speed with which Pechenganikel was again producing nickel matte was remarkable.

This rapid development was paralleled in most of post-war Soviet industry. The fourth five-year plan, which commenced in 1946 and aimed to exceed pre-war output figures by 1950, subjected all sections of the economy to immense pressures on productivity. The priority was on factories rather than housing, with the central authorities primarily intent on re-establishing heavy industrial sites.[96] Also, a new factor that would increase the importance of Soviet heavy industry, including nickel production, came into play. After the collapse of the wartime enemies Germany and Japan, relations between the Soviet Union and the Western powers soured quickly, and by the summer of 1947 the two blocs that were to characterize the Cold War polarization were forming. As the Cold War grew colder, the Soviet industry grew stronger, and was, by 1950, in a good position to embark on the coming arms race.[97] With its now well-established position in the armaments industry, nickel production was among the sectors that would have high priority. The role of nickel as a strategic metal in the Soviet economy was further augmented with the introduction of steel alloys containing nickel in jet engines, satellites, rockets and other space-age technologies.

It is not surprising, therefore, that activity in Nikel was intense during the last three years of the fourth five-year plan (1948, 1949 and 1950). The extraction of ore had become increasingly mechanized, and by 1949 the management could declare that 'the Kaula mine is now an example of full mechanization of all basic processes in mining'.[98] Obviously, replacing manual labour with mechanized techniques allowed for a substantial rise in extraction productivity, and the ambitious goals envisioned in Soyuznikelolovoproekt's plans from 1945 seemed attainable. While the first phase of the project had been to re-establish pre-war industrial capacity at Nikel, the second phase foresaw a doubling of produced ore to 420,000 tons annually, and production of nickel matte to 12,000 tons.[99] It would take the combine until 1952 to approach an ore production of 420,000 tons, but the output of nickel matte exceeded 12,000 tons already in 1950:

The numbers in table 1 show a formidable increase in both ore extraction and matte production, although, when looking at the ore extraction numbers, one might have expected the amount of produced nickel matte to be higher. This lack of correspondence between the increase in extracted ore and output of matte was due to several factors, but mainly that the nickel content in the extracted ore was decreasing, the further into the mountain the drillers proceeded. For a while, production norms for nickel matte could be fulfilled through intensified mining, that is, simply providing more ore for the smelters and convertors. However, it was clear to the management that the decreasing nickel content would, over time, mean that the combine needed its own enrichment unit, to help increase nickel content per weight unit of ore. To this end, an experimental enrichment plant was installed in 1950, with a prospective production start in 1953.[100] By 1953, the ore field was expanded with two additional mines, in the Kammikivi and Kotselvaara deposits but a fully fledged enrichment plant was not in place until 1958.[101]

In terms of production and keeping in mind the difficulties faced after the Soviet takeover, the years between 1948 and 1950 must be seen as a breakthrough period for the Pechenganikel combine. Many problems were ameliorated, most prominently in the logistics. In 1948, the

Table 1 Production of Nickel Ore and Nickel Matte in Nikel 1948–53 (All Production Figures in Tons)

	1948	1949	1950	1951	1952	1953
Ore	109,125	170,402	293,136	367,000	411,500	471,800
Matte	6,312	9,460	13,022	13,769	15,175	16,390

Sources: Annual reports from Pechenganikel 1948–53 in RGAE, f. 9037, op. 1

combine's transport fleet was thoroughly renewed through the transfer of almost 150 new vehicles (tractors, cars and trucks of various sizes).[102] As a consequence, in 1949, the transport section managed to fulfil its plans for the first time, despite a dramatic heightening of norms.[103] Thus, a major bottleneck was removed from the chain of production. As the metallurgical side of production (smelting and converting of ore) became more developed and efficient at Pechenganikel, the combine prioritized shipping nickel matte rather than the much bulkier raw ore to Monchegorsk. This shift had advantageous economic effects as the transport of nickel matte was about ten times cheaper than moving raw nickel ore of equivalent nickel content.[104]

That the combine was able to make this type of decision is a reflection of it becoming more and more a complete industrial enterprise, and less and less of a post-war rebuilding site. In the annual reports from the combine in the last three years of the 1940s, a sense of higher standards is evident. The once-numerous complaints about lack of supplies and other difficulties give way to a more business-like and pragmatic tone, with increased weight on developmental issues rather than the incessant need to patch up an industrial process in constant crisis. In turn, the industrial progress and gradual normalization of production provided more room for activities not necessarily connected to heightened productivity. An example of this is how the metallurgical plant in 1949 undertook a major effort to bring tidiness *(navedenie kultury)* to the workplace and its immediate surroundings by clearing off litter and industrial debris.[105] Although Nikel was still far from a comfortable place to live, the combine management could from this time on give consideration to other things than covering the minimum needs for industrial production and survival.

Already in this period, the first signs of concern about the damaging effects of industrial production began to appear, and as such can be seen as a forerunner of the environmental engagement that was later to be focused on the Pechenga industry. In 1949, the management reported that the metallurgical plant was not sufficiently ventilated. As a result, the working environment around the smelters was filled with waste gases,[106] highly harmful if inhaled over time. This issue was again taken up in the report for 1950, as the ventilation problem had not been solved.[107] Also in the mines there were health concerns related to the prevalence of silicosis among the miners. The management did not report the number of cases, but the problem was deemed serious enough for them to require a central investigation into the causes and possible prevention of the disease.[108] The devastating impact on both human health and the surrounding natural environment of industrial activity in Pechenga was later to become a prominent feature of how Nikel was perceived from the outside, both in neighbouring countries to the west and elsewhere in Russia.

For the time being, however, a main concern of those working at the combine was still the deplorable state of their living quarters. Although the industrial progress was palpable, housing problems had neither been accorded high priority, nor solved. A certain minimum had been achieved with the increase in average living space per inhabitant from 2.45 square metres in 1946 (see above) to 4 square metres by 1948.[109] After this, however, the improvement of housing seemed to be at a standstill, and when the average living space per person in 1951 still hovered at 4.69 square metres, Minister Lomako in Moscow intervened. A ministerial order (*prikaz*) issued in May that year included a detailed list of house-construction materials that were to be shipped to Nikel. The *prikaz* meticulously defined which individuals and which organizations were responsible for the safe transport of these supplies to Nikel,[110] which was indicative of Lomako's wish to ensure accountability. The housing problem lay not only in the shortage of square metres itself, but also that many families were either living in overcrowded apartments or occupying rooms never meant for accommodation at all. In 1950, sixty families were sharing an apartment with another family, twenty families were living in communal kitchens, and sixty-six families were dwelling in basements.[111] In many ways, living conditions were the one sector of life in Nikel that was the hardest to improve. Even after Lomako's intervention, housing in Nikel remained problematic. As of 1953 a total of 308 people were still living in basements, while the average living space was still below five square metres (ranging from 4.5 to 4.85 square metres depending on type of housing) – far below the nine square metres defined as sufficient in Soviet sanitary norms.[112]

* * *

The frantic activity in Nikel during its first six years as a Soviet possession confirms that Pechenga was far more than just an accidental booty. Clearly, the Soviet Union coveted the area, as became evident from June 1940 onwards (see Chapter 3), for more than strictly geostrategic reasons. As we have seen, the new Soviet owners in Nikel put in substantial efforts intended to transform Kolosjoki swiftly from a battleground to a productive industrial community. This was accomplished even though communications between Nikel and the rest of the Soviet Union made logistics extremely difficult – far more difficult than when the area was still Finnish. If geography is not only a function of location, but also a reflection of accessibility, it is fair to say that Pechenga was a very different geographical place when it became part of the Soviet Union. The Soviet transformation of Nikel was largely a matter of coping with the area's increased level of isolation and trying to overcome logistical problems.

One might argue that the speed with which Nikel was resurrected was merely a reflection of the standard Soviet approach to industrial projects, and even more so during the fourth five-year plan. And indeed, Soviet industry, both in the country as a whole and on the Kola Peninsula, was undergoing a massive and high-speed rebuilding programme after the Second World War. It is also true that, since the years of collectivization and industrialization in the 1930s, the typical Soviet manner of running projects had become one of 'shock-working' and campaigns in line with Stalin's wish to 'foster utopian industrial schemes by terrorizing doubters and encouraging enthusiasts'.[113] As we have seen, the stakhanovite movement in Nikel worked just that way. However, these Soviet precedents cannot account fully for why the nickel industry in Pechenga was included in the overall economy with such haste. After all, the area could have been left alone, at least for a while, until the rest of the economy was on firmer ground and the new border with Norway was firmly established.

We must seek the explanation for Nikel's speedy transformation in the deep appreciation of the industrial value of the area among Soviet leaders. Not only was it clear to them that the ore deposits in Pechenga were of potentially vast proportions. Nikel/ Kolosjoki was also seen as a repository of the knowledge and mining methods and equipment exclusive to the world's foremost nickel producer, the International Nickel Company of Canada. From the very moment that Soviet experts – those three Severonikel engineers (see Chapter 3) – laid eyes on the nickel plant in Kolosjoki in March 1940, it became obvious that Petsamon Nikkeli OY's plant and mines could be useful as more than just another source of the strategic metal. It could also provide instruction for other enterprises within Soviet mining, in terms of the physical organization of the mining and in terms of equipment. There is evidence that Soviet authorities in the early phase of rebuilding in Nikel emphasized the need to preserve Canadian equipment and technological solutions.[114] However, as the nickel plant became more and more a part of the Soviet economic system, the foreign technology also became a problem in and of itself, as supplies of spare parts and maintenance instructions were difficult to come by in the isolated Soviet industry.[115] Nonetheless, economic factors, including the desire for foreign technology, clearly had served to motivate the Soviet acquisition. Thus, the pace at which Nikel was developed after the war further underscores the argument made in the previous chapter about the importance of including economic motivations when assessing the Soviet wartime demands for the Petsamo region.

Limitations in power supply represented a main impediment to further heightening the economic significance of Nikel. Capacity at the electrical furnaces and convertors could not be fully exploited if there was only one high-voltage power line stretching from the Tuloma power station, some 150 km away. Pechenganikel needed its own electricity source and began to look in the direction of the demolished power station in Jäniskoski for a solution. In the next chapter, we will examine how Jäniskoski, which was still Finnish territory after the Finnish–Soviet armistice agreement in September 1944, became a part of the Pechenganikel operation. Thus, we return from the predominantly Soviet account in this chapter to another dimension in Nikel's history, and one that once again brought the area onto the international scene.

5

Finland builds Soviet power

From the very start, it was clear to the Soviet Union that the nickel operation in Pechenga would require comprehensive electrification for it to become a successful venture. The remoteness of Nikel made external power supply too costly. Maintaining a high-voltage power line from Tuloma, for example, was not a viable long-term solution. The wear and tear exacted by the harsh climate would necessitate frequent repairs in a difficult terrain. Energy sources would have to be found in closer proximity to the smelting plant.

It was Kolenergo, an energy enterprise subordinated to the Ministry of Power Stations (Minelektrostantsii) that provided electricity in Murmansk oblast. Besides the Tuloma works, Kolenergo's most important installation was a group of hydropower plants on the river Niva, close to the aluminium industry in Kandalaksha in the southern part of the peninsula. But the Niva plants could hardly solve any of the problems in Pechenga: they were too far away. In general, the industrialization of the Kola Peninsula brought with it a dramatic increase in power demand, a demand with which Kolenergo could not keep pace. The lack of power sources threatened to halt industrial development, especially within the power-intensive metallurgical sector.[1] The future of Pechenganikel hinged on finding a good local solution to the energy question.

Power supply had been an issue also while Petsamo was under Finnish control. Canadian–Finnish Petsamon Nikkeli OY did not have to look far, though, as the nearby Pasvik River had an abundance of rapids that could be utilized for power generation. However, much of the river constituted the national border with Norway. That meant that

Figure 7 The Jäniskoski power plant shortly before demolition in October 1944. Photo: Archive Rune Rautio.

most of the rapids were the shared property of two states, and, more importantly, that one of two river banks was not Finnish territory. Constructing a hydropower plant along the border would involve negotiations with the Norwegian state for access to the western river bank to shore up the dams. Fortunately for the Finns, then, the upper section (30 kilometres) of the 145-kilometre-long Pasvik River, from the outlet of Lake Inari at Virtaniemi to the river bend in the Rajakoski area, was fully on Finnish territory (see Map 5).

This stretch contained several exploitable whitewater portions: the Kaitakoski, Jäniskoski, and Rajakoski rapids. The Finnish government decided, in agreement with Petsamon Nikkeli OY, that the Jäniskoski rapids were best suited, and in 1938 construction work began at the site. The planned completion a year later was, as we saw in Chapter 3, interrupted by the Winter War, and it was not until summer 1942 that power from Jäniskoski became available to the then German-controlled nickel plant in Kolosjoki.[2]

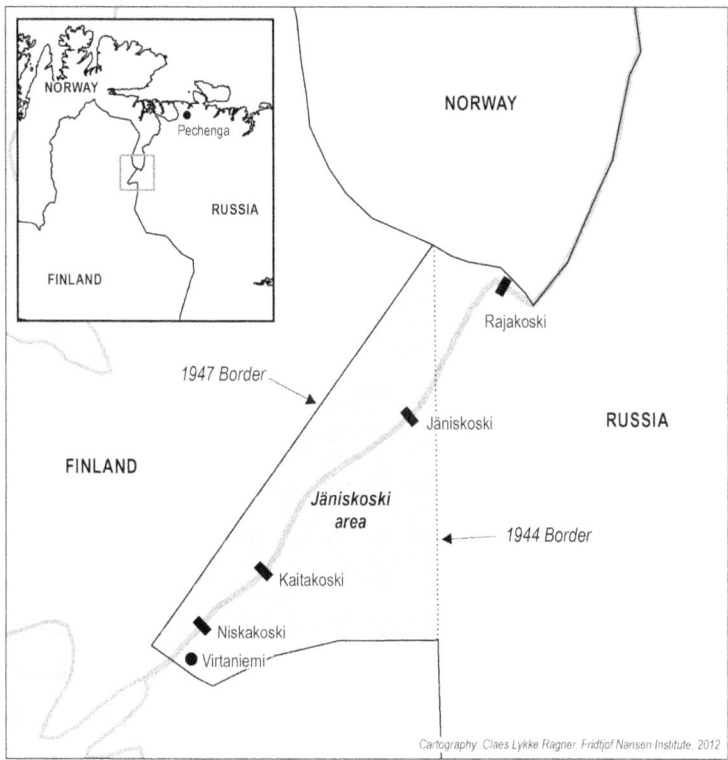

Map 5 The Jäniskoski area.

True to their scorched earth policy, the Nazi forces blew up the Jäniskoski power plant as well as the upstream regulatory dam at Niskakoski before retreating from the Northern Front. For the Soviet Union, however, the German destruction was not necessarily the biggest problem. When Petsamo had become Pechenga in 1944, the upper stretches of the Pasvik River, with the Jäniskoski power plant, remained Finnish, since they were not defined as lying within the Petsamo territory. Consequently, the new Soviet owners of the highly power-demanding nickel production site were faced with a 145-kilometre-long borderline along the Pasvik River, of which some 110 kilometres were shared with Norway and about 30 kilometres with Finland. Soviet territory did include both shores on two short stretches, both with rapids.

At the river bend at Rajakoski, a small triangle included full access to both shores. Then there was the small enclave of 3.6 square kilometres called Borisoglebskii (for the Russian Orthodox saints Boris and Gleb) just south of the river outlet at Kirkenes. This area, containing a small wooden chapel built in 1565 by the missionary monk Trifon, had in 1826 been retained by Tsarist Russia when the borders with Norway were established. The sacred patch of land had then passed, with Petsamo, into Finnish hands in 1920 and then back to the Soviet Union in 1944. Both areas would later be developed for energy purposes. For the time being, however, the initial focus of the Soviet authorities was the almost completed but severely damaged power plant at Jäniskoski.

In the following, we will discuss the Soviet endeavours to negotiate territorial hurdles and secure sufficient energy for Pechenganikel and the settlements connected to it. This process involved some forceful, albeit peaceful, acquisition of land, as well as lengthy negotiations between northern neighbours. In the three decades following the Second World War, no fewer than seven hydroelectric power plants were to be built on the Pasvik River, five of them Soviet. These were all essential to the development of Soviet industry and communities on the Kola Peninsula. In this chapter, the focus is on the first one in Jäniskoski, which provided Pechenganikel's history with yet another international episode. The Jäniskoski power plant, which was to be rebuilt with Finnish labour, was positioned in a sensitive border area, and both strategic and economic concerns entered into the equation. Pechenganikel's representatives thus had to manage labour and supplies in a very complicated environment.

After showing how the Soviet Union acquired Finnish land and labour, we will turn to three challenges that reveal the complicated nature of the project – problems of security, problems of Soviet supply, and ultimately problems relating to the Soviet takeover of the completed power station. Contrary to popular perceptions of the Soviet system as centrally organized and unified by a common purpose, we will see how various government agencies steered by their own agendas found themselves in frequent conflict with one another.

Jäniskoski is secured

Soon after the armistice agreement in 1944, Soviet authorities approached the Finnish government to discuss the future of the Jäniskoski power plant. As noted, the Jäniskoski area, comprising 176 square kilometres between Muotkavaara and southwards to Lake Inari, was still Finnish territory.[3] It was not ceded to the Soviet Union together with Petsamo in 1944, as is often assumed. This frequent misconception that the Jäniskoski area was part of Petsamo is possibly due to the fact that it was, as we will see, transferred to the Soviet Union in the spring of 1947, only two and a half years after Petsamo became Pechenga. In the interim, however, the Soviet Union would have to negotiate with Finland if they were to get any electricity generated from its rapids.

The Soviet position vis-à-vis Finland in the post-war years was one of massive strength. Between September 1944 and September 1947, the Allied Control Commission, headed by Leningrad party leader Andrei Zhdanov and manned for most of the time by 280 Soviet officials plus a minuscule British representation,[4] inhabited the Hotel Torni in Helsinki. From this stately abode (in fact the tallest building in Finland) the numerous Soviet representatives were able to influence the course of Finnish politics while overseeing that the requirements of the 1944 armistice were met. Among the burdens that weighed heavily on the Finnish post-war economy were comprehensive war reparations to the Soviet Union. For a small economy like that of Finland, meeting the Soviet demands – which not only were substantial but also accompanied by harsh and arguably unreasonable terms[5] – was very difficult. Under the strain of having to acquiesce to the strict and highly influential Zhdanov,[6] a large portion of Finnish post-war production went straight into the Soviet economy. In the words of Juho Kusti Paasikivi, who had returned to domestic politics to become Finland's first post-war prime minister in 1944, '[t]he Russians want nothing less than the shirts off our backs.'[7]

In this situation, there seemed little that Finland could do to prevent the Soviet Union from having its way in the upper Pasvik valley. In April

1946, the Finnish government gave the Soviet Union concession rights to the power plant in Jäniskoski. However, it soon became clear that the concession rights alone would not be enough. Under the circumstances, Pechenganikel's owners saw a chance not only of getting the rights to the electrical power from Jäniskoski, but of acquiring the entire area, and thus being able to exploit the waterfalls without interference from a Finnish operator.

For their part, Finnish leaders did not seem overly concerned about retaining that one little slip of land. The Jäniskoski area was on numerous occasions mentioned by leading Finnish politicians as potential compensation in return for the restoration to Finland of what were seen as more important areas, such as Viipuri (Vyborg), the Saimaa Canal and Porkkala (see Map 2).[8] A reciprocal arrangement along these lines was not within reach, however, as Moscow made it clear that it would not consider territorial adjustments or any reduction of war reparations in the ongoing negotiations.[9] The Soviets had no intentions of being lenient in their approach to the defeated Finnish counterpart.

Early in 1947, the Soviet Union and Finland reached agreement in three areas that were all relevant, directly or indirectly, to solving the problems of power supply in Nikel. Only one of these agreements was part of the overarching post-war settlements, namely the matter of so-called Nazi assets: At the Potsdam Conference in July/August 1945, the Soviet Union had reserved the right to claim ownership over Nazi assets left in Germany's co-belligerent states during the war, including Finland. This meant that the Finnish state was forced to accept, as part of its war reparations, a sizeable debt to the victorious eastern neighbour. By early 1947, Finland and the Soviet Union were in the process of agreeing on a sum and the terms of Finnish payment.

Parallel to these negotiations, two other items were prominent in Soviet–Finnish talks. Although they were both matters formally unrelated to the post-war settlement, they make sense only when seen in relation to the Nazi assets. Firstly, there was the matter of the Jäniskoski power station. As mentioned, Finland had granted the concession rights for the power plant to the Soviet Union already in April 1946. However, the demolished facility needed complete rebuilding before it could provide electricity for Pechenganikel. The Finnish semi-statal power company Imatran Voima was offered the job and conducted in early 1947 contract talks with Pechenganikel representatives. Secondly, the Soviet Union showed interest in more than just the power plant itself and indicated the possibility of Finnish cession of the whole Jäniskoski area. As mentioned, this area was not considered part of Petsamo and had therefore not been included in the 1944 armistice. However, its relevance to Pechenganikel's power supply made it highly attractive to Soviet interests.

As the three parallel negotiations progressed, the possibility of what might be called an all-Finnish solution became evident. Within ten days of these three-front talks, the Soviet Union had arranged not only for the complete refurbishment of the Jäniskoski power plant, but also for full payment for this project as well as the inclusion of the Jäniskoski area in Soviet territory. On 25 January 1947, the rebuilding of the Jäniskoski power plant was secured in what was referred to as a 'non-governmental' agreement[10] between Pechenganikel and Imatran Voima, whereby Imatran Voima was to undertake full reconstruction of the Jäniskoski facility and the control dam at Niskakoski, both still on Finnish territory.[11] Only ten days later, on 3 February 1947, Finland and the Soviet Union concluded the two other negotiations.[12]

Firstly, Finland agreed to increase the Soviet land mass, not as a part of war reparations, but by *selling* real estate to the Soviet Union. The Jäniskoski territory, including all buildings and installations situated there was transferred from Finland to the Soviet Union for the sum of 700 million Finnish marks. Secondly, the lengthy deliberations about Nazi assets came to an end. Finland and the Soviet Union agreed upon the sum of 6.5 billion Finnish marks, or USD 48 million, to be owed by Finland to the Soviet Union.[13] One clause in the agreement stipulated that the 'German money' was to be spent in Finland, thereby ensuring the Finnish workforce and producers some demand for their services and goods. Consequently, the Soviet Union had a fund in Finland that it could use in the rebuilding efforts after the war, which came in handy in the upper Pasvik valley. The costs of both Imatran Voima's reconstruction project at Jäniskoski and the purchase of the Jäniskoski area itself were to be covered by the fund. In sum, the Soviet Union acquired land from Finland and paid for Finnish companies to rebuild the power plant, all with garnished German marks.

As we see, the result of protracted negotiations between the Soviet Union and Finland was a conglomerate of agreements that must be considered very beneficial to Moscow and, of course, to Pechenganikel. While barely removing a kopek from their coffers,[14] Soviet authorities would be provided with a completely refurbished power plant, within Soviet borders. A more reliable source of electricity for both the power-demanding industrial processes in Nikel and the growing population in the cold river valley was, as we saw in Chapter 4, a key element in ensuring the future of Pechenganikel. With the first phase of the Soviet rebuilding of Pechenganikel nearing completion, the single high-voltage power line from Tuloma, 154 kilometres away, could not meet the projected demands. It is therefore no exaggeration to say that the Soviet Union came very cheaply by the solution to a major problem in its newly acquired territory.

Agreement with Finland had been reached, but there remained many practical problems to be solved before Imatran Voima could start reconstructing the power station. After all, the Finnish company had agreed to a project in an area that was soon to be Soviet territory. The complexity of the operation required Soviet representation in Finland for direct communication between Pechenganikel and Imatran Voima. To carry out this task on behalf of Pechenganikel, Boris Mefodievich Kleshko was sent by Mintsvetmet to Helsinki, where he would establish an office and oversee the process. Through his and others' correspondence with Soviet government agencies on various levels, the many obstacles en route from the 'non-governmental' agreement between Pechenganikel and Imatran Voima to completion of the rebuilding project in Jäniskoski become apparent. This documentation will be at the centre of the following discussion.[15]

Clash of cultures

Although Boris Kleshko was Pechenganikel's representative in Helsinki, this did not imply that he was in touch with his nominal principal. In fact, the Pechenganikel management was initially kept on the sidelines in this international affair. Negotiations were taken care of from Moscow, and Kleshko was appointed by and answered to Mintsvetmet and Glavnikelkobalt.[16] This arrangement, which limited the number of Soviet individuals in direct contact with Finnish counterparts to a minimum, was in line with the Stalinist policy of restricting Soviet citizens' interaction with the outside world. Any direct involvement of Pechenganikel employees was deemed undesirable. In the same vein, the Soviet borders in Nikel's immediate surroundings were tightly shut after the war. Of course, the sealing off of the Soviet hinterland was not a new phenomenon. However, with the emergence of post-war tensions in East–West relations, border controls were made even tighter throughout the Soviet Union, as was also observed in the Pasvik valley.[17] Consequently, one of Kleshko's foremost tasks in Helsinki was to negotiate not only with his Finnish counterparts, but also with his own authorities about how to arrange for Finnish workers to lawfully enter the Jäniskoski area, which soon would be included in the territory of the Soviet Union. The building project at Jäniskoski would involve a host of Soviet ministries and directorates with different and at times conflicting objectives. Accommodating the various Soviet interests was to prove at least equally difficult as mediating between Finnish and Soviet interests.

Kleshko's immediate task after arriving in Helsinki was to negotiate the necessary sets of agreements between Pechenganikel and the companies that would provide services and equipment for the rebuilding project. This encounter between Soviet officials and private Finnish companies may be described as a clash of cultures. Evidently, the private-sector Finnish actors did not feel bound by agreements between the Soviet Union and the Finnish state, and they related to their Soviet customer as they would to any other actor requesting their services. Especially on the issue of payment, differences came to the fore. The Soviets held that the deliveries to Jäniskoski were to be made according to 1938 price levels, as was the case with the Finnish state's war reparations to the Soviet Union (see footnote 5). Soviet Deputy Attaché of Commerce (*zamtorgpred*) to Finland, I. A. Andrianov, pointed out that the rebuilding project was to be funded by former German assets in Finland. To him it seemed only logical that also deliveries destined for Jäniskoski should be priced accordingly. Having met with resistance both on this point and concerning other terms of delivery from private Finnish companies, Andrianov and Kleshko turned to Finnish authorities. The head of the trade department in the Finnish Ministry of Foreign Affairs, Nykopp, was not immediately willing to accept the Soviet claims, stating that the Jäniskoski project could not be part of the reparations scheme with its 1938 price requirements, but as a regular case of Finnish export to the Soviet Union.

Nykopp pointed out that Pechenganikel was being offered Finnish deliveries at prices below or equal to the prices paid by other recipients of Finnish goods and services (here he mentioned British and Belgian customers). Unfazed by this, Andrianov continued, as Kleshko relates:

> Later Comrade Andrianov pointed to the unreasonable demands concerning price, advance payment and time-limits on orders from firms Kone, Strömberg and Tampella. Comrade Andrianov again motivated his criticism in the fact that the rebuilding of Jäniskoski is funded by former German assets. He pointed out that the Soviet Union did not charge the Finnish government any interest for two years [since the Potsdam conference 1945] and that therefore the increase of prices and demands for advance payment, from our point of view, should not take place. Concerning time-limits we pointed especially to the firm Tampella, which suggests unreasonably lengthy delivery terms on equipment that, as far as we know, can be produced in a significantly shorter period of time given the company's production capacity. We emphasized the less than forthcoming attitude towards us in the companies Strömberg and Tampella. This is exemplified by the fact that when the firm Strömberg set an 'unbinding' delivery time

on generators to 18 months, they explained that the word 'unbinding' could mean that the delivery time was anything from 18 months to eight years. Further, when we pointed out that their prices were high, they answered that 'if it is too expensive for you, order from someone else'.[18]

Kleshko's summary of this conversation tells us several things. Firstly, the Finnish nation, including individuals in private companies, did not necessarily view their Soviet neighbours with sympathy. Especially Strömberg's explanation of the term 'unbinding' indicates that the company would be more than happy to lose the contract with the Soviet customer. Secondly, Andrianov showed a striking lack of understanding of the principles of a market economy. His argumentation for the logic of low prices demonstrates scant awareness of how profit is the governing measure for any market-oriented company. Also, the fact that he chose to bring this up with a Finnish public servant to rectify what he felt was wrong, suggests that he expected Nykopp to be able to order private companies Tampella, Strömberg or Kone to accept the Soviet demands.

Boris Kleshko, who was the day-to-day Soviet manager of the Jäniskoski project, seems to have been more realistic in his approach to Finnish counterparts. Already in March 1947, he had written a report to his superiors in Mintsvetmet, asking them to confirm his autonomy from the Soviet trade representation (Torgpredstvo) in Helsinki, including Andrianov. Kleshko made it clear that the Torgpredstvo was delaying the project significantly.[19] Two months later, in the middle of May, he received confirmation from Moscow that he had every right to enter necessary agreements with Finnish companies, but that this would also have to be cleared with Torgpredstvo and the Ministry for Foreign Trade (Vneshtorg).[20] This dual message from Mintsvetmet, in which it was also stated that time was of the essence, was probably a way of allowing Kleshko to pursue the course he thought best, without formally disregarding the principle of Vneshtorg's and Torgpredstvo's supremacy in issues involving foreign trade. Whatever the case, it is evident from the documentation that negotiations began moving more smoothly once Kleshko had been given a freer rein.

By the end of June, Kleshko could report satisfactory progress in his talks with the Finnish companies. He had received bids on various parts for the power plant from Strömberg, Tampella, Kone and the Swedish firm Arbro; and Imatran Voima and Tampella had agreed on transport issues.[21] At the construction site, preparatory work was well underway, with 190 workers setting up housing barracks and clearing off remnants of the demolished power plant. Kleshko, however, was still not happy with the situation. Reporting from Jäniskoski, he impatiently pointed out that progress was held up unnecessarily, and it was not the Finnish companies that were to blame. In several matters, different Soviet government agencies, with competing agendas and interests and, not least, varying degrees of commitment to the Jäniskoski project, had been complicating progress at the construction site. As the Jäniskoski power plant project developed, more and more Soviet agencies became involved, and internal Soviet bickering became more intense. This was the case with the Ministry of Internal Affairs (MVD), which was, among other things, responsible for keeping Soviet borders secure.

Figure 8 Construction work in Jäniskoski. Photo: Archive Rune Rautio.

Problems of security

The question of how to organize the border zone in a secure manner caused friction among Soviet actors like the MVD, MID and Mintsvetmet. The Soviet–Finnish treaty on the transfer of Jäniskoski had been concluded already by 3 February 1947, but the area would for practical purposes remain open to Finnish citizens until the new borders were formally established. These new borders could be agreed only after a joint Finnish–Soviet border commission had completed its assignment, scheduled for fall 1947.[22]

The problem was that the Jäniskoski territory could not be sealed off, as would otherwise have been the Soviet reflex upon acquiring new land. Finnish workers had to be allowed onto Soviet territory, and the Soviet hinterland also had to be accessible for transports between Liinahamari and Nikel to the construction site. The solution, as communicated by Deputy Minister of Foreign Affairs Andrei Vyshinskii to Deputy Minister of Internal Affairs Ivan Serov, was to define the Jäniskoski area as a 'special border zone' until the completion of construction work. Vyshinskii ordered Serov to arrange for the establishment of a border crossing regime, including regulations for passports and other permits for the Finnish guests.[23] Serov certainly did not take the task lightly. Every Finnish citizen who wanted to enter Jäniskoski had to, in addition to an identification card, be equipped with a personal permit (*propusk*), either for multiple entries or for a one-time visit. The permit, written in both Finnish and Russian, was to bear a photo, as well as a stamp from both Kleshko and the Imatran Voima project manager, Gustav Telestam. Lists of all individuals who had received permits were to be stamped and approved by the Soviet embassy in Helsinki. The lists were then to be forwarded in three copies to the main office of the Karelian–Finnish border guard section in Petrozavodsk.[24] One of the copies was intended for the border control point at Virtaniemi, where the Jäniskoski workers would cross.

This arrangement hardly made for expediency: it had been constructed solely with the motivation of keeping Imatran Voima's workers under tight control. Predictably, Kleshko was not happy with the visa arrangements, and argued in a report to Moscow that needless waste of valuable time and money resulted from it:

> In the practical processing of documents difficulties of the following nature arise: The recruitment of the workforce for the construction site takes place in Rovaniemi, where there is a special office for worker recruitment. The worker must, upon arriving at the office and after having given the necessary information about himself, produce a photo to be used in the permit. The information and the photo are then sent to Imatran Voima in Helsinki, where, after the personal information from the worker is filled into the permit, the photo will be attached to the document. The permit is then given the necessary signature and stamps, before it is sent to Pechenganikel's representation in Helsinki for the Russian part of the processing. After the appropriate coordination with the consular department at the Soviet embassy in Helsinki, the permit is returned to Rovaniemi to be issued to the worker. Under these generally complicated conditions, the document spends six to seven days on its roundtrip, and while the worker is waiting for his permit, he demands payment according to medium wages and, in some cases, also room and board while in Rovaniemi. If we assume that payment will be handed out to a thousand workers (for the duration of the project) according to Finnish medium wages, which is around 800 Finnish marks per day, our budget for this should be four to four and a half million Finnish marks. And this only because we chose the order of document processing described above.[25]

From Kleshko's point of view, anything that would slow the project down was a problem. And, as an unusually outspoken industrialist, he was not beyond making this point to his superiors in Moscow. Kleshko proposed an arrangement that would cut down the waiting period in Rovaniemi by a couple of days, but there can be little doubt that he would have preferred to see the whole process thoroughly changed and sped up. One way around the strict regime, of course, was simply not to adhere to it, and send workers to Jäniskoski without the required documentation. This took place to some extent, probably because Imatran Voima had not been informed prior to the sudden introduction of the new regime when the Soviet Union officially took over the Jäniskoski territory on 15 August 1947.[26] For a while, the border guards felt pressured to admit workers without proper identification.[27] Deputy Minister Serov in MVD complained to Lomako's deputy and Head of Glavnikelkobalt Semyon Petrov that the Finnish ID cards were of varying types, old and in many cases not valid. In addition, the lists of workers had only been signed by Imatran Voima. They had neither been stamped by the Soviet consulate nor signed off by Pechenganikel's office in Helsinki. Serov was not at all comfortable with this and pointed out that the lack of control offered possibilities for 'undesirable persons' to trickle over the border. Petrov, who was obliged by bureaucratic necessity to take MVD's position seriously, relayed these worries to Kleshko, and ordered him to enforce Finnish compliance with Soviet regulations immediately.[28]

Further problems that would involve several ministries arose later that same year. On Saturday evening 8 November 1947, sometime between 7.30 and 9.45 pm, Jäniskoski was struck by fire. This incident was to give rise to several issues connected to the unclear legal status of the Jäniskoski territory. While the available documents do not allow for a conclusion as to the causes of the fire, there is some evidence to suggest that two boys of about twelve years of age, Veikko Nissi and his brother (presumably accompanying their parents in Jäniskoski), and the twenty-two-year-old Niilo Karjalainen were the perpetrators. This party of three had been preparing and enjoying a pancake meal in room 4 of barracks no. 2, using a woodstove that had been set up there. However, the pancakes were illicitly prepared, inasmuch as this particular woodstove only one day earlier had been checked and deemed unusable due to fire hazard.[29] Karjalainen left the premises as the last one, at around 7.30 p.m. He later maintained, during questioning, that there was then no sign of a fire spreading in the building. He had thoroughly put out the stove with snow, he claimed. At 9.45 pm, as the night watchman Kosti Ansimov approached the barracks, he saw a person running from the entrance door towards the nearby canteen, shouting that the building was burning. This person, who was never identified, could have caused the fire, and his observed presence may have exonerated Karjalainen and the Nissi brothers. The origin of the fire, which caused damage amounting to almost 400,000 Finnish marks, as the flames completely consumed the barracks and its contents, was never firmly established.[30]

Whatever or whoever set fire to barracks no. 2, the incident brought to the fore several worries held by Imatran Voima, worries that were shared by Mintsvetmet and Kleshko in the Pechenganikel office in Helsinki. As we have seen, the area had been declared a special border zone for the duration of the Finnish reconstruction project. Soviet border control was enforced from 15 August 1947, and all Finnish citizens were required to show several identification cards before entering. This, however, was not sufficient to define Jäniskoski as part of the Soviet Union in legal terms. Neither was the territory Finnish. As a piece of land with no sovereign, or rather in-between sovereigns, Jäniskoski was neither a Finnish responsibility nor a Soviet one. One effect of this was that Jäniskoski lacked various basic communal services. There was no fire protection other than a small brigade organized by the construction workers. Nor was there a regular police force in place. The investigation of the fire was conducted by the closest one came to a police officer in the area, namely a 'keeper of order' (*blyustitel poryadka*). This was a man named Kamara, who in the words of the very sceptical Soviet engineer Goncharov had been 'almost democratically elected' among the Finnish workers.[31]

Perhaps the most serious lack in this *terra nullius* was the unwillingness of any insurance company to provide its services there. Consequently, all damage to equipment and building materials, as the uninsured property of Pechenganikel, would mean a loss only to Pechenganikel. That did not, however, solve the problem of private property. Imatran Voima's employees were naturally worried that their personal belongings might disappear in flames or be damaged in some other way, with no compensation possible. The same applied to the privately owned store in Jäniskoski, which in addition to the contents of its shelves had a storehouse 'worth about 1.5 million Finnish marks'.[32]

Imatran Voima had brought these problems up before the fire, in September 1947,[33] but a solution did not seem to be forthcoming. With the fire, the situation had become untenable, and Imatran Voima demanded that some administrative changes be made by the Soviet side to allow for the presence of a police force and insurance of goods and equipment on the territory. More precisely, Imatran Voima called for a *Finnish* police force and a *Finnish* insurance agency, with the implication that it was *Finnish* law that was applicable and that *Finnish* courts had jurisdiction. The company went so far as to say, while hinting at a decline or complete halt in recruitment if workers could not insure their belongings, that 'in the opposite event, work done by Finnish labor [in Jäniskoski] will become impossible'.[34] Engineer Goncharov, who was one of Kleshko's subordinates in Helsinki, agreed with the Finnish company at least partly. He said nothing about which nation's laws should apply, but he voiced particular concern about the lack of a police force in Jäniskoski and emphasized that the quasi-policeman, the *blyustitel poryadka*, 'does not have the necessary authority to exert force against anti-social or criminal elements, and, most critically, elements that are hostile to us [i.e. the Soviet Union]'.[35] With this, Goncharov brought up the possibility of Jäniskoski becoming an arena for anti-Soviet activity.

The engineer did not elaborate further on the issue, but he likely had intelligence-collection or possibly sabotage in mind. It is also altogether conceivable that Goncharov was pointing to the possibility of hostile elements among the workers, knowing that jurisdictional matters were handled by the ministries most concerned with national security, the MID and the MVD. Goncharov might have found it useful to 'push the border-security button', so to speak. That Soviet state interests were on the line would, he may have hoped, raise some eyebrows in Moscow.[36] Incidentally, there is nothing to suggest that Soviet industrial actors, of which Goncharov was one, were overly worried about the Jäniskoski workforce being infiltrated by hostile elements.[37] The Soviet offices in Helsinki, and other concerned Soviet agencies, maintained impeccable relations with Imatran Voima throughout their cooperation. However, they were fretting about the security of the site itself and tried to draw attention to this problem by hinting that the integrity of the Soviet border could be at risk.

Petrov in Glavnikelkobalt became Imatran Voima's spokesman within the Soviet apparatus with regard to insurance and policing. He wrote a letter to MID, in which he stated that a police force and insurance services in Jäniskoski were essential to the future success of the project. He echoed, sincerely or not, the worries that had been relayed to him by Goncharov: 'This situation has already caused serious concern. At this point there are 600 workers on the construction site, and in 1948 the number will increase to 1500. Among them may be criminal, antisocial and hostile persons.' He also made it clear to MID that Imatran Voima seriously doubted the possibility of finishing the project if the problems were not solved.[38] As we see, the Glavnikelkobalt leader made a point of the potential threat to Soviet security. Again – the industrially inclined Petrov and his subordinates in Helsinki brought up the security factor, most likely for effect. Set on pushing the Jäniskoski project forward, they might have chosen to feed MID a fabricated but plausible threat that they hoped would speed up the settlement of the jurisdictional issues.

Petrov, however, knew that this would not take care of the immediate concerns. Aware that solving the problem of jurisdiction would require a lengthy process between the two states,[39] and probably also that Imatran Voima's request for a *Finnish* official police force in Jäniskoski was unrealistic, Petrov took measures to alleviate the situation temporarily. He had discussed the problems with Kleshko when the latter gave a personal report in Moscow, and followed up in writing with a clear order: 'From now until the Ministry of Foreign Affairs has solved the problem of jurisdiction in the acquired territory, a fire brigade and watchman force must be kept at the expense of the construction project [Pechenganikel] and be made up of Finnish citizens specifically appointed by you [Kleshko].'[40] Thus, Petrov came up with a short-term solution that would provide for a respite, and keep the project afloat. However, his order did not reach Kleshko until three months later,[41] and the unclear situation in Jäniskoski lingered on.

Jurisdictional problems would recur many times before the power station was ready to deliver its first watts to the Pechenganikel smelter. While the Jäniskoski territory was subjected to strict border control at the crossing point at Virtaniemi, and, of course, even stricter control at the inner border at Nautsi, Soviet border troops never policed the area itself. The Soviet stance, which did not falter, was that only Soviet law was applicable in the area, both for individuals and for businesses. All that the frustrated Finnish firm could do was what their Soviet customer suggested: strengthen their watchman force to prevent damage and theft. This was again the remedy when the Finnish project manager Gustav Telestam brought the problem up in early fall 1948, after a shipment of nails had been stolen and a company car had been wrecked by a drunken employee. Telestam complained that

> [i]n the current situation there exists no law whatsoever on the Jäniskoski territory and therefore no criminal offence may be punished. The firm [Imatran Voima] may not bring cases of theft of or damage to the property of the construction project to court, as this is Soviet property (Pechenganikel's). Finnish courts may not deal with crimes in Jäniskoski as it is not Finnish territory.[42]

Telestam rounded off by repeating the threat that 'if "Russian laws" are to be observed in Jäniskoski, then the Finns might leave the whole project'.[43] Imatran Voima, however, never abandoned the Jäniskoski power plant. Quite the contrary, the company would later, as we shall see, take upon itself another construction project not far from Jäniskoski. It seems, then, that for Imatran Voima the negative aspects – lack of law enforcement (and law, for that matter), haphazard fire protection and no insurance – were outweighed by the positive ones – having long-term contracts with a Soviet customer.

When the next incident that brought jurisdictional problems to the fore occurred in 1949, Imatran Voima's approach to the matter was quite different. Again, Jäniskoski was the scene of a fire, or rather attempted arson. On the evening of Tuesday, 28 June, an unknown person had assembled kindling, piled it in the wood storage house and lit it. Only the watchful eye of Maria Lehtola, the woodcutter's wife, and a concerted effort to put the flames out, prevented a potentially disastrous fire.[44] Kleshko wrote a letter to project manager Gustav Telestam, stating that Imatran Voima, as the party responsible for the rebuilding project needed to strengthen security at the construction site. He also, naturally, brought up the disturbing fact that this fire had been a premeditated act, and asserted that 'various criminal elements with an obvious ambition to cause damage to our construction are seeping into the building site'.[45] Kleshko was seconded by Petrov, who emphasized that intensified measures would be of the essence in securing the site now that the rebuilding project was nearing conclusion.[46] Telestam's reaction to the Soviet demand for better security, to be provided by his company, was one of concurrence: he accepted, on behalf of Imatran Voima, the main responsibility for keeping the construction site safe, and listed the many security measures that had been put in place, pointing especially to a fire truck received from Pechenganikel. He disagreed with Kleshko, however, about the nature of the attempted arson. In Telestam's view, it was not a result of planned sabotage against the construction site but had been caused by 'the insanity of a psychopath or the actions of a pyromaniac-like person'.[47] Telestam underscored that there were limits to the level of security that Imatran Voima could achieve:

> Although we are formally responsible for the totality of the construction, we do not have the means to fully eradicate the possibility of premeditated sabotage to the building project. There is no official police force on the construction site – only two so-called keepers of order. True, they are in close collaboration with Finnish police to prevent criminal elements from seeping in. This, however, does not give any guarantees that there will be no planned evil doings on the construction site.[48]

As we can see, the tone is quite different from the case in the aftermath of the previous fire in Jäniskoski. Telestam's admission of responsibility must have been the result of an agreement with his Soviet customer. Although it is not reflected in the available documentation, we may assume that Kleshko and Telestam at some point agreed that the only way to deal with dangers such as fires, crime and sabotage in Jäniskoski was to organize local security, rather than wait for a high-level Soviet–Finnish agreement.[49] We see from Telestam's letter that in 1949 there were two 'keepers of order', whereas there had been only one before. Assisted by Finnish police, these quasi-policemen vetted worker recruits, to prevent undesirable persons from entering the labor force. That Pechenganikel provided a fire truck represented, as Telestam stated, a marked improvement in fire safety. Also, the problem of insurance seems to have partly been taken care of in an agreement between the two parties. A letter from the Ministry of Metallurgic Industry (Minmetallurgprom)[50] to the Council of Ministers (the Soviet government) in January 1949 stated that 16.2 per cent of all wages paid to the Finnish workers were to be set aside for insurance purposes.[51] In this way the personal items of Imatran Voima employees were insured, if not by an insurance company. This did not cover the property of the construction site as such, however. Thus, practical problems arising from the obscure jurisdictional status of Jäniskoski were dealt with – directly between the two parties Pechenganikel (Kleshko) and Imatran Voima (Telestam) – as best as one could in the absence of a bilateral agreement on jurisdiction between Finland and the Soviet Union.

When preventive security measures failed, however, there was no obvious solution to the question of responsibility for Pechenganikel's property. As mentioned, there would be no compensation for losses, and damages were to be borne by Pechenganikel as the owner of all installations and equipment in Jäniskoski. When a third fire struck the construction site in June 1950, Petrov, the leader of Glavnikelkobalt, had had enough. A barracks and its contents worth two million Finnish marks had burnt to the ground, and Petrov wanted the losses covered in full by Imatran Voima, as the company was responsible for security. Knowing that there were no provisions for such a claim in the January 1947 agreement between Imatran Voima and Pechenganikel, Petrov asked the Ministry of Foreign Affairs for advice.[52] MID answered that the matter should be taken up directly with Imatran Voima, and that, if the company was not forthcoming, the claim could be brought to arbitration in the court of commerce in Helsinki.[53] There is no documentation that the issue was presented for arbitration, which would indicate that agreement was reached with Imatran Voima. Be that as it may, the Soviet claims show the increasing unease and irritation on the part of Petrov and his fellow industrialists as the Jäniskoski project was nearing completion. The closer to being finished, the more valuable the power station became to the Soviet Union – and the more was at stake. Another manifestation of this was Petrov's lack of trust in Finnish security, for other reasons than just future fires:

> All possible security measures have been taken. However, when considering that this security is handled by Finns, among whom there are, without a doubt, elements that are hostile to the USSR, such security renders itself completely useless and in reality, meaningless. The situation at the construction site today demands urgent organization of reliable security, and this can be achieved only if we get our border troops, located in the area, to keep the power station safe.
> … The local commander considers this possible, provided he receives orders to that effect.[54]

As we see, Petrov again, in early 1950, brought up the question of possible sabotage against Jäniskoski, this time more sincerely than before. To Petrov's dismay, central agencies like the MID and the Ministry for State Security were unwilling to provide for a Soviet watchman force for Jäniskoski. He therefore – after most of the Finns had left and there was no Finnish security in place – had to see an almost completed power station remain unguarded.[55]

The Soviet central authorities' relaxed approach to the security situation in Jäniskoski indicates that a Finnish threat was never deemed imminent. In fact, border controls seem to have been stricter for Soviet citizens than for Finns. While allowing Finnish citizens to access Jäniskoski under a simplified border crossing regime, Soviet citizens involved in the project were closely scrutinized. In August 1950, all employees at the Pechenganikel office in Helsinki had their multiple-entry visas to Jäniskoski annulled, with the somewhat absurd effect that these Soviet citizens had to request their own government (the Council of Ministers) for permission to re-enter what was Soviet territory, so they could oversee the transfer of the power plant from Imatran Voima to Pechenganikel upon completion.[56] Whether this was an expression of the traditional Soviet fear of an inner enemy is hard to say, but it certainly demonstrated the zeal of the border control bureaucracy!

Problems and politics of supply

Although the Jäniskoski project was run by Imatran Voima, its success very much depended on the Soviet side fulfilling its part of the deal. According to the agreement between Pechenganikel and Imatran Voima, all basic construction material, machinery and other equipment was to be delivered from the Soviet Union, with the exception of high-technology components like turbines and generators.[57] Delivery of machinery and heavy-duty materials like cement, TNT and iron for reinforcement was no trifling matter in a country severely damaged by war, especially not when the recipient was located in remote Jäniskoski. It is therefore not surprising that logistical factors played a central part in the progress, or lack thereof, in Jäniskoski's rebuilding.

One early problem that illustrates some of the key challenges that would plague the Jäniskoski project was the Soviet inability to provide explosives to the construction site. Many of the structures that were left after the German departure could not simply be lifted away. Heavy rubble would have to be blasted away with TNT, to be delivered from the Soviet side of the border. The lack of TNT led to several delays – and, as Kleshko was aware, delays meant higher expenses. Kleshko decided to go straight to the top with his complaints, using his access to Politburo member and at this point minister of foreign trade Anastas Mikoyan and the head of Mintsvetmet, Lomako:

> Despite the telegram that General Savanenkov sent to comrade Vyshinskii with copy to comrade Petrov on 20 May, about the numerous conversations between Pechenganikel's representative

comrade Kleshko and comrades Petrov, Mironov, Galper and Gurevich, the question of explosives remains unresolved. The firm Imatran Voima is asking for TNT daily, explosive work is not being conducted, the construction site is being developed as much as possible without explosives. But this is absolutely impossible, and the consequence is that the best time of year for construction work in the north is not taken advantage of. All the while Imatran Voima is paying out substantial wages [that will be added to the bill]. We have ordered support equipment for the power station, but this has still not reached Finland. The reason for this is that we have until recently not been given concrete instructions from Mashinoimport [Soviet government agency for the import of machinery] on the issuance of the orders, allegedly because of lacking [import] quotas. At the same time, because of accelerating inflation in Finland, the firms are starting to change their initial offers, increasing the prices.[58]

Here we see Kleshko's ability to use his connections in the upper echelons of the Soviet government structure in his efforts to speed up the process. This early problem of delivery of TNT alludes to both the practical issues of supply delivery and the lack of coordination and sometimes direct political competition that complicated dealing with these practical challenges throughout the construction process.

The question of access to Jäniskoski was the first hurdle. Here, the confluence of difficult conditions and political infighting complicated matters. The road from Liinahamari via Nikel to Jäniskoski was by no means an easy ride. We have already observed the difficulties experienced by Pechenganikel in getting supplies from the rest of the Soviet Union to Nikel. Moving provisions further on to the power station added another obstacle. To reach Jäniskoski from Nikel, some 95 kilometres of rough unpaved road had to be negotiated (see Map 1). Conditions not only rendered transport as such problematic; they also made maintenance a constant requirement. The long harsh winter would cause many potholes that appeared after the snow melted in spring. The summer season was just barely long enough for maintenance crews to shoddily repair the roads before the winter snows were back. Whoever was given the responsibility for keeping the road clear would have his work cut out for him. The task fell, by governmental decree, to the Ministry of Internal Affairs (MVD).[59] The MVD, however, asked the Council of Ministers to charge Pechenganikel with the task until a proper organization *(upravlenie)* could be set up and equipped.[60] Pechenganikel's burden was already substantial, and the road remained unusable for most of the winter 1947/1948. When combine director Trofimov claimed that conditions were unusually difficult that winter, this was not accepted by Petrov in Glavnikelkobalt, who pointed out that the Finns dealt far more successfully with similar problems on the other side of the border.[61] Petrov had been informed by Kleshko's subordinate in Helsinki, engineer Lebedev, who reported that

> [the] unsightly shape of the road [between Jäniskoski and Nikel] is due to a complete lack of attention to this problem from the people who are responsible for keeping it in usable condition. The attempt to plead exceptional circumstances, a snow-rich winter and the like is unfounded, as a road of not 100 kilometers, but 500 kilometers (Kemi-Jäniskoski) – in equally severe climate – has for the duration of the winter been kept in mint condition – traffic has not been stopped even for an hour – with the help of 5 vehicles with ploughs and about 100 workers.[62]

The significance of keeping the Nikel–Jäniskoski transport route open for traffic becomes apparent not only by the attention given to the matter by the Council of Ministers,[63] but also by the fact that the route was the only line of communication between Jäniskoski and the rest of the Soviet Union. If Soviet supplies, such as cement, explosives, excavators and other heavy machinery, were to have a chance of reaching the construction site on time, the road simply had to be in working order.

When Lebedev's colleague, engineer Nikitin, visited Jäniskoski between 19 February and 27 March 1948, he was aghast at the lack of improvement. The consequences were clear: Without excavators, cranes and tractors, all the heavy cement rubble left after the German retreat would have to be removed manually *(vruchnuyu)*. This meant that the schedule was significantly pushed back, which again led to a correspondingly delayed start in actual rebuilding efforts. Nikitin did not go easy on Pechenganikel director Trofimov, who reportedly 'left an impression of complete lack of interest in speeding up the project'. Not only was the road in bad shape, the scant equipment that actually reached the construction site from Pechenganikel was 'frequently incomplete and in need of immediate repairs'.[64] Throughout 1948, the inability to supply the construction site with necessary equipment – cement mixers, heaving mechanisms and other machinery – meant that much of the work had to be done by hand, resulting in an 'enormous waste of time and money'.[65] It may seem somewhat surprising that keeping a stretch of road open and transporting supplies to Jäniskoski proved to be insurmountable for Pechenganikel. However, as we saw in Chapter 4, at that time the combine was struggling to meet its own demands, due, inter alia, to transport difficulties from the port of Liinahamari to Nikel. In addition, Pechenganikel was but the last link in a long chain of suppliers, a chain that by no means could be described as infallible. It therefore seems that Trofimov and his combine received an undeservedly heavy share of the blame for delays in Jäniskoski.

The Pechenganikel director did defend himself. A report written by him and Kleshko in July 1948 clearly described the causes for an estimated three-month delay in Jäniskoski. All negative aspects of the project were ascribed to Soviet factors. Some of the equipment that had been shipped from within the Soviet Union was in such bad shape that it was with a sense of shame and embarrassment *(stydno)* they handed it over to the Finnish workers. And, of course, the transport route from Liinahamari to Jäniskoski was simply not up to standard: 'The condition of the road is threatening the shipment of goods to Jäniskoski and without extraordinary and radical measures supplies to the construction site will be disrupted.' The reason for this, as Trofimov and Kleshko saw it, lay not with Pechenganikel, but with the MVD's Directorate for Main Roads (UShossDor) whose employees had, 'despite systematic help from the combine' worked too slowly. Kleshko and Trofimov suggested an alternative route: to direct the transport of Soviet supplies through Finland instead.[66] Trofimov's denial of his own guilt was not accepted. In the summer of 1948, he was subjected to disciplinary measures of an unknown nature, and towards the end of the year he was replaced.[67]

When the agreement between Imatran Voima and Pechenganikel was reached in January 1947, the Council of Ministers had resolved that the first phase of energy production at the power station would commence in the fourth quarter of 1949.[68] However, a decree, even a governmental one, is merely a reflection of intention – not of reality. As we have seen, transport was one major obstacle to smooth completion of the plan. Moreover, the supplies that reached Jäniskoski were frequently inadequate in quantity as well as quality. In a report to the Soviet embassy in Helsinki, Kleshko left no doubt as to where the problems originated:

> We [the Soviet side] have not fulfilled any of our obligations to deliver the necessary construction mechanisms, equipment, building materials etc. on time …. The equipment and materials that have been brought to the construction site from the Union, have all been delayed – in conflict with the agreement – up to 1 year or longer. … The quality of the equipment and materials is frequently low, despite the fact that the governmental decree contains a specific order that all equipment that is shipped to Jäniskoski should be of export quality. … As a result of the complete absence of mechanization, the extremely heavy and labor-intensive removal of cement and iron rubble is done manually. … Manual labor of course prolongs the duration of work and markedly increases the costs of the project.[69]

With remarkable candour, Kleshko put the blame for the problems on his own – the Soviet suppliers. In his view, the Finnish workers and managers of Imatran Voima were doing their very best with the limited means of production they were being supplied with. This assessment of the Finns was shared also by Kleshko's superiors in Moscow.[70]

It might have come as a relief to some of the Soviet culprits then, that the Swedish firm ASEA, which had been commissioned to build two generators for the Jäniskoski power plant, announced that delivery would be delayed for seven and fourteen months for the first and second generator respectively.[71] This meant that the project would be given longer time to complete preparatory work. The starting date for the power plant was pushed back to August 1950 for the first aggregate; full production with two generators was to commence by the end of 1951.[72]

However, this did not mean that the problems experienced on the Soviet side were forgotten. Pechenganikel's director Trofimov, as we have seen, was replaced in late 1948. Now the combine, which until then had played little more than a nominal role as Imatran Voima's formal customer *(zakazchik)*, would become more involved. Petrov in Glavnikelkobalt dissolved Pechenganikel's Moscow office, which had been set up to handle orders from Soviet suppliers. Although this office had done its job, Petrov wrote, the very fact of its existence had led the Pechenganikel combine to 'neglect its duties to manage and control the construction of the power station'. Petrov instructed the new Pechenganikel director A. A. Ilin not only to observe developments in Jäniskoski with a watchful eye, but also to keep Kleshko and his colleagues in Helsinki on a tight leash. Pechenganikel was thus accorded a much more central position in the project from late 1948 onwards, in the hope that this more immediate control would prevent further problems. The combine was even given the immediate responsibility for project funding, except for payments in foreign currency.[73]

Another aspect of stricter control was the involvement of the party apparatus – or more precisely, that the party apparatus meddled. The Jäniskoski power plant had originally been a concern for government agencies, rather than a matter for the Communist Party. The ministries, directorates and various enterprises handled the project purely as an industrial venture. Most importantly, the workers – Imatran Voima's Finnish employees – were not to be subjected to the regular ideological indoctrination, which would normally be a task for the agitprop section of the Party.[74]

However, the supply problems and the ensuing delays caught the interest of local Bolshevik officials. The secretary of the Murmansk regional (oblast) party committee Verbitskii in June 1948 wrote a letter to Lomako in Mintsvetmet and the Minister of Power Plants Zhimerin insisting that work on the power line from Jäniskoski to Nikel be intensified. The committee apparently felt justified, by virtue of its ideological supremacy, in making this pressing request, even though it had not been directly involved in the Jäniskoski project. Verbitskii even proposed that the ministries take action and order their directorates to finish the power line by the end of the year.[75] Petrov, as the head of Glavnikelkobalt, was given the task of explaining that this was not possible due to lack of resources.[76] On 30 June 1948, the Pechenga local party committee *(raikom)* issued a resolution titled 'On the progress of adhering to the agreement on deliveries of equipment and materials to the construction of the Jäniskoski power station'.[77] The Pechenga party committee was obviously not pleased with how the Soviet suppliers had acquitted themselves, and was also pushing for speedy completion of the planned power line from Jäniskoski to Nikel. Their initiative was politely acknowledged by Petrov's deputy in Glavnikelkobalt, Mironov.[78]

Lower-level party organizations, exemplified here with the *oblast* and regional committees, did not cause commotion in the ministries or directorates. Forthcoming explanations of why their suggestions were inapplicable were enough to fend them off. The Party loomed much larger, however, once the Central Committee became involved. When the oblast committee reported directly to Politburo member Georgi Malenkov about the difficulties in the North,[79] Petrov in Glavnikelkobalt felt inclined to write a detailed report on the progress in Jäniskoski.[80] Tevosyan, at that time minister of metallurgical industry, forwarded Petrov's report to Malenkov, and added that 'orders have been given to ensure timely transport of spare parts, instruments and materials, and the execution of this is subjected to extraordinary control measures [*osobyi kontrol*]'.[81] One of the control measures involved, as mentioned, was punitive sanctions against Pechenganikel director Trofimov, a fact that also was reported to the Central Committee.[82] It was obviously important for Tevosyan to assure Malenkov that his ministry was on top of the situation, capable of handling the difficulties that had arisen. We may assume, then, that the attention from the Party served as a reminder to the industrialists that the ideological realm, controlled by the Bolsheviks, was always poised to meddle in their affairs, with the attendant sometimes difficult personal consequences.[83]

Kleshko versus Vakava

The presence of a looming party apparatus and the potentially devastating punishment for straying from its ideological path could be used as a means of applying pressure in conflicts within the Soviet system. The linchpin in the Jäniskoski project, Boris Mefodievich Kleshko, was to find himself at the receiving end of menacing slander, in an episode that must have weighed heavily on him. Tellingly, the accusations came from within his own ranks, and were charged with an ideological venom that required Kleshko's staunchest defence.

The conflict was connected to the problems of equipping the Jäniskoski reconstruction site with sufficient machinery. The erratic Soviet supplies not only were a source of internal Soviet bickering, but also caused irritation in Imatran Voima. Engineer Telestam, the Finnish project manager, aired his frustration to engineer Lebedev:

> You keep telling me to speed up the work, while at the same time, as you know, without machines that should have been here a year ago it is very hard to speed up anything. ... I take every measure to complete the maximum amount of work, but the absence of machinery for such a long period will inevitably influence the completion rate of the work program.[84]

Telestam's frustration with transport arrangements and the occasionally chaotic Soviet handling of these, was not limited to the freight of goods via the Liinahamari-Jäniskoski road. Another important transport route for Jäniskoski went through northern Finland. Some cargo from the Soviet Union and all the supplies from non-Soviet providers were trucked some 370 kilometres from Rovaniemi to the construction site.[85] The long freight distance and the heavy cargo made for a lucrative contract and fierce competition among several Finnish transport agencies – and one Soviet one – for the job. Vakava, a Soviet agency operating in Finland, got the contract. Telestam repeatedly pointed out to Kleshko, and rightly so, that he had broken his most holy of principles – to keep all Pechenganikel's costs to a minimum – in contracting Vakava for all freights from the south.[86] Telestam's taunting, however, was a minor problem compared to what Kleshko would experience at the hands of this Soviet firm. In the spring of 1949, Kleshko's relationship to Vakava came to take an ominous turn, potentially threatening his name, reputation and position.

Vakava had been established in late winter 1947, around the time the Jäniskoski reconstruction project was being developed. As a Soviet firm, run by the Administration for Soviet Property in Finland (USI Finland),[87] Vakava was bound to win the bid for the Jäniskoski transport assignment. It would be politically difficult – if not impossible – for Kleshko not to award his compatriots the contract. However, Kleshko was, as noted, deeply committed to curtailing Pechenganikel's expenses as much as possible. Matters were therefore complicated by the fact that Finnish transport agencies were offering to do the job at a lower price. To make things worse, in this context Vakava acted as a subcontractor, and hired in turn a Finnish firm, Lapin Kuletus, to do the actual cargo trucking for them. Vakava's sole contribution, then, was that of a price-increasing middle man.[88]

Gustav Telestam had urged Kleshko to opt for the Finnish firm Pohjolan Likkenen. It is possible that Telestam did this for reasons of personal gain – apparently, he had a business interest in the company – but Pohjolan Likkenen's price was in fact substantially lower than that offered by Vakava. Kleshko found himself between a rock and a hard place: should he go with the cheapest bid, thereby sticking by his principle of sparing Pechenganikel as many costs as possible, or should he silently accept Vakava's uncompetitive and inflated price? Kleshko chose the middle ground. Political necessity forced him to offer Vakava the contract, but on several occasions from 1947 to 1949 he tried to pressure Vakava's price down. Kleshko kept receiving new and lower bids from Finnish transport agencies – even one from Vakava's hired operator Lapin Kuletus – and used these as pretexts for negotiations with Vakava. Finally, in May 1949 the issue was brought to a head. Kleshko, having recently been informed of Vakava's considerable profit margin in their deal with Lapin Kuletus, demanded substantial price cuts. Vakava gave in slightly, but not enough. Kleshko's negative reaction was unsurprising, and serious enough that the Vakava management felt the contract was in danger of being annulled.[89] Kleshko was evidently no longer their ally.

There are several aspects of this episode that stand out. For one, the Soviet envoy Kleshko found himself in a business conflict with two other Soviet envoys: deputy head of USI Finland Maslov and the general director of Vakava, Avanesov. Secondly, one Soviet company operating abroad, Vakava, was basically squeezing another Soviet company operating at home, Pechenganikel, for as much foreign currency as possible. This was done through a highly capitalist and unproductive method – the subcontractor's use of hired labour. Truly, this was an episode very illustrative of the lack of logical coordination between Soviet entities that were meant to be acting for a common cause. Even more striking were the methods used by Vakava and USI Finland to put pressure on Kleshko when their price demands were questioned.

Maslov in USI Finland attacked Kleshko for his allegedly close ties to Gustav Telestam, who 'wanted to give the contract to a private capitalist company, in pursuit of his personal interests', and stated that 'for incomprehensible reasons comrade Kleshko supported him in this question'.[90] The intimations that Kleshko's loyalties lay with his capitalist friend Telestam rather than with Pechenganikel were serious, and were repeated in even more blunt language:

> [T]he clique of shrewd businessmen *[kuchka deltsov]* headed by Telestam ... became interested in transferring the contract from our firm to untrustworthy private chauffeurs ... in order to make it easier to perform certain operations aimed at their own private gain at the expense of 'Pechengo-Nikel' [*sic*]. Why comrade Kleshko supports this group of Finnish shrewd businessmen in the question of transport to Jäniskoski is unknown to us.[91]

As if this was not enough, it was made clear that it was not only Vakava that was in danger of losing its contract due to Kleshko's disloyalty. Another Soviet firm, Suomen Petrooli (literally Finnish Petrol), had been commissioned by Vakava to provide fuel for Lapin Kuletus, and thus been given entry into the Western market, in competition with 'major English and American oil companies (Shell, Nobel-Standard, Gulf-Oil) and the Finnish Trustivapaa Bensini'.[92] Obviously, this opportunity to beat the capitalists at their own game would be lost if Vakava no longer had the contract. Kleshko was consequently seen as an obstacle to Soviet success in Finland, and in effect as siding with the enemy.

In the Soviet context, these allegations, however vaguely presented, could prove very dangerous. Although it was never directly stated that Kleshko had crossed the line – such ominous questions were only hinted at – the implications were that he was no longer trustworthy and that he had developed strong ties to his capitalist partners in Finland. Upon receiving information about the conflict, Glavnikelkobalt ordered Kleshko to renew the contract with Vakava immediately, albeit at the same time asking the Directorate for Soviet Property Abroad to instruct Vakava to lower the price to a minimum. Kleshko was recalled to Moscow for meetings.[93]

It must have been a worried Kleshko who headed home to the Soviet capital. After all, his position as a loyal defender of Soviet interests abroad had been cast in doubt. Kleshko must have decided that attack was the best form of defence, a defence he put down on paper: In six closely written pages he thoroughly refuted the accusations made against him as completely unfounded. He characterized USI Finland and Vakava's accounts of the conflict as 'entirely slanderous, ... gravely distorted, biased and incorrect'. He denied having threatened annulment of the contract with Vakava, but willingly pleaded guilty to having been 'guided by an aspiration towards the maximum cut of transport costs', while never forgetting 'to give preference to our Soviet firm [Vakava]'. Kleshko systematically demonstrated how Vakava had been a more expensive alternative to Finnish firms, and especially emphasized how the enterprise made large profits from the contract, as they paid the Finnish partner Lapin Kuletus considerably less than what they received in direct transport fees. In fact, Kleshko stated, 20 per cent of the total price went to Vakava, thus making it 'a case where one Soviet firm receives a profit at the expense of another Soviet firm – Pechenganikel'. Kleshko rounded off his well-argued defence with a reiteration of his main points:

> Finally, I find it necessary to once again stress that the letters from comrade Maslov and comrade Ivanov concerning me are of a slanderous nature. I hold that I have, during my work with the firm Vakava, taken a correct position in constantly striving for price cuts in a rather significant post on the budget – transport – and this is a position I will continue to take.[94]

Fortunately for Kleshko, this defensive strategy worked. His superiors in Glavnikelkobalt did not doubt his commitment to Pechenganikel's cause, and – as far as the documentary evidence is concerned – chose to disregard all vague accusations of disloyalty and fraternization with his capitalist contacts in Finland. Instead, from the documentation available to him, Petrov considered it proven that Finnish firms were cheaper than Vakava and that Kleshko had acted correctly in demanding price cuts. Petrov also deemed it unreasonable that Vakava's position as a subcontractor should lead to higher transport tariffs than what could otherwise be obtained on the Finnish market.[95]

Thus, Kleshko's position was intact. His counterparts in Vakava and USI Finland had not managed to prompt any punitive reaction against him. Obviously, Kleshko's own defence played an important part in this, but it is also probable that he was well-connected in the higher echelons of Soviet party-state, and thus to a large degree protected from his rivals' malicious intent.[96] Further, it was probably important for Petrov to keep the episode within the industrial domain, and outside of the ideological sphere. If, say, a Communist Party Control Commission were to pick up on the accusations against his trusted envoy to Finland and find Kleshko guilty of disloyalty to Soviet interests, that would also reflect badly on Petrov himself.[97] Thus, it was in Petrov's interest to contain the conflict by resolving it quickly.

Most importantly, however, the episode shows the internal rivalry and lack of coordination between various Soviet agencies. We have seen how this played out in the border zone arrangements and jurisdiction questions in Jäniskoski. Especially among the traditionally strong sectors like defence and foreign affairs, infighting was frequent and sometimes fierce. In the Vakava case, the Soviet bickering became exposed to outsiders, the Finns, and the otherwise rather uncomplicated question of transport to Jäniskoski became a matter of contention between Vakava and Kleshko, with the latter being put in a potentially perilous position.

The storm blew over, however, and Kleshko eventually became the object of great appreciation. By mid-1950, the conclusion of the Jäniskoski project was in sight. Imatran Voima's job was nearing its end, and the Soviet customer was very pleased with the result. Already in 1949, the question of a special reward for Telestam had come up.[98] A. I. Petrov, the mining engineer who by then had taken over the reins at the Pechenganikel combine, also included Kleshko, his engineers Lebedev and Nikitin and the Helsinki office accountant Golovanov in a request for a trip to the ultimate Soviet spa experience: he recommended that the four be sent to 'the southern coast of the Crimea' for a month, and that Telestam be given two trips accompanied by his wife.[99] But before they were able to enjoy such balmy rewards, Kleshko, Telestam and colleagues would have to make sure the power station was safely transferred to its Soviet owner, Minelektrostantsii.

A problematic takeover

The handing over of the power station would be a bumpy process. Originally, a gradual Soviet takeover was foreseen to start in summer 1950, when the first turbine and generator were scheduled for installation and initial production. A Soviet management group of nine engineers would be appointed, and another eleven workers in support functions would accompany them. A few Finnish engineers, in addition to Swedish representatives from the firms delivering the turbine and generator (ASEA and Karlstad Mekaniska Verkstad), would for a short period overlap with their Soviet colleagues to ensure a smooth transition.[100] This proved far more complicated than expected. The main problem was that neither the Ministry of Metallurgical Industry nor Pechenganikel, as metallurgical agencies, had suitable personnel among their cadres. These would have to come from within the ranks of the Ministry of Power Stations (Minelektrostantsii) or be recruited directly from technical schools (ordered by the Ministry of Higher Education).[101] As seen in previous chapters, properly educated personnel were not easy to come by and were prized assets in the Soviet economy. The compartmentalized nature of the various sectors meant that a transfer of qualified labour was no simple matter – every sector would instinctively make it a priority to fend for its own interests and keep its own skilled people. Again, the Soviet system's ability to coordinate its efforts for the good of Jäniskoski was put to the test, and again it failed.

On 13 July 1950, experiments began. The power station was up and running by 31 July, as planned, and from now on, Jäniskoski delivered electrical power to Pechenganikel. However, while the Finns and Swedes had met their contract obligations, the Soviet customer was not fully prepared to take possession of the property. Kleshko reported on the lack of Soviet personnel in his usual brusque style:

> It must be remarked, that the status of the power station's operational personnel is extremely unfortunate, as in fact there is no operational personnel at all. Work at the station has gone awry from the very first moment. The turbine specialists and electricians at the control panel are all Finnish. … The absence of even just one [Soviet] turbine operator is a big oversight from our side, both during the installation and now. Svan, the main fitter from the Swedish firm KMV [Karlstad mechanical workshop] has already left, and in fact never gave any practical demonstrations, advice or information to anyone, either

about the assembling or on how to operate the turbine. He repeatedly asked: 'When will the fellow, to whom I may explain, demonstrate and show everything to in detail, arrive?' Such a person, unfortunately, did not arrive before Svan left. … It is necessary, at least now, to solve the most serious question of bringing the Jäniskoski station up to full strength with an operational staff. The power station is good – and good hands are necessary from the very beginning.[102]

Thus, Pechenganikel's first electricity from Jäniskoski was actually provided by a group of Finnish engineers. When the time came for the formal handover of Jäniskoski, the takeover commission's chairman Ryaboshapko wanted a postponement. The power station was simply not finished, he stated.[103] Ryaboshapko was the head of Kolenergo, Minelektrostantsii's subordinate organization providing electricity on the Kola Peninsula. Kolenergo would, after the takeover was finalized, operate Jäniskoski and be responsible for providing Pechenganikel with much-needed electricity.

It is remarkable how Kolenergo and Minelektrostantsii were reluctant to complete this takeover, while Glavnikelkobalt and Pechenganikel were equally intent on an expedient transfer. For the Ministry of Metallurgical Industry, a source of worry was that the longer the takeover was delayed, the costlier would the project become. Until all Finnish personnel had left, their wages, which constituted a 'significant sum in Finnish marks', had to be covered by Pechenganikel and the ministry.[104] On the other hand, Minelektrostantsii and Kolenergo wanted to avoid taking over an undermanned power station, especially one as remote as Jäniskoski. Ryaboshapko's request for a delay in the takeover commission's trip to Jäniskoski was turned down, and from 13 to 26 December the commission assessed Imatran Voima's work. This, however, did not mean that Minelektrostantsii was ready to take responsibility.

The transfer of Jäniskoski from Pechenganikel to Kolenergo dragged on well into 1951. Matters were sped up when the Ministry of Metallurgical Industry was once again reorganized and divided into two separate ministries on 23 December 1950.[105] Petr Lomako was reinstated as minister of non-ferrous metallurgy, and soon thereafter personally intervened in the Jäniskoski question. In a letter to the Council of Ministers, Lomako emphasized that all work, apart from installation of the final turbine and generator, had been completed. The only reason the Finns could not be sent home was lack of Soviet personnel to operate the station. He requested the Council to immediately order Minister Zhimerin in Minelektrostantsii to take responsibility for Jäniskoski, and to provide the necessary operational personnel.[106] Minelektrostantsii was still unwilling, however, and agreed to become the new owner of Jäniskoski only 'in principle' *(v printsipe)* and under a series of conditions. Lomako, clearly annoyed at these refusals and the fact that his own ministry was paying unnecessary amounts of Finnish currency to Imatran Voima due to the long takeover process, wrote another letter to the Council of Ministers:

> The Ministry of Power Stations makes its takeover of Jäniskoski power station subject to extraordinary and unfounded demands, which they expect the Ministry of Nonferrous Metallurgy to fulfill. The Ministry of Non-ferrous Metallurgy has built the power station in Jäniskoski to the extent foreseen in the contract with the Finnish firm and in accordance with the Finnish–Soviet agreement of 3 February, 1947. Inasmuch as the Ministry of Power Stations in principle agrees to take over Jäniskoski power station, it also has to complete all work that comes in addition to what has been done by the Ministry of Nonferrous Metallurgy under the agreement with the Finns. With this in mind, the Ministry of Nonferrous Metallurgy asks that no further tasks in the subsequent building of the Jäniskoski power station be laid upon it from the moment of transfer to the Ministry of Power Stations.[107]

Although the work at Jäniskoski was more or less completed, Lomako knew that a significant number of construction projects still were in the pipeline. Apart from the fitting and installation of the second generator and turbine, due in summer 1951, the Jäniskoski settlement had to be transformed into a village within the Soviet command system *(rabochaya poselka)*. This meant, in addition to supplying all the support services needed to operate the power station, building a village hospital and a school, and organizing a telegraph, postal system and necessary commercial services.[108] Despite resistance, the Council of Ministers decreed that responsibility for Jäniskoski be transferred to Minelektrostantsii on 1 May 1951. With this, Pechenganikel was free to worry exclusively about the further development of its own mining operation, and Mintsvetmet was relieved of further responsibilities in Jäniskoski. And, of course, Boris Mefodievich Kleshko and his subordinates in Helsinki were able to congratulate themselves on a job well done. Moreover, they had paved the way for new power station projects in the Pasvik valley – projects that would not be tackled by them, but by Minelektrostantsii.

Expansion and coexistence

The heading for this concluding section is taken from Adam B. Ulam's seminal work on Soviet foreign policy.[109] Ulam sees two main trends, expansion and coexistence, as descriptive of Soviet foreign policy at large. This was also true in the foreign policy 'microcosm' of the Pasvik valley. While expanding Soviet national territory, Soviet interests coexisted with both their Finnish and later their Norwegian neighbours, inasmuch as they took advantage of both Finnish and later Norwegian expertise on hydroelectric power. In turn, this coexistence led to a further expansion of Soviet industrial potential, as it was essential for providing energy to the power-demanding nickel refining processes on the Kola Peninsula.

Already in September 1948, about halfway into the Jäniskoski project, the question of further development of hydroelectric power on the Pasvik River had been brought up. Semyon Petrov, head of Glavnikelkobalt, visited the construction site, and in a conversation with Gustav Telestam asked whether the river had other whitewater sections suited for the purpose. This was the right person to ask: prior to the Soviet acquisition of Petsamo, Telestam had looked into the matter for Petsamon Nikkeli OY. He was quickly able to give an assessment of the various rapids in the river, and recommended that the Rajakoski rapids, located only 12 kilometres northeast of Jäniskoski, be exploited for power production.[110]

From a Soviet perspective, there was little doubt that the Jäniskoski power plant alone would be insufficient to meet the projected power demands of the Kola nickel industry. By 1949, when Pechenganikel had completed the first phase of its reconstruction (see Chapter 4), production had to be kept at half capacity, due to low energy supplies.[111] The future thirst for industrial power would be even harder to quench. According to the Leningrad-based planning agency Gidroenergoproekt, Pechenganikel and Severonikel combined would require 1,000 million kilowatt hours a year by 1954/55, whereas Kolenergo, if no new power sources were developed, would be able to provide only 600 million kilowatt hours.[112] A shortage of 400 million kilowatt hours would have to be made up for, and Jäniskoski was only one of many steps on the way to full coverage.

Throughout the Jäniskoski project, future construction of a power plant at Rajakoski was discussed. Gustav Telestam and Imatran Voima were centrally placed in these discussions, and at the end of the Jäniskoski project their services were again commissioned by the Soviet Union. It was of the essence to start soon, so as to be able to make use of machinery, buildings and workers already in place at nearby Jäniskoski.[113] However, as a semi-public enterprise, Imatran Voima required a decree from the Finnish government. As in the Jäniskoski case, this was taken care of through an agreement between the Soviet and Finnish Governments. The agreement was signed on 13 June 1950, and provided for Imatran Voima's construction of dams, as well as delivery and fitting of all electrical equipment.[114] Now the Finns would have to get used to another Soviet counterpart, as the Council of Ministers had left the responsibility also for this project in Minelektrostantsii's hands.[115]

Rajakoski power station was completed early 1956. Soon thereafter, the construction of yet another power station was requested by the Soviet Union. This time it was the Kaitakoski rapids, some 10 kilometres south of Jäniskoski, that were to be exploited. When the power station in Kaitakoski was completed in 1959, that marked the end of a twelve-year period of intense Soviet electrification of the upper Pasvik valley, by Finnish hands (see Map 1).[116] For a little while at least, Pechenganikel had been secured a sufficient supply of electricity.

* * *

As we have seen in this chapter, the Soviet Union was well-positioned to solve pressing energy concerns in the Pechenga area. The socialist state used its leverage as victor, from the elevated quarters in the Hotel Torni in Helsinki, to acquire access to the Pasvik River. Importantly, this was all done with Finnish consent and within the boundaries of international law. The Jäniskoski area, containing three exploitable rapids, was legally purchased – not acquired by military means – from Finland. The company Imatran Voima was paid in Finnish marks, although the money was taken from the Soviet war booty – the 6.5 billion marks left in Finland by Germany. This arrangement was obviously also in Finland's interest. For Imatran Voima, long-term projects like Jäniskoski and Rajakoski must have been lucrative. For the Finnish state, it was an efficient way of reducing monetary obligations to the Soviet Union, and thereby diminishing Soviet influence over the Finnish economy. The positive effects on employment rates in northern Finland must also have played a part. Furthermore, the well-being of Imatran Voima, as a semi-public enterprise, was important to the Finnish state. The fact that both the Soviet Union and Finland signed an agreement for yet another power plant to be built on the Pasvik River as the Jäniskoski project came to an end shows the beneficial effects of the collaboration for both sides.

Within the Soviet apparatus there existed many tensions. First of all, concerns over border security in agencies like MVD were pitted against the industrial ambitions of the metallurgical sector. While MVD and the border guards were set on containing Soviet territory as much as possible, Glavnikelkobalt and Mintsvetmet (and Minmetallurgprom) worked for expedient and uncomplicated access to Jäniskoski for

Finnish workers. When it came to the construction site itself, however, it was the industrialists that were worried about security, especially when the power station was nearing completion. Site security was seen as separate from border security and was therefore not considered to be a concern for Soviet border troops. The result was a mongrel arrangement: a strictly contained area without police and law, and with an extremely unclear jurisdictional status. Nevertheless, the fact that Jäniskoski was at all rebuilt – and by a Finnish company at that – shows that the Soviet industrial sector carried considerable weight, also when faced with the Soviet security establishment.

Perhaps more notable was the widespread infighting between various Soviet agencies in matters far less significant than the question of jurisdiction. The history of Jäniskoski illustrates how the Soviet system, contrary to socialist ideals of collective unification, was in fact rife with bickering and conflicting interests. On the enterprise or directorate level, attempts at shunning responsibility were frequent. One example was Kolenergo's refusal to take responsibility for the almost completed Jäniskoski power station; another was UShossDor's foot-dragging on maintenance of the Nikel–Jäniskoski transport route, despite clear instructions from the Council of Ministers. On the individual level, personal disagreements, as in the case of Kleshko's opposition to the Soviet transport agency Vakava, could result in libellous letters being sent to superiors in Moscow.

This, of course, does not mean that the Soviet command structure was necessarily unable to complete complicated tasks. Although we see a system that was sometimes paralysed by abdication of responsibility and an ensuing inertia, the intensity with which some individuals like Kleshko and Petrov worked to fulfil their assignments was remarkable. Naturally, it was also in their personal interest to see the power station completed, but they worked for this goal with a fervour that went beyond the call of duty. In many ways, Kleshko's individual abilities and efforts made the Jäniskoski project viable. We should not forget that the Soviet Union was a country devastated by the Second World War. Getting just one truckload of supplies to remote Jäniskoski could be considered a feat. The sources suggest that this feat was to a large extent the personal accomplishment of Boris Mefodievich Kleshko.

Kleshko, more than anyone else also in the Jäniskoski sources, exemplifies a remarkable willingness to criticize shortcomings within the Soviet system. His candour and brusqueness lay far from the propagandistic picture of Soviet superiority that was both presented to the outside world and prepared for internal consumption. He repeatedly and openly praised the efforts of capitalist Finns, while at the same time voicing disapproval of his own Soviet suppliers. Numerous documents written by various actors in the metallurgical complex suggest that Kleshko belonged to a group of Soviet industrialists who in many respects stood intellectually closer to their Finnish counterparts than they did to Soviet actors who did not share their motivation. The unifying factor between the Kleshko-type Soviet industrialist and his Western (in this case Finnish) counterpart, it seems, was a deep commitment to getting the job done. In that sense, then, the case of Kleshko shows that the Soviet system did in fact foster highly industrious leaders, some of whom were appointed to head important projects.

For an operator within the Soviet command structure, getting the job done could at times require creative solutions. Superior Soviet bodies like the Council of Ministers or the State Planning Committee (Gosplan) would demand progress, while also creating seemingly impassable hurdles to the very same progress. This was experienced daily by factory managers in the Soviet industrial sector.[117] Jäniskoski was no different: Firstly, while the border control was to remain watertight, enough workers had to be allowed to enter the area. Secondly, Kolenergo was ordered to take the reins in Jäniskoski, but Kolenergo already had a shortage of hands and no men to spare. These examples illustrate further what was mentioned about decrees from the central level: they were often an expression of Moscow's intentions, and not necessarily in keeping with the possibilities on the ground. Nevertheless, the central level was rarely directly ignored, even in small matters.[118]

From 1947 to 1951, Imatran Voima contributed to solving Pechenganikel's energy crisis by rebuilding the hydroelectric power plant in Jäniskoski. The Finnish company would lend its services to the Soviet Union in connection with two additional power plants on the Pasvik River– in Rajakoski (completed in 1956) and Kaitakoski (completed in 1959). In this way, the power plants of the Pasvik River became, as Pechenganikel already was, repositories for Western technology within the Soviet Union. Soon, Western input was to become even more pronounced, when Norway collaborated with the Soviet Union in building yet another two Soviet power stations in the valley. The last Soviet power plant, Hevoskoski, was completed in 1970. By that time, Pechenganikel had long been left to its primary tasks – producing and refining nickel.

6

Conclusion

What we know is that ... nobody knows anything. You can't know anything. The things you know you don't know. Intention? Motive? Consequence? Meaning? All that we don't know is astonishing. Even more astonishing is what passes for knowing.

Philip Roth, 2005[1]

These humbling words remind us that drawing conclusions is a dangerous sport. Much like the Stalinist leadership, historians are not omniscient and can therefore only present their own interpretations of past events. To assert that the interpretation offered here represents anything close to the full and absolute truth would be folly. Bearing this sobering insight in mind, I will nevertheless attempt in the following to make sense of the many twists and turns in the history of Petsamo, PNO, Pechenga and Pechenganikel.

In the first chapter of this book, I introduced several topics relevant to developments in Petsamo/Pechenga, most notably the economic and political nature of the Stalinist regime. In this concluding chapter, with hindsight to the narrative that has been presented in this book, I will readdress these topics. Finally, I offer some last remarks pertaining to the two aspects – Soviet economic ambitions and security concerns – that have helped frame the research presented in this book.

Pechenga and Soviet autarchy

When Finland's claim to Pechenga gained acceptance around the negotiating table in Tartu in October 1920, this was hardly seen as a strategic blunder by the Soviet delegation. The eastern slopes of the Pasvik valley had scant military significance. Topographically speaking, the territory might even become a burden in the event of an attack from the West: its low elevation would make it hard to defend. Neither was there anything to indicate that Soviet economic interests would suffer by the loss of this territory. There was apparently nothing in Pechenga that did not exist in abundance elsewhere in the former tsardom. For Finland, the acquisition of Pechenga primarily meant that, if functioning roads and railway tracks could be built, the young republic would no longer be partly trapped behind frozen waters in the Gulf of Bothnia or be dependent on passage through the narrow Danish straits when exiting the Baltic Sea. Finland would enjoy unrestricted access to the world oceans all year round.

Less than twelve months after Pechenga had become Petsamo, things started to change. With Talvia and Törnquist's geological expedition in 1921, a process that would furnish the territory with strategic importance was set in motion. Slightly more than ten years later, the economic potential of Petsamo was drastically upgraded. Major industrial players negotiated with the Finnish state for the right to exploit the massive mineral ore deposits identified there. Fanning the flames of interest, the ore that was to be drawn from Petsamo contained not just any metal: it contained nickel, a 'strategic metal'. Due to its remarkable heat and shock resistance, nickel was coveted by the world's producers of munitions, armoured steel plates and other means of war. I will argue that it was a deepening Soviet appreciation of Petsamo's nickel resources and the role the strategic metal could play in enhancing the country's international position that, in 1944, prompted Moscow to retake the land that had been relinquished twenty-four years earlier.

Commissar of Foreign Affairs Vyacheslav Molotov breached the Soviet line in the Petsamo matter when he made Moscow's claim to Finnish nickel output known to Finnish envoy Juho Kusti Paasikivi in June 1940. Though there probably exist documents explicitly stating why the Kremlin so surprisingly trumpeted its right to nickel matte from Petsamo – an area they had willingly handed back to Finland at the conclusion of the Winter War three months earlier – my archival research has not yielded such documentation. Consequently, I have been obliged to explain the Soviet turnaround circumstantially, from reasonable inferences from the available documentation and from what is known about the Soviet state and Soviet policies at the time.

In Chapter 3, I argued that rather than seeing Petsamo as a valuable buffer zone, the Soviet leadership was primarily interested in acquiring the territory both for the nickel itself and the industrial network that had been set up by Canadian-owned Petsamon Nikkeli OY. The information that kindled this interest – contained in reconnaissance reports from Soviet mining specialists who in panegyric terms praised the Petsamo nickel operation – was in all probability received and digested by the Kremlin leaders sometime during the late spring/early summer of 1940.

Also in a broader industrial context, the ambition to turn Petsamo into Pechenga makes sense. As noted in the introductory chapter, a Soviet campaign to explore and exploit Arctic natural resources – the 'settling of the North' (*osvoenie severa*) – had from the early 1930s been transforming the Siberian and Kola Peninsula tundra into industrially productive areas. In 1935, the Soviet authorities decided to establish nickel plants at three separate locations: one in northern Siberia, where they simultaneously established the city of Norilsk (Norilsk Nikel), one in Orsk on the southern slopes of the Urals (Yuzhuralnikel) and one on the Monche tundra south of Murmansk (Severonikel). Severonikel started production in 1939. The three mining engineers who examined the Petsamo mines and smelter in March 1940 were all stationed there. Having just contributed to the Severonikel upstart, they were well-attuned to the technological requirements and organizational demands posed by a nickel-producing venture. Their observations left no doubt that the nickel plant in Petsamo was well suited as an example for the juvenile Soviet nickel industry.

Of course, the Soviet thirst for nickel played out against a wider backdrop than merely that of industry. Acutely aware of its strategic properties, the Soviet leadership sought to be self-sufficient in nickel supply. This was an obvious ambition in 1940, in the early phase of the Second World War, but it was no less relevant in 1944, when the war could be seen to be ending. Despite having defeated Nazi Germany alongside the Western powers, the Soviet leadership remained distrustful of their wartime allies. A new and far more protracted conflict – the Cold War – was in the making. The lengthy competition for ideological supremacy that ensued drove the Soviet Union to speed up production in all branches, but especially in industries of military significance. Already the first post-war five-year plan from 1946 left no doubt that the Soviet leadership had every intention of demonstrating that productivity in their socialist state was superior to that of the capitalist world. For the nickel industry in Pechenga, this entailed a hasty rebuilding of the demolished production capacities so that the enterprise could serve Moscow's purposes.

A new and intensified period of frantic activity began. If the 1930s were a time for building socialism in the Soviet Union, the immediate post-war years can be seen as a time for *rebuilding* socialism, or the socialist production base. The switch from 'Petsamo' to 'Pechenga' was much more than just a name change. Everything changed, as the region was transformed to a Soviet municipality *(raion)* and its nickel industry became a Soviet enterprise.

From being a Finnish territory developed by an archetypical representative of Western capitalism – the Canadian-owned conglomerate International Nickel Company (Inco) – Pechenga became the scene of a radical reorientation towards the values of 'the vanguard of progressive humanity'[2] – towards socialism. Applying methods developed during the industrialization campaigns in the 1930s – shock-working, socialist competition, Stakhanovism, Marxist indoctrination and of course, the extremely ambitious five-year plans – the new owners of Pechenga rapidly and thoroughly Sovietized the area, making it their own. The result, a speedy recovery of production after wartime damages, was both predictable and impressive. Equally predictable, albeit not equally impressive, was the dire infrastructure of daily life in the new territory.

Totalitarian intent in a nested dictatorship

I would venture the assertion that both the propagated self-perception of Stalinism and the models of totalitarianism that were developed by Western scholars to understand it were ideal representations that failed to capture the multifaceted nature of Soviet society. In many ways, the totalitarian interpretation of Stalinism was a product of Stalinism itself, as it took the Soviet façade at face value. Informed as they were by empirical studies of publicly accessible official sources, later scholars made the same error as their objects of study: they mistook façade for reality.

As discussed in the introductory chapter, the Stalinist regime was neither omniscient nor omnipotent. Even for leaders fired by totalitarian intent, one day still has only twenty-four hours; it is simply not possible for a small group of people to run a country in all detail. True, the Politburo agendas were packed with trifles, and masses of documents bear the signature of Stalin or other Politburo members. However, that is not so much a symptom of achieved totalitarian rule as it is an indication of totalitarian *intent*. To the Soviet leaders, it was important to be perceived as omniscient. In this, they succeeded – in principle there were no matters too petty for Stalin or a Politburo member to meddle in. But achieving the ideal-type totalitarian rule was impossible. The complex reality of the vast Soviet empire precluded the full realization of such ambitions. If anything, the Kremlin's focus on trivial matters carried with it a danger of the leadership losing sight of more important strategic issues.

The oppressive Stalinist state was upheld by an immense hierarchical command system. In some ways, the Soviet governance system worked like other bureaucracies. Orders were executed according to directions from above, and individual promotions could be obtained through successful implementation of these orders. On the other hand, the system was infused with power mechanisms and a governance tradition that impeded both creativity and efficiency. Specific to the Soviet system were the repressive means at the disposal of the many 'smaller Stalins' in the 'nested dictatorship', reproducing not only discursive elements of propaganda from the Kremlin but also its coercive methods of suppression. Supervisors at all levels in the Soviet pecking order were potential, and sometimes fatal, threats to their subordinates.

Also, the inflexible top–down planning of all sectors of Soviet production made for many unintended distortions of targets and outputs further down the command structure. However hard the State Planning Committee tried, it simply could not replace the market mechanisms of supply and demand. The result was a Soviet bureaucracy that in some ways resembled other governance systems, but that, at least in certain crucial areas, was infinitely more dysfunctional in all its rigidities and arbitrariness.

The shortcomings of the planned economy were felt at all levels of Soviet life, but perhaps most acutely by the common man, woman and child. The company town of Nikel was no exception. Living in poor conditions, the work force of Pechenganikel was expected to pull the massive weight of resurrecting the enterprise from the rubbles of war. For many years, the housing situation barely improved, all the while the production of nickel matte was intensified and increased. This reflected the strong emphasis the Soviet authorities put on production targets, and their correspondingly feeble commitment to providing the necessities of everyday life for Soviet citizens.

That said, also the industrial sphere experienced massive difficulties within the framework of the Soviet command economy. In Pechenga, this was particularly evident in the logistics sector. The ships that were to deliver new provisions to the distant territory were erratic at best. The Pechenga roads and local means of transport, ranging from horse carriages to decommissioned army vehicles, all suffered from lack of supplies and maintenance. These difficulties certainly made life no easier for Pechenganikel's managerial staff, and improvements were hard to come by.

As late as the early 1950s, the same logistical obstacles were also threatening to undermine the rebuilding of the hydroelectric power plant in Jäniskoski, some 100 kilometres upstream the Pasvik River. Perhaps the main impediment to improvements lay not in the infrastructure itself, but in the Soviet governmental structure. Vertically organized by branches of production or control, Soviet ministries with their underlying agencies were closed systems that had little or no incentive to lend a helping hand to a 'neighboring' branch. Thus, for example, the Soviet highway management, which was subordinate to the Ministry of the Interior, gave no indication of interest in directing scarce resources to the maintenance of a distant road that led only to the isolated Jäniskoski power plant. That road was simply too unimportant to bother about – moreover, the continuing problems resulting from its impassable condition would reflect badly on someone else, in this case the Pechenganikel combine and the Ministry of Non-ferrous Metallurgy.

How, then, in a system seemingly devoid of positive material incentives, could such momentous feats as the rebuilding of Pechenganikel and restart of nickel matte production be achieved, a mere two years after a ruinous war? Clearly, the priorities of the Soviet leadership, with its immense authority and obvious interest in a speedy revival of Pechenga's industrial activity, should not be underestimated. However, that does not provide the full picture. The success of any reconstruction effort will always depend on the people who actually do the work. Though the power of decree and the activating effect of the stick were palpable, they cannot fully account for the eagerness of the Pechenganikel work force. Neither can the positive incentives that in fact did exist, such as higher salaries in the North and premiums for increased productivity. All these elements matter, of course, but the one decisive factor lay in the motivation of the workers and managers themselves. Accepting and adopting the incessant propaganda of socialist values, especially in the defiant post-war years, was probably inevitable for the common Soviet citizen. Thus, I would argue, Pechenganikel was resurrected by a group of people who *wanted* to rebuild socialism. To a large extent, this shared wish counterbalanced and even made up for some of the flaws of the Soviet planned economy.

In a similar way, the notion of a multitude of miniature Stalins wielding dictatorial powers on all levels of the 'nested dictatorship' has its limitations for explaining the apparent autonomy enjoyed by lower-level bureaucrats in the Soviet system. An example is provided by the personal conduct of Boris Mefodievich Kleshko, who was charged with overseeing the reconstruction of the Jäniskoski hydroelectric power plant. From 1947 to 1951, this civil servant was obliged to negotiate the expectations of his own superiors in the Ministry for Non-ferrous Metallurgy, handle organizational resistance and inertia from other Soviet branches of production and even confront the bourgeois representatives of Finnish capitalism. As a member of the Soviet political monoculture, he demonstrated an astonishing non-conformity not only when in the company of Finns, but even more so when facing foot-dragging Soviet bureaucrats who delayed his project. Refusing to yield to the pressure applied by fellow Soviet industrialists, he put himself in harm's way for the sake of the reconstruction of the Jäniskoski power plant. With his knowledge of how to work the Soviet system and ability to relate professionally to his Finnish partners, Kleshko defied the logics of the totalitarian model – all for the best of the Soviet state.

Thus, Kleshko's story serves as an example of how rigorous work ethics and professional pride could counter some of the worst effects of the dysfunctional Soviet system. It also bears witness to the limitations of the alleged absolute power of the Stalinist regime. In this case, the planned objective – rebuilding the Jäniskoski power plant – was achieved less by decree and more by Kleshko's individual aptness and unwavering ambition to get the job done. To allow myself a speculative counterfactual assertion: Had Kleshko's Soviet adversaries, the 'smaller Stalins' who attempted to pin him down as a supporter of the Finnish 'clique of shrewd businessmen' succeeded, he would probably have been removed from his office as a 'class enemy'. There is little doubt that this would have meant that electric power from the Jäniskoski turbines would have come much later.

* * *

The history of Petsamo/Pechenga was from 1921 bound to the local nickel ore. From the time of its discovery, the mineral resource transformed the area from a quiet wilderness into an object of great interest to the outside world. The attention directed towards the nickel resource in this northern periphery was motivated in many ways, but it was purely commercial concerns that steered the gaze of the world's foremost nickel producer to the Finnish–Norwegian borderland. Aiming to preserve its world monopoly, International Nickel Company of Canada industrialized Petsamo. Then, in the build-up to the German attack on the Soviet Union in June 1941, the Petsamo question became a contentious issue in Finland's troubled relations with the two authoritarian rival states. Now the commercially motivated attraction to the nickel resources became infused with a strong strategic component. Acutely aware of the military significance of nickel, the warring powers were keen not only to secure enough of the strategic metal for themselves, but also to limit enemy access to it.

The coming of peace did little to change the Soviet valuation of nickel. In the aftermath of the long war, the Kremlin was as determined as ever to create an indestructible defence of the socialist fatherland. The prime means to achieve this goal was to continue the massive industrialization that had started in the 1930s. Both by virtue of its substantial nickel ore and as a repository of Western technology, Petsamo became an attractive appendage to these efforts. In 1944, Petsamo was permanently annexed to the Soviet Union and given back its old name, Pechenga. The strategic significance of nickel only increased from then on. A major component in much war materiel, nickel was in high demand in the Soviet military-industrial complex. The arms race, fuelled by the ideological and geopolitical stalemate of the Cold War, made sure that the production network in Pechenga grew.

In the post-war decades, the once Finnish territory would witness, as mentioned in Chapter 5, another four Soviet hydropower plants on the Pasvik River (there are also two Norwegian power plants there). Infrastructure would make immense leaps forward, both in terms of roads and railway lines. In 1957, a year after the railway reached Nikel, the neighbouring town of Zapolyarnyi was established, centred around enormous open-air pits for the extraction of more nickel. As the rest of the Kola Peninsula, the Pechenga region was palpably affected by military presence, most notably the Northern Fleet, which immensely increased human presence in this once untouched wilderness.

With growth come growing pains. By the late 1970s, Sulphur dioxide emissions from the Pechenganikel smelters had disfigured and burnt large swathes of boreal forests in the vicinity of Nikel. By the time the Soviet Union entered its final era, acidic waste from the local production was long considered not only a Soviet problem; it was deeply affecting Pechenga's Nordic neighbours as well. Thus, from the relative comfort of Soviet isolation of the preceding decades, the nickel industry in Pechenga again entered the international scene, this time as a problem to be fixed rather than a property to be coveted. Thus, perhaps the most palpable part of Pechenga's sovietization was the environmental degradation that ensued after four decades of fervent and unrestrained socialist production. Little did geology student Hugo Törnquist know of the consequences, when he first laid hand on the nickel-rich rocks of Petsamo in 1921.

Notes

Chapter 1

1 Sergei M. Kirov (1957), *Izbrannye stati i rechi*, Moscow: Gosudarstvennoe izdatelstvo politicheskoi literatury, p. 66.
2 *Reka Paz*, or simply *Paz*, is the official Russian name of the river. However, in Soviet documents variations of the Norwegian form Pasvik and more often the Finnish form Paatsjoki are frequently used. In all probability, all forms stem from the Saami name *Baccevæj-dædno*. For a brief etymological discussion, see V. A. Matsak (ed.) (2005), *Pechenga: Opyt kraevedcheskoi entsiklopedii*, Murmansk: Prosvetitelskiy tsentr 'Dobrokhot', pp. 454–5. Being a native Norwegian speaker, I have chosen to use the Norwegian names for both the river and the valley it runs through: the Pasvik River and the Pasvik valley. Several other geographical names in this study, such as Petsamo/Pechenga and Kolosjoki/Nikel, will appear in both their Finnish and Russian forms. The shifts will be duly explained when they occur.
3 See Max Engman and Kasper Westerlund (eds) (2009), *Petsamo och havet*, Åbo: Uniprint, pp. 7–10. For a popular and illustrated account of the Petsamo corridor's significance as transport route in 1940–1, see Eric Björklund (1981), *Petsamotrafiken*, Danderyd: Åkeriförlaget.
4 See Henrik Meinander (2018), 'Finland', in David Stahel (ed.), *Joining Hitler's Crusade*, Cambridge: Cambridge University Press, pp. 17–45.
5 For this well-established interpretation of Stalin's reign, see Robert C. Tucker (1990), *Stalin in Power: The Revolution from above, 1929–1941*, New York: Norton. For an interesting introduction to Stalinism, see Richard Sakwa (1998), *Soviet Politics in Perspective*, London: Routledge, pp. 29–49.
6 This Kirov quote, which adorned the 'Soviet Arctic' pavilion at the All-Union Agricultural-Economic Exhibition (precursor of the later VDNKh) is cited in McCannon's work on the Soviet exploration of the vast northern areas of Eurasia: John McCannon (1998), *Red Arctic: Polar*

Expedition and the Myth of the North in the Soviet Union, 1932–1939, Oxford: Oxford University Press, p. 116.
7 Anne Appelbaum (2003), *Gulag: A History of the Soviet Camps*, London: Allen Lane, p. 87.
8 For an ambitious attempt at understanding Soviet industrialism and its environmental legacy, see Andy Bruno (2016), *The Nature of Soviet Power: An Arctic Environmental History*, Cambridge: Cambridge University Press. In his book, Bruno specifically studies the industrialization of the Kola Peninsula to gain insight into 'the environmental history of twentieth-century economic modernization in the Soviet Union' (p. 2).
9 For an account of the fourth five-year plan, which was designed for Soviet recovery from the war damages and to enable the socialist state to compete industrially and militarily with the West, see Alec Nove (1978), *An Economic History of the U.S.S.R.*, New York: Penguin Books, pp. 287–321.
10 Stephen Kotkin (1995), *Magnetic Mountain: Stalinism as Civilization*, Berkeley, CA: University of California Press, pp. 355 and 363.
11 In an article critical of Kotkin's attempt at explaining the essence of Soviet society, Mark Edele claims that Kotkin is too preoccupied with the state and leaves little or no room for other fields of human interaction that existed independently of the state. See Mark Edele (2007), 'Soviet Society, Social Structure, and Everyday Life', *Kritika: Explorations in Russian and Eurasian History*, Vol. 8, No. 2, pp. 349–73. While Edele's critique opens up to wider perspectives for future historical research on Stalinism, it does seem to overlook one of Kotkin's main findings: that Stalinism, in its many linguistic and physical reproductions, permeated all spheres of Soviet life and thereby constituted 'the fabric of society' (ibid., p. 364) that Edele finds to be missing from Kotkin's study.
12 Kotkin, *Magnetic Mountain*, p. 3. The totalitarian model was under attack already from the 1960s. However, that criticism was mainly directed at its application to the understanding of the Khrushchev era, and later to subsequent periods in Soviet history. Only with the Stalinism debate in the journal *Russian Review* was the totalitarian model claimed to be unsuited to a full understanding of Stalinism (see Edele, 'Soviet Society, Social Structure, and Everyday Life', p. 362). For an introduction to totalitarian models and the criticism levelled against them, see Sakwa, *Soviet Politics in Perspective*, pp. 156–60.

13 Edele, 'Soviet Society, Social Structure, and Everyday Life', p. 362.
14 As is evident from Edele's critique (see above), Kotkin by no means disregards the state and its influence over people's lives but rather demonstrates the degree to which Stalinist *discourse* became ingrained in people's imaginations and self-perceptions, constituting the foundation for what he calls the Stalinist civilization. Thus, Kotkin confirms not so much the totalitarian image of Stalin as a monolithic ruler as he identifies Stalinism as the hegemonic discourse that defined the boundaries of accepted speech and modes of action. As opposed to one of the fundamental premises of totalitarianism – that the population is passive and coerced (for a definition of totalitarianism, see Sakwa, *Soviet Politics in Perspective*, p. 158) – Kotkin emphasizes the active acceptance of Stalin and Stalinism among the Soviet population.
15 In his study of the Stalinist economy, Paul R. Gregory points out that '[a]lthough Lenin had argued that the party make only the most important decisions, Stalin spent as much time worrying about streets and monuments in Moscow, whether a highway should have two or four lanes, or the price of bread as about basic economic and foreign policy. By reserving the right to change any decision, no matter how trivial, all decisions ultimately ended up on his desk.' See Paul R. Gregory (2004), *The Political Economy of Stalinism: Evidence from the Soviet Secret Archives*, Cambridge: Cambridge University Press, p. 267; see also the listing of matters that were included in Politburo agendas in G. M. Adibekiv, K. M. Anderson and L. A. Rogovaya (eds) (2001), *Politbyuro TsK RKP(b): Povestki dnya zasedanii 1919–1952*, Moscow: Rosspen. Although this might suggest that Stalin and the Politburo were omnipresent, I will, as Gregory does (see following quotes), argue that this was in fact not the case.
16 The debate about how to understand Hitler's Germany, with its many parallels to the Stalinism debate, is presented and continued in Ian Kershaw (2000), *The Nazi Dictatorship: Problems and Perspectives of Interpretation*, 4th ed. London: Bloomsbury Academic. For a brief introduction to totalitarianism models and studies of Nazism, see pp. 23–6.
17 In his well-documented book, Gregory insists that Stalin and the Politburo in fact made 'pitifully few decisions' but that these were left to 'opportunistic agents' at lower levels. See Gregory (2004), *The Political*

Economy of Stalinism, p. 270. For 'nested dictatorship', see p. 156, and for the discussion of 'smaller Stalins', see pp. 269–70.

18 One example is provided by historian Vojtech Mastny, who already in a 1979 book appeared sceptical to the notion of Stalin's monolithic power. (See V. Mastny (1979), *Russia's Road to the Cold War: Diplomacy, Warfare and the Politics of Communism, 1941–1945*, New York, NY: Columbia University Press, p. xvi.) Mastny was later, with access to Soviet documentation, able to confirm his suspicions (see V. Mastny (1996), *The Cold War and Soviet Insecurity: The Stalin Years*, Oxford: Oxford University Press.) For a different view, also based on archival material available after 1991, see Vladislav Zubok and Constantine Pleshakov (1996), *Inside the Kremlin's Cold War: From Stalin to Khrushchev*, Cambridge, MA: Harvard University Press. Although Zubok and Pleshakov's portrayal of Stalin seems to implicitly confirm the totalitarian model, this is arguably a result of the authors' preoccupation with Stalin and his immediate surroundings. Rather than being an interpretation of Soviet decision making as such, therefore, the depiction of monolithic power seems to reflect the authors' Stalinocentric approach to the subject matter. I am grateful to Sven Holtsmark for pointing me in the direction of these authors.

19 Kershaw, *The Nazi Dictatorship*, p. 25.

20 Sakwa, *Soviet Politics in Perspective*, p. 159.

21 The vertically structured Soviet economy was organized according to branches of production. Ministries (or People's Commissariats) were responsible for not only the production of a certain commodity, but also all other activity associated with this production. For example, the Ministry of Non-ferrous Metallurgy (*Mintsvetmet*), which controlled the nickel industry in Pechenga, was charged with not only producing a certain amount of nickel each year, but also providing education, healthcare services and housing and so on. for the workers and their families. The Ministry of Power Stations (*Minelektrostantsii*) had corresponding responsibilities for the power stations that provided the nickel smelters with electricity, and for their employees. As we shall see, coordination between branches was difficult, as there were scant incentives for horizontal allegiances. For an introduction to the ministerial structure, see Alec Nove (1980), *The Soviet Economic System*,

London: George Allen & Unwin, pp. 62ff. For an example of Soviet compartmentalization and how this impeded necessary collaboration between the prison health services and civilian health services in post-Soviet republics, see Geir Hønneland and Lars Rowe (2004), *Health as International Politics: Combating Communicable Diseases in the Baltic Sea Region*, Burlington, VT: Ashgate, pp. 81–3.

Chapter 2

1 The city's name was St. Petersburg from its foundation in 1703 until 1914, when anti-German sentiments made a de-Germanization if its name necessary. The next ten years it bore the more Slavic-sounding name Petrograd, until Lenin's death in 1924 prompted its renaming to Leningrad. After the collapse of the Soviet Union in 1991 the city was again given its original name, St. Petersburg.
2 Osmo Jussila, 'Finland as a Grand Duchy', in Osmo Jussila, Seppo Hentilä and Jukka Nevakivi (1999), *From Grand Duchy to a Modern State: A Political History of Finland since 1809*, London: Hurst & Company, p. 93.
3 The provisional government's March Manifesto ensured the constitutional rights of Finland and other parts of the Tsarist Empire. However, the Manifesto was issued by a provisional government that saw itself as the heir to the Tsar's supreme power, and as in effect replacing the Tsar rather than abolishing Russian supremacy over Finland. See Jussila, 'Finland as a Grand Duchy', pp. 94–6.
4 Ibid., p. 95.
5 The shifting fortunes of Lenin's Bolsheviks during the spring and summer of 1917 were in fact less straightforward than this brief account suggests. Lenin himself spent most of the summer and early fall of 1917 in various safe houses in southern Finland, and, according to historian Richard Pipes, was convinced that 'the whole Bolshevik experiment was over and done with'. See Richard Pipes (1997), *Three 'Whys' of the Russian Revolution*, New York: Vintage, p. 48. For Lenin's somewhat farcical escape that summer and his stay in Finland, see Robert Service (2001), *Lenin: A Biography*, London: Macmillan, pp. 290–2 and p. 302.

6 As quoted from Lenin's collected works in Neil Harding (1996), *Leninism*, London: Macmillan, p. 204.
7 Ibid., pp. 204–5.
8 Robert Service (2005), *A History of Modern Russia from Nicholas II to Vladimir Putin*, Cambridge, MA: Harvard University Press, p. 69.
9 Seppo Hentilä, 'From Independence to the End of the Continuation War 1917–1944', in Osmo Jussila, Seppo Hentilä and Jukka Nevakivi (1999), *From Grand Duchy to a Modern State: A Political History of Finland since 1809*, London: Hurst, p. 101.
10 Hentilä, 'From Independence to the End of the Continuation War 1917–1944', p. 102.
11 Ibid., p. 103.
12 For the specifics of the Finnish case, see Hentilä, 'From Independence to the End of the Continuation War 1917–1944', pp. 101–6. For Lenin's thoughts on the national question and the world socialist federation, see Harding, *Leninism*; Service, *Lenin: A Biography*.
13 Heikki Ylikangas (1995), *Vägen Till Tammerfors: Striden mellan röda och vita i finska inbördeskriget 1918*, Stockholm: Bokförlaget Atlantis, pp. 23–4.
14 Hentilä, 'From Independence to the End of the Continuation War 1917–1944': on death tolls, see p. 110; on foreign participation in the war, see pp. 107–12.
15 On 'the many names of the 1918 war', see Hentilä, 'From Independence to the End of the Continuation War 1917–1944', pp. 113–15.
16 Ibid., pp. 105–6.
17 On the Finnish irredentist movement, and on Petsamo's role in shaping independent Finland, see Peter Stadius (2016), 'Petsamo: Bringing Modernity to Finland's Arctic Ocean Shore 1920–1039', *Acta Borealia*, Vol. 33, No. 2, pp. 140–65.
18 John H. Wuorinen (1965), *A History of Finland*, New York: Columbia University Press, p. 226.
19 Hentilä, 'From Independence to the End of the Continuation War 1917–1944', p. 116.
20 Wuorinen, *A History of Finland*, pp. 224–5.
21 Peace Treaty between the Republic of Finland and the Russian Socialist Federal Soviet Republic, signed at Dorpat, 14 October 1920, available

in English translation at www.histdoc. net/history/dorpat1920_en.html, accessed 25 March 2019, article 4. Excerpts of the treaty text, in a slightly different translation, are also available in Wuorinen, *A History of Finland*, pp. 485–91.

22 Peace Treaty between the Republic of Finland and the Russian Socialist Federal Soviet Republic, signed at Dorpat, 14 October 1920, available in English translation at www.histdoc.net/history/dorpat1920_en.html, accessed 25 March 2019, articles 6, 7 and 8.

23 Åsmund Egge and Vadim Roginskij (eds) (2006), *Komintern og Norge: DNA-perioden 1919–1923: En dokumentasjon*, Oslo (Unipub), doc. 34: letter from Mikhail Kobetskij to Lev Trotskij on usage of the Murmansk transit point, 21 October 1920. The document is collected from RGASPI, f. 5, op. 3, d. 152, ll. 1–2.

24 See Vesa Rautio (2000), 'Petsamo – 'Kaipaukseni maasta' globaalitalouden pyörteisiin' ('Pechenga – from 'the place where my heart belongs' to global boost and busts'), *Terra*, Vol. 112, No. 3, pp. 129–40, where it is stated that this solution was accepted at the personal behest of Finnish president Karlo Juho Ståhlberg. I am grateful to Rautio for providing me with an English translation of his article. Apparently, history professor and politician Väinö Voionmaa played an important role in convincing the Finnish government that a reduced settlement was favourable to Finland. See Stadius, 'Petsamo'.

25 Hentilä, 'From Independence to the End of the Continuation War 1917–1944', p. 139.

26 The 'pork barrel revolt' was named for the improvised podium, a pork barrel, on which the Finnish Red officer Jahvetti Moilanen (a.k.a. F. J. Myyryläinen) had stood when he called for Eastern Karelian Finns to join him in a raid across the border with Finland. The raid was in all likeliness instigated by the Finnish Communist Party. See Hentilä, 'From Independence to the End of the Continuation War 1917–1944', p. 140.

27 Yohanan Cohen (1989), *Small Nations in Times of Crisis and Confrontation*, Albany, NY: State University of New York Press, p. 339.

28 H. Peter Krosby (1968), *Finland, Germany and the Soviet Union 1940–1941*, Madison, WI: University of Wisconsin Press, p. 6.

29 The Petsamo area, with its northern untouched nature, had been romanticized in Finnish literature since the beginning of the century,

and was increasingly seen as part of Finland. See Rautio, 'Petsamo – "Kaipaukseni maasta" globaalitalouden pyörteisiin.'
30 Magnus Londen et al. (2008), *Come to Finland*, Helsinki: Edita Publishing, p. 116. For early tourism development in Petsamo, and its significance for newly independent Finland, see Stadius, 'Petsamo'.
31 Heikki Papunen, 'One Hundred Years of Ore Exploration in Finland', in Heikki Tanskanen (ed.) (1986), *The Development of Geological Sciences in Finland*, Espoo: Geological Survey of Finland, Bulletin 336, p. 176.
32 Alf R. Jacobsen (2006), *Nikkel, jern og blod*, Oslo: Aschehoug, p. 19. Törnquist was not the first to discover nickel ore in Petsamo. Findings of rocks containing nickel had been reported by the Russian geologist Konradi as early as in 1913, although there is no mention of further exploration in this instance. See Eero J. Hanski (1992), *Petrology of the Pechenga Ferropicrites and Cogenetic, Ni-bearing Gabbro-wehrlite Intrusions, Kola Peninsula, Russia*, Espoo: Geological Survey of Finland, Bulletin 367, p. 12.
33 Papunen, 'One Hundred Years of Ore Exploration in Finland', pp. 177–8.
34 Heikki Väyrynen (1938), *Petrologie des Nickelerzfeldes kaulatunturi-kammikivitunturi in Petsamo*, Helsinki: Commission Geologique de Finlande, Bulletin 116, p. 7.
35 Papunen, 'One Hundred Years of Ore Exploration in Finland', p. 176.
36 This Väinö Tanner should not to be confused with the Finnish Social Democrat leader who in the course of his career held four ministerial posts, including that of prime minister, and who not only bears the same name as the ethnologist, but also shares 1881 as year of birth.
37 Papunen, 'One Hundred Years of Ore Exploration in Finland', p. 176.
38 Ibid. It should be noted that snowfall at that time of year is an unusual occurrence in the European far north.
39 Ibid., p. 177.
40 Jari Eloranta and Ilkka Nummela (2007), 'Finnish Nickel as a Strategic Metal, 1920–1944', *Scandinavian Journal of History*, Vol. 32, No. 4, pp. 322–45, at p. 328.
41 Matt Bray (1994), 'INCO's Petsamo Venture, 1933–1945: An Incident in Canadian, British, Finnish and Soviet Relations', *International Journal of Canadian Studies*, Vol. 9, p. 176; Eloranta and Nummela, 'Finnish Nickel as a Strategic Metal', p. 330. Eloranta and Nummela note the possibility

42 Wuorinen, *A History of Finland*, pp. 285 ff.
43 John F. Thompson and Norman Beasley (1960), *For the Years to Come: A Story of International Nickel of Canada*, New York and London: G. P. Putnam's Sons and Longmans and Green & Co., p. 254.
44 Ibid., p. 254; Eloranta and Nummela, 'Finnish Nickel as a Strategic Metal', p. 330.
45 Bray, 'INCO's Petsamo Venture', p. 175.
46 Krosby, *Finland, Germany and the Soviet Union*, p. 27.
47 I will, for the sake of brevity, follow historian Matt Bray's example in using 'INCO', although that was not the company's official designation until 1976.
48 Thompson and Beasley, *For the Years to Come*, p. 253.
49 In 1932, according to H. Peter Krosby, INCO controlled about 85 per cent of world production. See Krosby, *Finland, Germany and the Soviet Union*, p. 27.
50 Eloranta and Nummela, 'Finnish Nickel as a Strategic Metal', p. 325.
51 Bray, 'INCO's Petsamo Venture', pp. 174–5. The reasons for INCO's takeover of Mond Nickel are described differently by Thompson and Beasley, *For the Years to Come*, who ascribe the re-organization of INCO leading to Canadian supremacy to the simple fact that the company's properties were located mainly in Canada (see p. 190), whereas INCO's acquisition of Mond Nickel was apparently prompted by the desire to avoid wasteful operations at the Frood mine in Sudbury, ON (see p. 205). The authors, unlike Bray, do not link the two episodes. In my view, however, the fact that INCO's re-organization took place *before* (on 31 October 1928) the acquisition of Mond (28 December 1928) does strengthen the likelihood of a linkage.
52 As quoted in Bray, 'INCO's Petsamo Venture', p. 175.
53 Eloranta and Nummela, 'Finnish Nickel as a Strategic Metal', p. 330.
54 Ibid., p. 330. We may assume that the Finnish preference for INCO as a partner in Petsamo was motivated by the company's extensive experience in developing mining industry in remote wilderness areas. For INCO's early days and the pioneer development of Ontario ores, see Thompson and Beasley, *For the Years to Come*.

that strategic foreign policy considerations may have prompted Finnish politicians to prefer non-Finnish investments to a domestic operator.

55 Eloranta and Nummela, 'Finnish Nickel as a Strategic Metal', p. 331.
56 As quoted in Bray, 'INCO's Petsamo Venture', p. 176.
57 See Eloranta and Nummela, 'Finnish Nickel as a Strategic Metal'.
58 As quoted in Bray, 'INCO's Petsamo Venture', p. 177.
59 For a brief introduction to the history of nickel as a usable metal, see Thompson and Beasley, *For the Years to Come*, pp. 1–5.
60 Ibid., p. 21.
61 As quoted in Thompson and Beasley, *For the Years to Come*, pp. 64–5.
62 Ibid., p. 121.
63 Eloranta and Nummela, 'Finnish Nickel as a Strategic Metal', pp. 322–45. Other metals listed as 'strategic', due to their importance in the armaments industries, were aluminium, copper, lead, tin and zinc.
64 This paragraph is based on various sections of Thompson and Beasley, *For the Years to Come*.
65 Bray, 'INCO's Petsamo Venture', pp. 177–8.
66 Krosby, *Finland, Germany and the Soviet Union*, p. 5.
67 Bray, 'INCO's Petsamo Venture', p. 178.
68 Eugen Autere and Jaako Liede (eds) (1989), *Petsamon Nikkeli. Taistelu strategisesta metallista*, Helsinki: Vuorimiesyhdistys – Bergsmannaföreningen r.y, p. 298 (English summary).
69 Stadius, 'Petsamo'.
70 The following description of Kolosjoki is based on Matsak, *Pechenga*, pp. 397–401, which in turn leans on Autere and Liede (eds), *Petsamon Nikkeli*, pp. 32–40, 164–6, 259, 260.
71 Stadius, 'Petsamo'.

Chapter 3

1 A version of this chapter was published as an article in *Journal of Slavic Military Studies* (2020).
2 For an intriguingly informative introduction to Finnish historiography on the war experience, see Ville Kivimäki (2012), 'Three Wars and Their Epitaphs', in T. Kinnunen and Ville Kivimäki (eds), *Finland in World War II: History, Memory, Interpretations*, Boston: Brill, pp. 1–46.

3 Boris Yartsev's formal position at the Soviet legation in Helsinki was second secretary, but his obvious association with Soviet intelligence ensured a key position in the early stages of Soviet–Finnish talks. See Max Jacobson (1961), *The Diplomacy of the Winter War: An Account of the Russo–Finnish War, 1939–1940*, Cambridge, MA: Harvard University Press, pp. 7–8.

4 Juho Kusti Paasikivi (1870–1956) was a Finnish diplomat and statesman whose political life was profoundly influenced by developments in the Russian empire and later the Soviet Union. He was Finnish prime minister for a brief stint in 1918 and later from 1944 to 1946, before he embarked on a ten-year long tenure of the Finnish presidency until his death in 1956. As we have seen, he negotiated the Tartu Peace Treaty with the Russian Soviet Federative Socialist Republic in 1920. He was well versed in Russian culture and language, having studied in his youth in St. Petersburg, and was a natural choice to lead the Finnish delegation in 1939. After the Second World War, Paasikivi would become the president of Finland. His life has spurred several biographies, and his own published story about events in his career (*Minnen I & II* – see bibliography) has informed this chapter.

5 Jacobson, *The Diplomacy of the Winter War*, pp. 115–16. In fact, as part of Molotov's preparatory work for the negotiations, the possibility of demanding cessation of Petsamo was discussed, though the demand was never presented to the Finnish delegation. See O. A. Rzheshevskii (ed.) (1999), *Zimnyaya Voina. Politicheskaya istoriya*, Moscow: Nauka, pp. 119ff.

6 Krosby, *Finland, Germany and the Soviet Union*, p. 7.

7 Numerous examples of this are presented in INCO's official history. See Thompson and Beasley, *For the Years to Come*.

8 This section is based on Bray, 'INCO's Petsamo Venture', pp. 179–80. The citations are quoted from Bray's work.

9 Robert Edwards (2006), *White Death: Russia's War on Finland, 1939–40*, London: Weidenfeld & Nicolson, p. 204; Rzheshevskii, *Zimnyaya Voina*, p. 166.

10 Carl Murray Wallace and Ashley Thomson (1993), *Sudbury: Rail Town to Regional Capital*, Toronto: Dundurn Press, p. 170.

11 Bray, 'INCO's Petsamo Venture', p. 180; Matsak, *Pechenga*, p. 400.

12 See Jacobsen, *Nikkel, jern og blod*, p. 50. According to Jacobsen, Collier was apprehensive about INCO's intentions with the sabotage proposal and allegedly feared it would enable the company to claim reparations from the UK after the war if British authorities condoned the action. Albeit a viable interpretation, Jacobsen's claim is insufficiently substantiated by sources to be considered more than a speculation.
13 Bray, 'INCO's Petsamo Venture', p. 181. Bray in this instance refers to Dr Johan Söderhjelm, who was the director of PNO at the time. Söderhjelm reported that Soviet pilots captured by Finnish forces had said they had been ordered to avoid damaging PNO installations.
14 See Krosby, *Finland, Germany and the Soviet Union*, p. 10. As does Bray (see previous footnote), Krosby refers to Söderhjelm for the claim that the mines and their surroundings were untouched.
15 Ibid., p. 10.
16 RGAE, f. 9037, op. 1, ed. khr. 148. This file in the Russian State Archive for Economic Affairs contains seven documents, of which three pertain directly to the fact-finding mission of the Soviet specialist team in March 1940: ll. 59–29, *Otchet o komandirovke na nikelevy rudnik Salmiyarvi v Finlyandii i dokladnaya zapiska po medno-nikelevym rudam 'Petsamo' v Finlyandii* (Report on trip to the Salmijärvi nickel mine in Finland and memorandum on the nickel ore 'Petsamo' in Finland, hereafter Petrov's report); ll. 20–11, *Dokladnaya zapiska po medno-nikelevym rudam Petsamo v Finlyandii (Pechengskye tundry)* (Memorandum on the copper-nickel ore in Petsamo, Finland, hereafter Rutshtein's first report); ll. 10–6, *Dokladnaya zapiska k voprosu rudnoy bazy nikelevykh mestorozhdenii Pechengskikh tundr (Petsamo-Tunturit) v Finlyandii* (Memorandum concerning the question of the ore occurrence on the Pechenga tundra in Finland, hereafter Rutshtein's second report). The first was written by mining engineer A. I. Petrov, the other two by the head of *Monchegorlag* Sh. N. Rutshtein, both at the Severonikel combine in Monchegorsk.
17 Veniamin Petrovich Pyatikovskii, *Preobrazhennyi Sever*, Murmansk: Murmanskoe knizhnoe izdatelstvo 1974, pp. 379–84.
18 RGAE, f. 9037, op. 1, ed. khr. 148, Rutshtein's first report, l. 7. Incidentally, the practical utility of a nickel ore occurrence depends largely on the relative content of nickel: the more nickel per weight unit of ore, the less enrichment is needed.

19 RGAE, f. 9037, op. 1, ed. khr. 148, Petrov's report, l. 53; Ibid., Rutshtein's first report, l. 13.
20 RGAE, f. 9037, op. 1, ed. khr. 148, Petrov's report, l. 46.
21 RGAE, f. 9037, op. 1, ed. khr. 148, Petrov's report, l. 42.
22 Ibid., Petrov's report, ll. 34–33.
23 RGAE, f. 9037, op. 1, ed. khr. 148, Petrov's report, ll. 30–29. Both the aspect of safety measures and the compactness of both living quarters and industrial installations are mentioned several times in Petrov's report.
24 Bray, 'INCO's Petsamo Venture', pp. 181–2.
25 As quoted in ibid., p. 182.
26 This heading is inspired by H. Peter Krosby (1967), *Petsamo in the Spotlight: A Study in Finnish–German Relations, 1940–1941*, Ph.D. thesis, Columbia University. Krosby's 1968 *Finland, Germany and the Soviet Union 1940–1941*, has informed much of this chapter.
27 Per G. Andreen (1980), *Finland i brännpunkten: mars 1940 – juni 1941*, Stockholm: Lindfors nya Bokförlag, p. 184.
28 *Dokumenty vneshnei politiki 1940-22 iyunya 1941*, vol. 1, Moscow: Mezhdunarodnye otnoshenya, doc. 478, Memo from conversation between Vyshinskii and UK ambassador Cripps, 2 November 1940, pp. 12–16 and ibid., doc. 530, Memo from conversation between Vyshinskii and Ambassador Cripps, 19 November 1940. See also Bray, 'INCO's Petsamo Venture', p. 188.
29 Germany's evolving interest in Petsamo is thoroughly documented and discussed in Krosby, *Petsamo in the Spotlight*.
30 According to Paasikivi, Molotov said in negotiations with the Finns that 'very significant military circles in our country are of the opinion that Petsamo should not have been returned to Finland'. See Juho Kusti Paasikivi (1958), *Minnen.1939–1940*, Stockholm: Albert Bonniers Förlag, p. 186.
31 The conversation is recorded in *Dokumenty vneshnei politiki 1940-22 iyunya 1941. Vol 1*, Moscow: Mezhdunarodnye otnosheniya 1995, doc. 216, Memo from meeting between Molotov and Paasikivi, 23 June 1940, pp. 363–4 and in Suomen Ulkoasiainministeriö (The Finnish Ministry of Foreign Affairs) (1941), *Finland Reveals Her Secret Documents on Soviet Foreign Policy: March 1940–June 1941*, New York: Wilfred Funk., doc. 14, pp. 50–1. For Paasikivi's personal account, see J. K. Paasikivi (1959),

Minnen II: Som sendebud i Moskva, Stockholm: Albert Bonniers Förlag, p. 162.

32 The discussion between Molotov and Paasikivi can be found in *Dokumenty vneshnei politiki,* vol. 1, doc. 227, Memo from meeting between Molotov and Paasikivi, 27 June 1940, pp. 379–80. It is also referred to in Suomen Ulkoasiainministeriö, *Finland Reveals Her Secret Documents*, doc. 15, Paasikivi's telegram to the Finnish MFA on 27 June 1940, p. 51. In the latter, Molotov is claimed to have said that the Soviet Union wanted the Petsamo area 'for all time'. This detail is not reflected in the Russian memo.

33 Incidentally, there is no reason to believe that the *nature* of the Soviet demand, which must be described as an infringement on Finnish sovereignty, was surprising to Paasikivi. Great-Power activities in Europe had for some time overstepped the boundaries set up by international law and abusive behaviour from the European totalitarian states must have been accepted as the norm at this time.

34 The Russian version of the treaty text is found in *Dokumenty vneshnei politiki*, vol. 1, doc. 73, Peace Agreement between the Soviet Union and the Republic of Finland, 12 March 1940, pp. 140–2. An English translation of this treaty is reprinted in Max Jakobson (1961), *The Diplomacy of the Winter War: An Account of the Russo–Finnish War*, Cambridge, MA: Harvard University Press, pp. 261–6.

35 Blücher quoted in Krosby, *Finland, Germany and the Soviet Union*, p. 12.

36 After the German attack on Poland in September 1939, access to raw materials for German industry was curtailed by enemy states. British and Canadian nickel producers, controlling well over 80 per cent of the world market aborted all trade with German consumers, most notably the industrial conglomerate I. G. Farbenindustrie, which had developed new methods for refining nickel matte (see P. T. Sandvik and J. Scherner (2016), 'Why Did Germany Not Fully Exploit the Norwegian Nickel Industry 1940-45?' in Hans Otto Frøland et al. (eds), *Industrial Collaboration in Nazi-Occupied Europe: Norway in Context*, London: Palgrave Macmillan, pp. 273–98). Consequently, Berlin sought to procure the metal elsewhere, and nickel from Petsamo became a prime target for German negotiators in German–Finnish trade talks from the spring of 1940 (See Krosby, *Finland, Germany and the Soviet Union*, pp. 12–15).

Similarly, nickel was very much part of the trade relations between the Soviet Union and Germany that were established in the aftermath of the Molotov–Ribbentrop Pact from August 1939. The German–Soviet trade agreement of February 1940 obliged Soviet industry to provide Germany with three thousand tons of nickel over the coming eighteen months. (See Schnurre's memo from 26 February 1940 in *Akten zur Deutschen Auswärtigen Politik* (1961), Baden-Baden: P. Keppler Verlag KG, Serie D, Bd.8, Nr.636, p. 643). That German authorities were aware of Petsamo's industrial potential and expected the Soviet Union to retain the territory after annexing it in November 1939 is reflected in a telegram to the Auswärtiges Amt of 10 January 1940, in Politisches Archiv des Auswärtigen Amts RZ 311, Bd.3, which discusses the Soviet capacity for nickel production. On the general Soviet–German economic collaboration in this period, see Heinrich Schwendemann (1993), *Die wirtschaftliche Zusammenarbeit zwischen dem Deutschen Reich und der Sowjetunion von 1939 bis 1941. Alternative zu Hitlers Ostprogramm?*, Berlin: Akademie Verlag.
37 See, for example, *Istoriya ordena Lenina. Leningradskoe voennogo okruga* (1974), Moscow: Voennoe izdatelstvo Ministerstvo oborony SSSR, p. 151; *Peterburgskii, Petrogradskii, Leningradskii voennyi okrug 1864-1999* (1999), St. Petersburg: Poligon, pp. 281–2; Ohto Manninen (2004), 'The Soviet Plans for the North Western Theatre of Operations in 1939-1944', *Finnish Defence Studies*, Helsinki: National Defense College, p. 13.
38 A. M. Vasilevskii (1973), *Delo vsei zhizni*, Moscow: Izdatelstvo politicheskoi literatury, p. 103.
39 For an account of the role IG Farben played in Germany's war, see Joseph Borkin (1979), *The Crime and Punishment of I.G. Farben*, New York: Pocket Books. For a more general discussion of the converging interests of the Nazi regime and private German economic interests, where IG Farben's central position is discussed, see Kershaw, *The Nazi Dictatorship*, pp. 47–68.
40 Eloranta and Nummela, 'Finnish Nickel as a Strategic Metal', p. 332.
41 Ibid., pp. 332–5.
42 Krosby, *Finland, Germany and the Soviet Union*, p. 13.
43 Andreen, *Finland i brännpunkten*, p. 93 and p. 185; Ibid., pp. 30–1.
44 Whether the Finnish Ryti government at this point was already making well-contemplated and independent decisions with a view to secure

German support against the Soviet threat is part of the Finnish postwar debate. As this study is not designed to provide direct answers to questions posed in this debate, the author has sought to remain neutral in the following description of events.

45 Krosby, *Finland, Germany and the Soviet Union*, p. 29; Bray, 'INCO's Petsamo Venture', p. 182.
46 Robert Stanley listed several other conditions for his acceptance, mostly to avoid INCO being seen as aiding and abetting enemy Germany in time of war. See Bray, 'INCO's Petsamo Venture', pp. 184–5.
47 The paragraphs describing the process in London and Canada are based on Bray, 'INCO's Petsamo Venture', pp.183–7. Prime Minister King's telegram stands as quoted there, at p. 187.
48 Records from the many consultations between Paasikivi and Molotov/Vyshinski in the interim peace period bear witness to Finnish persistence in the Petsamo question and the resulting Soviet impatience. See for example *Dokumenty vneshnei politiki*, vol. 2, doc. 496, Memo from conversation between Vyshinskii and Paasikivi, 12 November 1940; Ibid., doc 531, Memo from conversation between Molotov and Paasikivi, 19 November 1940; Ibid., doc. 649, Memo from conversation between Vyshinskii and Paasikivi, 14 January 1941; Ibid., doc. 663, Memo from conversation between Vyshinskii and Paasikivi, 24 January 1941.
49 See for example *Dokumenty vneshnei politiki*, vol. 2, doc. 547, Memo from conversation between Molotov and German trade negotiator F. Schnurre, 25 November 1940.
50 Andreen, *Finland i brännpunkten*, pp. 215–16.
51 Krosby, *Finland, Germany and the Soviet Union*, pp. 152–64; Andreen, *Finland i brännpunkten*, pp. 216–17.
52 Finnish resistance to finding a conclusion to the negotiations had several pretexts, most notably connected to how positions in the new Soviet-Finnish venture should be divided between the states. See *Dokumenty vneshnei politiki*, vol. 2, doc.676, Memo from conversation between Vyshinskii and Paasikivi, 12 February 1941.
53 Anthony F. Upton, *Finland in Crisis 1940–1941: A Study in Small-Power Politics* (Ithaca, NY: Cornell University Press, 1965), p. 213.
54 See for example *Dokumenty vneshnei politiki*, vol. 2, doc. 649, Memo from conversation between Vyshinskii and Paasikivi, 14 January 1941; Ibid.,

doc. 676, Memo from conversation between Vyshinskii and Paasikivi, 12 February 1941. See also Suomen Ulkoasiainministeriö, *Finland Reveals Her Secret Documents*, doc. 60, p. 89 and doc. 67, p. 94. Paasikivi's many telegrams from Moscow in this period are littered with reports of barely hidden invasion threats from the Soviet Ministry of Foreign Affairs.

55 On Finland's deepening association and eventual 'brotherhood in arms' with Nazi Germany between March 1940 and June 1941, see Meinander, 'Finland', pp. 17–45. The path towards, and the nature of, Finland's co-belligerence with the *Wehrmacht* has been fiercely debated among Finnish historians. Crucially for non-Finnish speakers, the resulting voluminous historiography is almost exclusively written in Finnish. However, an extremely interesting and informative introduction to interpretations and the widening scope of historical research in this area is to be found in Kivimäki, 'Three Wars and Their Epitaphs'. This anthology, which contains contributions on the most central fields of research within Finnish wartime history, goes some way in alleviating the problems raised by linguistic barriers.

56 Suomen Ulkoasiainministeriö, *Finland Reveals Her Secret Documents*, doc. 74, pp. 99–105.

57 Krosby, *Finland, Germany and the Soviet Union*, pp. 170–84.

58 See, for example, Meinander, 'Finland'.

59 Krosby, *Finland, Germany and the Soviet Union*, p. 182.

60 Ibid., p. 179; Jacobsen, *Nikkel, jern og blod*, p. 142.

61 Krosby, *Finland, Germany and the Soviet Union*, p. 190.

62 Ibid., pp. 191–7.

63 Ibid., pp. 190–9. The Führer's evaluation of the importance of Finnish nickel (i.e. nickel from Petsamo) to the German war industry was emphasized in his conversation with Molotov in November 1940 where Hitler several times stressed the economic (as opposed to political) significance of Finnish timber and nickel. See *Dokumenty vneshnei politiki*, vol. 2, doc. 511, Memo from conversation between Molotov and Hitler, 13 November 1940. Incidentally, the obvious importance of Petsamo to Germany, which must have been well known to Soviet and Allied forces, begs the question of why Petsamo was left relatively undamaged by bombardment when in German hands. One possible explanation might be found in the comprehensive air defence systems

put in place there by the *Wehrmacht*. Reputedly, anti-aircraft defences were stronger in Petsamo than at 'any other spot on the eastern front' (See Krosby, *Finland, Germany and the Soviet Union*, p. 199). This interpretation is supported by reports from the German forces on site, that states that air raids against landing strips in Luostari, Nautsi and Kirkenes, as well as against Kolosjoki and the hydropower plant in Jäniskoski, were unsuccessful due to the powerful ground-to-air weaponry on site. See Kansallisarkisto (National Archives of Finland), Daily Report, 16 September 1942 and 31 October 1942, Kriegstagebuch Nr. 5 der 6. Gebirgsdivision, Ia, 1.4.42-15.5.42, F40-362: A fully satisfactory answer to this question, however, requires further research.
64 Matsak, *Pechenga*, p. 401.
65 Krosby, *Finland, Germany and the Soviet Union*, pp. 200–01.
66 Jacobsen, *Nikkel, jern og blod*, pp. 206, 210.
67 Hentilä, 'From Independence to the End of the Continuation War 1917–1944', pp. 209–11.
68 Krosby, *Finland, Germany and the Soviet Union*, p. 200.
69 Jukka Nevakivi, 'From the Continuation War to the Present 1944–1999', in Osmo Jussila, Seppo Hentilä and Jukka Nevakivi (eds), *From Grand Duchy to a Modern State: A Political History of Finland since 1809*, London: Hurst & Company, 1999, pp. 219–21.
70 Matsak, *Pechenga*, pp. 401ff.
71 *Dokumenty vneshnei politiki 22 iyunya-1 yanvarya 1942* (2000), Moscow: Mezhdunarodnye otnosheniya, doc. 328, Memo from conversation between Stalin and Eden, 16 December 1941, pp. 501ff; N. I. Baryshnikov (2001), 'Problema Petsamo v sovetsko-finlyandskikh otnosheniyakh (1939-1944gg.)', in M. N. Suprun (ed.), *Voina v Arktike (1939-1944gg.)*, St. Petersburg: Izdatelstvo Pravda Severa, pp. 22–32; Bray, 'INCO's Petsamo Venture', p. 188.
72 Krosby, *Finland, Germany and the Soviet Union*, p. 13; Bray, 'INCO's Petsamo Venture', p. 181.
73 Krosby, *Finland, Germany and the Soviet Union*, p. 8.
74 As quoted in ibid., p. 33. It should be noted here, that Petsamo did play a strategically important role as a transit area in the interim peace period between March 1940 and June 1941. In this period, tonnages of crucial goods, and even military equipment, were transported via Liinahamari and

onwards to southern Finland and Sweden. This, of course, may have had an impact on Soviet assessments of Petsamo's value. For more on the role of this transport route, see A. Aitamäki (2009), 'Linhamar som ett andningshål mot väst – Godstrafiken längs Ishavsvägen under freden mellan vinter- och forsättingskriget', in M. Engman and K. Westerlund (eds), *Petsamo och havet*, Åbo: Uniprint, pp. 94–110; Björklund, *Petsamotrafiken*.

75 Upton, *Finland in Crisis 1940-1941*, pp. 106–7.

76 Apparently, German newspaper *Frankfurter Zeitung* reported in late December 1939 that Soviet authorities had demanded that Petsamo be returned as part of their negotiations with Finland before the Winter War. The Soviet information agency TASS issued a denial of these allegations in January 1940. See *Dokumenty vneshnei politiki*, vol. 1, doc. 21, TASS Disclaimer 18 January 1940, pp. 43–4. In early May the same year, TASS disclaimed information relayed by news agency Reuter to the effect that the Soviet Union had designs on Petsamo. See ibid., doc. 136, TASS Disclaimer, 4 May 1940.

77 N. I. Baryshnikov (2001), 'Problema Petsamo v sovetsko-finlyandskikh otnosheniyakh (1939-1944gg.)', in M. N. Suprun (ed.), *Voina v Arktike (1939-1944gg.)*, St. Petersburg: Izdatelstvo Pravda Severa, pp. 22–32.

78 Sven G. Holtsmark (2003), 'Fra periferi til krigsteater. Nordområdene i sovjetisk militær tenkning i mellomkrigstiden', *Forsvarsstudier*, Vol. 4, pp. 76–9.

79 In the Spring 1940, German officials applied some pressure on Soviet counterparts to make good on their commitment for the delivery of nickel, as stipulated by the German–Soviet trade agreement. See, for example, *Dokumenty vneshnei politiki*, vol. 1, doc. 104, memo from meeting between I. F. Tevosyan and Herman Göring, 29 March 1940, pp. 197–200, where Göring calls for 'speedy deliveries of metal – especially nickel'.

80 Paasikivi, *Minnen II*, pp. 162ff.

81 It is worth noting that German forces were still not present in Kirkenes when Molotov made his first Petsamo demands. Not until early July 1940 did *Wehrmacht* soldiers relieve the Norwegian border guards there. See Fredrik Fagertun (ed.) (2016), *Nenne Rachløw Isachsen: Min krigsdagbok*, Stamsund: Orkana forlag, p. 11. Their imminent arrival must nevertheless have been an obvious element behind Soviet assessments.

82 Arguably, the Red Army leadership did not see Petsamo as providing much of a buffer, for topographical reasons. The leader of the General Staff of the Red Army A. I. Antonov pointed out, in July 1945, that Petsamo was extremely exposed to areas in the immediate west. With many potential anchorages for navy vessels and a plethora of bays appropriate for harbouring sea planes, the Varanger Peninsula and Fjord were well suited for enemy operations. As Antonov put it, Varanger 'is hanging over the whole Pechenga area' (*'navisaet nad vsei Pechengskoi oblastyu'*) (See Memo from Red Army General Staff, 14 July 1945 in Sven G. Holtsmark (ed.) (1995), *Norge og Sovjetunionen. En utenrikspolitisk dokumentasjon*, Oslo: J. W. Cappelens forlag, doc. 277, pp. 360–2. The Russian original can be found in *Sovetsko-norvezhskie otnosheniya 1917-1955. Sbornik dokumentov* (1997), Moscow: Elia-Art-O, doc. 277, pp. 385–6). One possible inference from this statement is that Antonov opined that Petsamo was one more area that needed protection – not an area that could provide protection in and of itself.

83 RGAE, f. 9037, op. 1, ed. khr. 148, dispatch note to Rutshtein's second report, dated 17 July 1944. Rutshtein had at this point been transferred to the southern Urals working at the *Yuzhuralnikel* combine.

84 Upton, *Finland in Crisis 1940-1941*, p. 106.

85 J. Eloranta and I. Nummela (2007), 'Finnish Nickel as a Strategic Metal 1920-1944', *Scandinavian Journal of History*, Vol. 32, No. 4, p. 334; Bray, 'INCO's Petsamo Venture', p. 189.

86 For an intriguing account of Soviet industrialization of the North, see Andy Bruno, *The Nature of Soviet Power*. Bruno devotes a full chapter to the nickel industry in Monchegorsk and Pechenga (pp. 170–219).

87 The Soviet urgency in 'settling the North' was reflected by Stalin when he stated: '[t]he Arctic and our northern regions contain colossal wealth. We must create a Soviet organization which can, in the shortest period possible, include this wealth in the general resources of our socialist common structure.' As quoted in John McCannon, *Red Arctic*, p. 33.

88 As quoted in Pyatikovskii, *Preobrazhennyi Sever*, p. 389. Leningrad party chief Kirov was, until his untimely death in 1934, also head of the party organizations in Karelia and Murmansk as these were subordinated Leningradskaya oblast at the time.

89 RGASPI, f. 017, op. 88, d. 322. The Kirov quote is from his *Stati i rechi* (articles and speeches) from 1934, p. 66 and serves in this document as an epigraph to a photo file containing city snapshots of urban environments on the Kola Peninsula.

90 Kirov's significance in the Soviet industrialization of the Kola Peninsula in the 1930s, both before and after his death in 1934, is widely acknowledged in Soviet literature. One of many examples is found in M. I. Sukharev (1979), *Sever industrialnyi: Deyatelnost KPSS po rukovodstvu industrialnym razvitiem Evropeiskogo Severa SSSR na zavershayushchem etape sotsialisticheskogo stroitelstva 1946–1958*, Murmansk: Murmanskoe knizhnoe izdatelstvo, p. 39.

Chapter 4

1 For the purposes of this chapter, the term 'sovietization' indicates merely the transfer of territory and industrial installations from Finland to the Soviet Union, and the inclusion of these elements into the Soviet production system. It does not, then, bear the meaning of the term when applied to the chronologically parallel process in post-war Eastern Europe, where the future People's Democracies, and their populations, were forced into the ideological and economic fabric of the Kremlin's monolithic power (see, for example, Zubok and Pleshakov, *Inside the Kremlin's Cold War*, pp. 128–37; Anne Appelbaum (2012), *Iron Curtain: The Crushing of Eastern Europe 1944–1956*, London: Allen Lane). The sovietization of the mainly Saami population remaining in Petsamo after the war is not dealt with in this study.

2 From I. G. Ubarov's account of the Soviet seizure of Kolosjoki. Ubarov took part in the final battle for the town. See Matsak, *Pechenga*, pp. 408–9.

3 In the armistice of September 1944, the Soviet takeover of Petsamo was agreed upon. Later, on 8 October, the arrangement that regulated the Soviet payment of compensation to INCO was signed and attached as a protocol. For partial texts of both, see Matsak, *Pechenga*, pp. 895–8, and for the text of the protocol, see Thompson and Beasley, *For the Years to Come*, p. 249.

4 Bray, 'INCO's Petsamo Venture', p. 188.
5 Thompson and Beasley, *For the Years to Come*, p. 245.
6 Bray, 'INCO's Petsamo Venture', p. 189.
7 Ibid., p. 189.
8 The process of transferring the compensation to INCO is accounted for in Thompson and Beasley, *For the Years to Come*, pp. 246–53.
9 In March 1946, the People's Commissariat for Non-ferrous Metallurgy, like all other People's Commissariats, was renamed and became the *Ministry* for Non-ferrous Metallurgy, or Mintsvetmet in its Soviet abbreviation. As Alec Nove has pointed out, the shift from 'People's Commissariat' to 'Ministry' was only a matter of linguistic preference, and carried no organizational significance (Nove, *An Economic History of the U.S.S.R.*, p. 294). The Ministry for Non-ferrous Metallurgy was in a state of constant re-organization from 1939 to 1947. Minister Petr F. Lomako, however, was sitting safely in his chair from 1940, except for the periods when Mintsvetmet was merged with the Ministry of Ferrous Metallurgy into what was called the Ministry for Metallurgical Industry (see next chapter). In 1957, responsibility for industry and other sectors was taken over by regional economic councils (Sovnarkhozy) (See RGAE, f. 9022, op. 31, ll. 6–7, introduction (by V. V. Solovyev) to fond 9022, *Narkomat-Ministerstvo Tsvetnoi Metallurgii SSSR*). The Sovnarkhozy were abandoned after Khrushchev's fall from grace, and in 1965 the ministerial structure was re-established.
10 RGAE, f. 9037, op. 1, ed. khr. 113, ll. 5–1. This file contains four separate communications (*VChgramma*) conducted via the provisory telephone lines of staff headquarters of the 14th Army in Nikel.
11 At this time, however, the Jäniskoski power plant was a Finnish concern, as it had not been included in the territory ceded to the Soviet Union in September. How this changed, and how Pechenganikel was provided with electricity, we will see in the next chapter.
12 RGAE, f. 9037, op. 1, ed. khr. 113, ll. 5–1, telegram (VChgramma) from Gribin to Mintsvetmet, dated 21 November 1944.
13 The unskilled labour needed to clear up after the German exit was mainly provided by soldiers who had fought in the Red Army and were kept in service for this purpose. See Rautio, 'Petsamo'.

14 RGAE, f. 9037, op. 1, ed. khr. 113, ll. 3–2, telegram (VChgramma) from Gribin to Mintsvetmet, dated 21 November 1944.
15 Matsak (ed.) (2005), *Pechenga*, p. 411.
16 RGAE, f. 9037, op. 1, ed. khr. 113, ll. 3–2, telegram (VChgramma) from Gribin to Mintsvetmet, dated 21 November 1944.
17 GKO had in the war years effectively replaced the ministerial structure and was the superior Soviet executive body until it was dissolved on 4 September 1945. Nove, *An Economic History of the U.S.S.R.*, p. 288.
18 RGAE, f. 9037, op. 1, ed. khr. 113, ll. 1v–1b, message from Lomako to Mikoyan referring to the dispatches from Pechenganikel, from November 1944.
19 In his reply to Pechenganikel, Lomako stated that the matter of the misplaced persons in Kirkenes would be decided by the end of November by the leader of GKO Smorodinov and by Golikov, who was responsible for repatriations in GKO. See RGAE, f. 9037, op. 1, ed. khr. 113, ll. 5–4, telegram from Mintsvetmet to Shchelkunov and Gribin, dated 27 November 1944.
20 See for example Marianne Neerland Solheim (2005), 'Slavene fra øst: Sovjetiske krigsfanger i Norge 1941–45', *Defence Studies*, Vol. 5, Oslo: Institute for Defence Studies, pp. 137–48.
21 RGAE, f. 9037, op. 1, ed. khr. 113, ll. 1v–1b, message from Lomako to Mikoyan referring to the dispatches from Pechenganikel, from November 1944.
22 Ibid., ll. 3–2, telegram (VChgramma) from Gribin to Mintsvetmet, dated 21 November 1944.
23 Many US-produced Studebaker trucks had been transferred to the Soviet Union during the war, earning a reputation for reliability in harsh conditions. Some had even been used as transportation and launching pads for Katyusha rockets.
24 RGAE, f. 9037, op. 1, ed. khr. 113, ll. 5–4, telegram from Mintsvetmet to Shchelkunov and Gribin, dated 27 November 1944.
25 RGAE, f. 9037, op. 1, ed. khr. 113, ll. 3–2, telegram (VChgramma) from Gribin to Mintsvetmet, dated 21 November 1944. For the record, 100 grams of vodka is only enough to fill one rather small tea cup and can therefore hardly be seen as an invitation to excessive alcohol consumption.

26 Matsak, *Pechenga*, pp. 415 and 411.
27 Soyuznikelolovoproekt (later Gipronikel institute) was founded in 1934 as part of the Soviet non-ferrous metallurgical complex and was charged with designing industrial sites all over the Soviet Union. See Andrew R. Bond (1996), 'The Russian Copper Industry and the Noril'sk Joint-Stock Company in the Mid-1990s', *Post-Soviet Geography and Economics*, Vol. 37, No. 5, p. 296 (footnote 19).
28 Matsak, *Pechenga*, pp. 411–12.
29 RGAE, f. 9037, op. 1, ed. khr. 175, l. 61, from protocol of meeting between Soyuznikelolovoproekt, Glavnikelkobalt and dept. of construction of Mintsvetmet, Moscow, 27 July 1945 (ll. 62–51).
30 Ibid., ll. 64–63, Decision of Mintsvetmet 'on the approval of the project plan for the Pechenganikel combine', 7 September 1945.
31 Krosby, *Finland, Germany and the Soviet Union*, p. 198. The German production figures are calculated from Krosby's table 1.
32 RGAE, f. 9037, op. 1, ed. khr. 175, l. 58–57, from protocol of meeting between Soyuznikelolovoproekt, Glavnikelkobalt and dept. of construction of Mintsvetmet, Moscow, 27 July 1945 (ll. 62–51).
33 Ibid., ed. khr. 113, ll. 5–4, telegram from Mintsvetmet to Shchelkunov and Gribin, dated 27 November 1944.
34 Matsak, *Pechenga*, p. 410.
35 RGAE, f. 9037, op. 1, ed. khr. 175, l. 61 and l. 53, from protocol of meeting between Soyuznikelolovoproekt, Glavnikelkobalt and dept. of construction of Mintsvetmet, Moscow, 27 July 1945 (ll. 62–51).
36 Ibid., ll. 64–63, Decision of Mintsvetmet 'on the approval of the project plan for the Pechenganikel combine', 7 September 1945.
37 RGAE, f. 9039, op. 1, ed. khr. 418, annual report for 1946 from the direction of construction in Nikel to Glavalyuminstroi.
38 RGAE, f. 9037, op. 1, ed. khr. 175, ll. 32–29, expense budget No 1 for the recruitment of workers to the rebuilding of Pechenganikel.
39 *Organizatsionnyi nabor (orgnabor)* or organized recruitment is a term stemming from the forced industrialization of the 1930s, applied to the process of recruiting workers from collective farms to industrial enterprises. In the post-war years, *orgnabor* was used to supply remotely located, high-priority heavy industrial sites with unskilled labour. See Lloyd E. Lee (1991), *World War II: Crucible of the Contemporary World: Commentary and Readings*, Armonk, NY: M.E. Sharpe, p. 261.

40 One well-documented example of this is the development of the steelworks in Magnitogorsk in the Southern Urals, where the number of inhabitants rose from below 100 in 1929 to a massive 250,000 by 1932. See Kotkin, *Magnetic Mountain*, pp. 72ff.
41 RGAE, f. 9037, op. 1, ed. khr. 175, ll. 32–29, expense budget No 1 for the recruitment of workers to the rebuilding of Pechenganikel.
42 Ibid. Komsomol is short for *Vsesoyuznii Leninskii Kommunisticheskii Soyuz Molodezhi* (VLKSM), the youth movement of the Soviet Communist Party. Its members were routinely mobilized when needed in larger construction projects and other efforts of limited duration.
43 Matsak, *Pechenga*, p. 412.
44 RGAE, f. 9039, op. 1, ed. khr. 418, annual report for 1946 from the direction of construction in Nikel to Glavalyuminstroi, l. 53.
45 Matsak, *Pechenga*, p. 411; RGAE, f. 9037, op. 1, ed. khr. 164, monthly technical mining reports from the Pechenganikel combine.
46 Matsak, *Pechenga*, p. 412.
47 RGAE, f. 9039, op. 1, ed. khr. 418, l. 61, annual report for 1946 from the direction of construction in Nikel to Glavalyuminstroi.
48 Matsak, *Pechenga*, p. 412.
49 Leonid A. Potemkin (1965), *U severnoi granitsy. Pechenga sovetskaya*, Murmansk: Murmanskoe knizhnoe izdatelstvo, pp. 188–90; RGAE, f. 9039, op. 1, ed. khr. 418, annual report for 1946 from the direction of construction in Nikel to *Glavalyuminstroi*, ll. 60–61.
50 This directorate was also in charge of building processes in the nickel industries, after the re-organization process in *Narkomtsvetmet* that started in 1939 and led to the demise of *Glavnikelolovo*. For details, see RGAE, f. 9022, op. 31, l. ff, introduction (by V. V. Solovyev) to fond 9022, *Narkomat-Ministerstvo Tsvetnoi Metallurgii SSSR*.
51 For Shchelkunov's positions, see Matsak, *Pechenga*, p. 412; For Berdnikov's reports, see RGAE, f. 9039, op. 1, ed. khr. 418, annual report for 1946 from the direction of construction in Nikel to *Glavalyuminstroi* and f. 9037, op. 1, ed. khr. 186, annual report for 1946 from Pechenganikel to Glavnikelkobalt.
52 RGAE, f. 9037, op. 1, ed. khr. 186, l. 20, annual report for 1946 from Pechenganikel to Glavnikelkobalt.
53 RGAE, f. 9039, op. 1, ed. khr. 418, ll. 70–76, annual report for 1946 from the direction of construction in Nikel to *Glavalyuminstroi*.

54 RGAE, f. 9037, op. 1, ed. khr. 186, l. 3, annual report for 1946 from Pechenganikel to Glavnikelkobalt.
55 Ibid., l. 6.
56 RGAE, f. 9037, op. 1, ed. khr. 200, l. 20, letter from head engineer Berdnikov to Mintsvetmet and Glavnikelkobalt, attached to the Pechenganikel technical report on metallurgical production from December 1946.
57 RGAE, f. 9039, op. 1, ed. khr. 418, ll. 82–83, annual report for 1946 from the direction of construction in Nikel to *Glavalyuminstroi*.
58 Matsak, *Pechenga*, p. 417.
59 RGAE, f. 9037, op. 1, ed. khr. 186, l. 9, annual report for 1946 from Pechenganikel to Glavnikelkobalt.
60 Matsak, *Pechenga*, p. 417.
61 RGAE, f. 9039, op. 1, ed. khr. 418, l. 78, annual report for 1946 from the direction of construction in Nikel to *Glavalyuminstroi*.
62 Ibid., ll. 78–79.
63 RGAE, f. 9037, op. 1, ed. khr. 186, l. 12, annual report for 1946 from Pechenganikel to Glavnikelkobalt.
64 Ibid., ll. 8–9.
65 The title *stakhanovets* honoured Donbas coalminer Aleksei G. Stakhanov who, in August 1935, allegedly raised the productivity of his work-team far beyond the figures in the plan document. This achievement was soon after held up as an example for other workers in the state-induced campaign of the 'stakhanovite movement'. For an interesting description of how this was practised, and the problems it caused, see Kotkin, *Magnetic Mountain*, pp. 207–14; about shock-workers, see pp. 90–3.
66 RGAE, f. 9037, op. 1, ed. khr. 186, l. 10, annual report for 1946 from Pechenganikel to Glavnikelkobalt.
67 Ibid., l. 11.
68 Ibid., l. 16.
69 Åsmund Egge (1993), *Fra Aleksander II til Boris Jeltsin. Russland og Sovjetunionens moderne historie*, Oslo: Universitetsforlaget, p. 209.
70 Kotkin, *Magnetic Mountain*, pp. 208 and 213.
71 RGAE, f. 9037, op. 1, ed. khr. 186, l. 12, annual report for 1946 from Pechenganikel to Glavnikelkobalt.
72 RGAE, f. 9039, op. 1, ed. khr. 418, l. 79, annual report for 1946 from the direction of construction in Nikel to *Glavalyuminstroi*.

73 RGAE, f. 9037, op. 1, ed. khr. 186, l. 12–13, annual report for 1946 from Pechenganikel to Glavnikelkobalt.
74 Ibid., l. 5.
75 RGAE, f. 9022, op. 27 ed. khr. 259, ll. 123–124, decree No 406 from the minister of non-ferrous metallurgy, 9 October 1946.
76 The commission report dated 30 November 1946 is reprinted in Matsak, *Pechenga*, pp. 419–20.
77 RGAE, f. 9022, op. 27, ed. khr. 284, l. 37, decree No 46 from the minister of non-ferrous metallurgy, 7 February 1947.
78 Ibid., ed. khr. 330, l. 151, attachment to decree No 70a from the minister of non-ferrous metallurgy, 27 February 1948. The nickel-related enterprises subordinated to Glavnikelkobalt are listed here: The Yuzhuralnikel combine, the Severonikel combine, the Dashkenkobalt ore processing facility, the State Union nickel factory 'Rezhskii', the State Union nickel factory 'Ufaleiskii', the Installation No. 5 (*Ustanovka No. 5*), the Elizavetinskoye ore processing facility, the research institute Gipronikel in addition to the Pechenganikel combine.
79 At the end of 1947, the company town Nikel was still far from able to offer acceptable housing to all its inhabitants. On the positive side, the combine had organized the construction of an additional 5,551 square metres of living area, and partly provided the housing with central heating and water supply. This had made it possible for 139 families to move from basements and dugouts, 54 families from condemned barracks, 127 families from the various settlements around Nikel, and the resettlement of 173 families previously living in dorms, communal kitchens and overcrowded apartments. Nothing is said about the size of these 493 families, but it is obvious that the additional square metres of living space could not have offered anywhere near a comfortable living situation. Even though the combine had set aside over 60 per cent of its investment budget for housing purposes, the problem was not solved. The situation was further aggravated by unstable foundations under the Finnish prefabricated houses. Some of them were literally falling to pieces. See RGASPI, f. 017, op. 88, d. 867, ll. 16–17, report 1947 from the Murmansk *oblast* party committee, 4 February 1949, and RGAE, f. 9037, op. 1, ed. khr. 227, ll. 18–24, Pechenganikel annual report (supplementary note) for 1947. We return to the problem of housing in the concluding section of this chapter.

80 RGASPI, f. 017, op. 88, d. 477, l. 5, annual report 1946 from the Murmansk *oblast* party committee.
81 RGAE, f. 9037, op. 1, ed. khr. 227, ll. 5–6, Pechenganikel annual report (supplementary note) for 1947.
82 RGASPI, f. 017, op. 76, d. 720, ll. 11–20, Murmansk *oblast* party committee's overall party budget and financial report for 1946.
83 See Kotkin, *Magnetic Mountain*, pp. 198ff.
84 RGASPI, f. 017, op. 88, d. 477, l. 10, annual report 1946 from the Murmansk *oblast* party committee.
85 Ibid., d. 760, l. 3, information dispatch about the plenary session in Murmansk oblast committee of the Communist Party, 23 May 1946.
86 Ibid., d. 867, ll. 26–28, report 1947 from the Murmansk oblast party committee, 4 February 1949.
87 Ibid., d. 760, ll. 8–9, information dispatch about the implementation of the Central Committee's decree on organizing all-Union socialist competitions for the fulfilment and overfulfilment (*perevypolnenie*) of the five-year plan for rebuilding and developing the national economy of the Soviet Union, 20 July 1946.
88 RGAE, f. 9037, op. 1, ed. khr. 227, ll. 11–12, Pechenganikel annual report (supplementary note) for 1947.
89 A wide range of variation over the theme of socialist competition was developed. There was the internal race between individual workers at enterprises, but also between larger groups of workers. Then there were the competitions between whole enterprises, and between similar work brigades at different enterprises. Many of these competitions were combined with reaching a set production target before the envisioned end date, or before a certain date, for example the Constitution Day (5 December) or Stalin's birthday (18 December).
90 See for example Paul R. Gregory and Robert C. Stuart (1981), *Soviet Economic Structure and Performance*, 2nd ed., New York: Harper & Row, p. 181.
91 For a brilliant and hugely interesting analysis of this phenomenon, see various sections in Kotkin, *Magnetic Mountain*.
92 RGAE, f. 9037, op. 1, ed. khr. 227, l. 13, Pechenganikel annual report (supplementary note) for 1947.
93 RGASPI, f. 017, op. 88, d. 867, l. 19, report 1947 from the Murmansk *oblast* party committee, 4 February 1949.

94 Matsak, *Pechenga*, p. 411. The author does not provide a source for this statement, but if nothing else, its inclusion in his text bears witness to the perceived dichotomy between 'Western' and 'Soviet' industrialism. The author's main point seems to be that the workers in Nikel proved the pessimistic Western specialists wrong, and through extraordinary enthusiasm and work ethics rebuilt the industry there much faster than expected.
95 RGAE, f. 9037, op. 1, ed. khr. 331, ll. 15–16, Pechenganikel annual report (supplementary note) for 1949.
96 Nove, *An Economic History of the U.S.S.R.*, pp. 290–3.
97 For a discussion of the fourth four-year plan (1946–50), see ibid., pp. 287ff.
98 RGAE, f. 9037, op. 1, ed. khr. 331, l. 15, Pechenganikel annual report (supplementary note) for 1949.
99 Ibid., ed. khr. 175, ll. 64–63, from protocol of meeting between Soyuznikelolovoproekt, Glavnikelkobalt and dept. of construction of Mintsvetmet, Moscow, 27 July 1945 (ll. 62–51).
100 RGAE, f. 9037, op. 1, ed. khr. 390, l. 15 and ll. 31–32, Pechenganikel annual report (supplementary note) for 1950.
101 O. Ya. Galushko (1985), '40 let trudovoy vakhty gorno-metallurgicheskogo kombinata "Pechenganikel"', *Tsvetnaya Metallurgiya*, No. 9, pp. 1–3.
102 RGAE, f. 9037, op. 1, ed. khr. 265, l. 2, Pechenganikel annual report (supplementary note) for 1948.
103 Ibid., ed. khr. 331, l. 18, Pechenganikel annual report (supplementary note) for 1949.
104 Ibid., ed. khr. 390, l. 26, Pechenganikel annual report (supplementary note) for 1950.
105 Ibid., ed. khr. 331, l. 17, Pechenganikel annual report (supplementary note) for 1949.
106 Ibid., l. 18.
107 Ibid., ed. khr. 390, l. 96, Pechenganikel annual report (supplementary note) for 1950.
108 Ibid., l. 97. The combine management called for the realization of an initiative from the Leningrad Institute on Occupational Diseases (Leningradskii institut profzabolevanii) to do research on silicosis and its prevention. Silicosis is caused by inhalation of silica, a fine dust that is

raised in the air as a result of pneumatic drilling or mining by explosives (both methods used in Nikel), and is characterized by shortness of breath, fever, and cyanosis (bluish skin). Silicosis increases susceptibility to other pulmonary diseases, such as tuberculosis, and may lead to emphysema, often with a fatal result.

109 Ibid., ed. khr. 265, l. 52, Pechenganikel annual report (supplementary note) for 1948.
110 RGAE, f. 9022, op. 27, ed. khr. 371, ll. 58–61, Order from the Ministry for Non-ferrous Metallurgy No. 186, May 1951 'on measures for immediate support to the Pechenganikel combine'.
111 RGAE, f. 9037, op. 1, ed. khr. 390, l. 96, Pechenganikel annual report (supplementary note) for 1950.
112 Ibid., ed. khr. 552, ll. 77–79, Pechenganikel annual report (supplementary note) for 1953.
113 Service, *A History of Modern Russia*, p. 217.
114 RGAE, f. 9037, op. 1, ed. khr. 175, ll. 58–57, from protocol of meeting between Soyuznikelolovoproekt, Glavnikelkobalt and dept. of construction in Mintsvetmet, Moscow, 27 July 1945 (ll. 62–51).
115 Ibid., ed. khr. 331, ll. 26–27, Pechenganikel annual report (supplementary note) for 1949.

Chapter 5

1 RGASPI, f. 017, op. 88, d. 867, l. 23, annual report from the Murmansk oblast party committee for 1948, 4 February 1949.
2 Krosby, *Finland, Germany and the Soviet Union*, p. 5 and pp. 91–2.
3 This patch of land did not have a specific name but will in the following be referred to as the Jäniskoski area or territory, as it was named in Soviet documents. In reality, Jäniskoski (lit.: The Hare Rapids) is the name of whitewater parts in the upper Pasvik River but will here be used to denote both the area as a whole and the settlement connected to the power station that was built there.
4 Nevakivi, 'From the Continuation War to the Present', p. 230.
5 One example: the war reparations were to be delivered at 1938 selling prices. By 1952, when the last Finnish delivery was made to the Soviet

Union, the actual market prices on Finland's delivery had almost doubled. See Nevakivi, 'From the Continuation War to the Present', p. 229.
6 Zhdanov was intent on staying within the formal boundaries of his mandate by not meddling directly in Finnish decision making. See Nevakivi, 'From the Continuation War to the Present', p. 226. However, the Soviet colonel general was a force to be reckoned with. His position in Finland during the time of the Allied Control Commission's presence there has been referred to as 'above all Finnish law and thereby in a position resembling that of a Governor General'. See Risto E. J. Pentitilä (1994), 'Finland's Security in a Changing Europe: A Historical Perspective', *Finnish Defence Studies*, Vol. 7 (1994), Helsinki: National Defence College, p. 15.
7 As quoted in Nevakivi, 'From the Continuation War to the Present', p. 229.
8 Both Paasikivi (who left the post of prime minister to become president in 1946) and his successor Mauno Pekkala brought up this possibility. See Tuomo Polvinen (translated and edited by D. G. Kirby and Peter Herring) (1986), *Between East and West: Finland in International Politics, 1944-47*, Minneapolis, MN: University of Minnesota Press, pp. 212–18.
9 Nevakivi, 'From the Continuation War to the Present', p. 240.
10 Imatran Voima was partly controlled by the Finnish state as a provider of the common good electricity. Pechenganikel was, of course, completely state-owned. An agreement between these two actors therefore hardly qualified for the term 'non-governmental'.
11 Robert M. Slusser and Jan F. Triska (with the assistance of George Ginsburgs and Wilfred O. Reiners) (1959), *A Calendar of Soviet Treaties, 1917–1957*, Stanford, CA: Stanford University Press, p. 423.
12 That the two latter agreements were concluded on the same day is apparent from a record of a conversation between the head of the legal department in the Soviet Ministry of Foreign Trade, A. S. Korolenko, and the Finnish representative engineer Gylling (Gjuling). See RGAE, f. 9037, op. 1, ed. khr. 257, ll. 48–49. Also, the Soviet party organ *Pravda* referred to the simultaneous agreements the day after, on 4 February 1947. See Potemkin, *U severnoi granitsy*, p. 264. A brief account of the treaty establishing the Jäniskoski area as Soviet territory is given in Slusser and Triska, *A Calendar of Soviet Treaties, 1917–1957*, p. 225.

13 See Nevakivi, 'From the Continuation War to the Present', p. 229.
14 The agreement between Pechenganikel and Imatran Voima did foresee that all construction equipment and basic construction material were to be provided from the Soviet Union. These supplies were of course not free of charge, neither was their transport. The costs were, however, minuscule compared to total expenses involved in the Jäniskoski project.
15 In RGAE, f. 9037, op. 1 a total of six files of about 120 to about 220 pages each contain correspondence between various Soviet institutions involved in aspects of the Jäniskoski operation.
16 That the Pechenganikel management was not fully informed about proceedings in the Jäniskoski project becomes apparent in a letter from the combine director V. I. Trofimov to Glavnikelkobalt, dated 19 March 1947. The director complained that he had received big shipments of equipment and materials destined for Jäniskoski, and that the cargo was put to Pechenganikel's expense, whereas he had no information about how and when to transport the cargo further, or with whom to communicate about this. He concludes the letter by requesting a copy of the agreement between his own company and Imatran Voima – almost two months after the agreement had been concluded, and well over a month after Boris Kleshko had established Pechenganikel's offices in Helsinki. See RGAE, f. 9037, op. 1, ed. khr. 257, l. 1. For Boris Kleshko's arrival in Finland, see ibid., l. 16.
17 Historical accounts of the emergence of the Cold War and its consequences are too numerous to detail here. For the specific observation of the Soviet tightening of the Norwegian–Soviet border, see Hanne Brusletto (1994), 'Forhandlinger mellom Norge og Sovjetunionen om kraftutbygging i Pasvikelven 1945–1963. Norsk-sovjetisk brobygging under den kalde krigen', MA thesis in history, University of Oslo, fall 1994, p. 25.
18 RGAE, f. 9037, op. 1, ed. khr. 257, ll. 68–69, notes from meeting between Andrianov, Kleshko and Nykopp, 18 April 1947. The firms metioned were contracted to deliver turbines (Tampella), generators (Strömberg) and salmon ladders (Kone).
19 Ibid., ll. 16–20. Kleshko's first report to Semyon M. Petrov, head of Glavnikelkobalt and deputy minister of non-ferrous metallurgy, dated 18 March 1947.

20 Ibid., l. 6, letter from Petrov to Kleshko, dated 13 May 1947.
21 Ibid., ll. 97–98, letter from Kleshko to Petrov, dated 23 July 1947.
22 The treaty was ratified by Finland 21 February and by the Soviet Union 3 March. It entered into force on 18 April 1947, on the exchange of acts of ratification in Moscow. The joint Finnish–Soviet border commission established as part of the treaty was ordered to complete its work by 1 October 1947. See Slusser and Triska, *A Calendar of Soviet Treaties, 1917–1957,* p. 225.
23 RGAE, f. 9037, op. 1, ed. khr. 257, ll. 65–66, letter from Vyshinskii to Serov, 2 April 1947.
24 Ibid., ll. 88–89, letter from Serov to Petrov, 12 July 1947.
25 Ibid., ll. 136–137, report from Kleshko, 29 November 1947.
26 Ibid., ed. khr. 318, ll. 21–25, letter from Imatran Voima to Kleshko, 17 September 1947. See also ibid., ll. 63–64, letter from Kleshko to Petrov, 23 March 1948. Kleshko here explains the lack of proper documents mostly as a result of practical difficulties in getting all the formalities right.
27 Ibid., ll. 63–64, letter from Kleshko to Petrov, 23 March 1948. Here Kleshko informed Petrov that also workers who only had documents that were approved by Imatran Voima would be allowed to pass through until 5 March 1948, by agreement with the local commander of the Soviet Border Control, Lieutenant Colonel *(podpolkovnik)* Kaganchuk.
28 Ibid., ll. 18–19, letter from Petrov to Kleshko, 28 February 1948.
29 Barracks no. 2 was not meant to contain woodstoves. Room 4 had been equipped with one because it had been used as a vaccination locale while typhoid fever raged among the workers. The medical staff had used the stove to heat water, presumably for sterilization purposes. However, when the woodstove was checked on 7 November, it was established that it had not been installed in accordance with fire regulations, and the room was temporarily sealed off. See RGAE, f. 9037, op. 1, ed. khr. 257, ll. 177–179, letter from Imatran Voima to engineer Goncharov, 24 November 1947.
30 The information about the fire, the night watchman's observations and the woodstove's condition stem from the interrogation protocol made by 'keeper of order' (*blyustitel poryadka*) F. Kamara. See RGAE, f. 9037, op. 1, ed. khr. 257, ll. 180–182, Imatran Voima's interrogation protocol from

the investigation of the fire at the Jäniskoski construction site (translated from Finnish into Russian), 12 November 1947 and ibid., ll. 177–179, letter from Imatran Voima to engineer Goncharov, 24 November 1947. There is no documentation that the pancake-makers were found guilty of starting the fire, and both the interrogation protocol and Imatran Voima's letter to Goncharov seem to indicate a lenient attitude towards the three. For the cost of damages, see also ibid., l. 183, value assessment of barracks no. 2.

31 RGAE, f. 9037, op. 1, ed. khr. 257, l. 176, letter from Goncharov to Petrov, 27 November 1947.

32 Ibid., ll. 177–179, letter from Imatran Voima to engineer Goncharov, 24 November 1947.

33 Ibid., ed. khr. 318, ll. 21–25, letter from Imatran Voima to Kleshko, 17 September 1947.

34 Ibid., ed. khr. 257, ll. 177–179, letter from Imatran Voima to engineer Goncharov, 24 November 1947. This letter repeats the content of RGAE, f. 9037, op. 1, ed. khr. 318, ll. 21–25, letter from Imatran Voima to Kleshko, 17 September 1947.

35 RGAE, f. 9037, op. 1, ed. khr. 257, l. 176, letter from Goncharov to Petrov, 27 November 1947. Goncharev used the phrase '*vrazhdebnye nam element*'.

36 This would probably have little effect in the Soviet capital. There is evidence to suggest that, rather than taking defensive measures in Jäniskoski, Soviet intelligence agencies saw the Jäniskoski project as an opportunity to recruit agents among the Finnish workers. According to the Finnish security police, this did in fact take place, to some extent. See Brusletto, 'Forhandlinger mellom Norge og Sovjetunionen', p. 123.

37 One example is provided by the following incident: Earlier in 1947, Kleshko and the Deputy Attaché of Commerce Andrianov had been invited to a conversation with a certain Rautelin, chairman of the Finnish construction workers' union and himself a member of the Finnish Communist Party. Rautelin urged his Soviet comrades to keep a keen eye on the Imatran Voima organization, and especially on the head of supplies, who according to Rautelin was a former White officer (*byvshii feldfebel*). He also suggested that a representative from his union be hired by Pechenganikel to agitate for a proper proletarian spirit (*kulturno-*

massovaya rabota) at the construction site. There is no documentation to indicate that these warnings and suggestions were taken seriously. See RGAE, f. 9037, op. 1, ed. khr. 257, ll. 81–82, transcript of conversation with the chairman of the Finnish construction workers' union.
38 RGAE, f. 9037, op. 1, ed. khr. 257, l. 174, letter from Petrov to Vetrov (head of MID's 5th European department), 25 December 1947.
39 Ibid.
40 RGAE, f. 9037, op. 1, ed. khr. 257, l. 191, letter from Petrov to Kleshko, 25 December 1947.
41 Ibid., ed. khr. 318, l. 65, letter from Kleshko to Petrov, 31 March 1948.
42 Ibid., ed. khr. 319, ll. 41–50, Technical report from visit to Jäniskoski, 4 August–9 September, 1948, made by engineer A. I. Nikitin, l. 49.
43 Ibid.
44 RGAE, f. 9037, op. 1, ed. khr. 376, ll. 70-71, Investigation protocol after attempted arson in the woodstore (translated from Finnish into Russian), undated.
45 Ibid., l. 72, letter from Kleshko to Telestam, 4 August 1949.
46 Ibid., l. 73, letter from Petrov to Kleshko and Petrov (director of Pechenganikel), 30 August 1949.
47 Ibid., l. 84, letter from Telestam to Kleshko, 2 September, 1949.
48 Ibid.
49 According to information given by Finnish authorities to the Norwegian security police (when Norway embarked on a similar power plant project some years later), Finnish law was applicable in Jäniskoski for offences committed against Finnish individuals and property. Offenders were to be transported out of Jäniskoski to the nearest police station (in Ivalo). Offences against Soviet property or Soviet individuals, however, were to be brought before a Soviet court. See Brusletto, 'Forhandlinger mellom Norge og Sovjetunionen', p. 122. In practice, as we have seen, all offences were dealt with by the 'keepers of order'.
50 The ministries of ferrous and of non-ferrous metallurgy were merged into one, the Ministry of Metallurgic Industry (Minmetallurgprom) in July 1948, and later, by a decree of 23 December 1950, re-established as separate entities. In the following, as the narrative skips back and forth in time, both sets of names will come up, as will both ministers. Tevosyan and A. Kuzmin held the post of minister of metallurgic

industry between July 1948 and December 1953, whereas Petr Lomako headed the Ministry of Non-ferrous Metallurgy before and after this intermezzo. To confuse matters even further, Minmetallurgprom, incorporating the two above-mentioned ministries, re-emerged in March 1950. For our purposes, however, the most important information is the level at which decisions were made, and not what that level (ministerial level) was officially termed at any given moment. For the numerous re-organizations of the metallurgical branch, see RGAE, f. 9022, op. 31, ll. 6–7, introduction (by V. V. Solovyev) to fond 9022, *Narkomat-Ministerstvo Tsvetnoi Metallurgii SSSR*.

51 RGAE, f. 9037, op. 1, ed. khr. 376, ll. 1–4, letter from Deputy Minister of Metallurgical Industry A. Piterskii to Chairman of the Currency Committee of the Council of Ministers A. N. Kosygin, 25 January 1949.

52 Ibid., ed. khr. 430, l. 20, letter from Petrov to P. Orlov (MID), 29 June, 1950.

53 Ibid., l. 37. letter from P. Orlov (MID) to Petrov, 25 August 1950.

54 Ibid., l. 11, letter from Petrov to Deputy Minister of Metallurgical Industry A. G. Sheremetevo, April 1950.

55 Ibid., l. 99, letter from Petrov to Deputy Minister of Metallurgical Industry G. G. Vodnev, November 1950.

56 Ibid. l. 97, draft letter from Petrov to Kuzmin, 5 November 1950, and ibid., l. 100, draft letter from Kusmin to Tevosyan, 5 November 1950.

57 Ibid. ed. khr. 319, ll. 52–54, Kleshko's report on Jäniskoski hydroelectric power station, 21 June 1948.

58 Ibid., ed. khr. 257, ll. 77–78, telephonogram from Kleshko and Artemev to Mikoyan and Lomako, received 23 June 1947.

59 Or, more precisely, the road became the responsibility of the Directorate for Main Roads (Upravlenie Shosseinykh Dorog – UShossDor), which was subordinated the MVD. See RGAE, f. 9037, op. 1, ed. khr. 318, l. 5, letter from Lomako to Minister of Internal Affairs Sergei Kruglov, 11 January 1948. UShossDor (or GUShossDor) had, as part of the MVD system, almost unlimited access to cheap labour from within the GULag system (see M. B. Smirnov (ed.) (1998), *Sistema ispravitelno-trudovykh lagerei v SSSR*, Moscow: Zvenya, p. 7). It is, however, unlikely that the stretch of road between Nikel and Jäniskoski was deemed appropriate for prisoner workers, due to its proximity to the border.

60 RGAE, f. 9037, op. 1, ed. khr. 318, l. 14, letter from Head Engineer at Glavnikelkobalt A. Mironov to Pechenganikel director Trofimov, 2 February 1948.
61 Ibid., l. 56, letter from Petrov to Trofimov, 3 April 1948.
62 Ibid., ll. 70–73, Lebedev's report from visit to Jäniskoski 24 January to 26 February 1948, 3 March 1948.
63 The degree of detail in central agencies' decision making was always considered to be high in the extremely centralized Soviet economy. With the opening of Soviet archives from the early 1990s this assumption has become even stronger. See for example R. W. Davies (2001), 'Making Economic Policy', in Paul R. Gregory (ed.), *Behind the Façade of Stalin's Command Economy: Evidence from the Soviet State and Party Archives*, Stanford, CA: Hoover Institution Press, pp. 61–80.
64 RGAE, f. 9037, op. 1, ed. khr. 318, ll. 99–104, Nikitin's report from visit to Jäniskoski 19 January to 27 March 1948, 27 April 1948.
65 Ibid., ll. 117–120, Lebedev's report from visit to Jäniskoski, 16 March to 27 April 1948, 29 April 1948.
66 Ibid., ed. khr. 319, ll. 3–7, report from Kleshko and Trofimov to Lomako and Petrov, 31 July 1948.
67 Ibid., ed. khr. 318, ll. 149–150, letter from Petrov to the Central Committee of the Communist Party, dept. of heavy industry, 31 August 1948. Trofimov was in late 1948 replaced as Pechenganikel director by a certain A. A. Ilin (a fact that is evident in the correspondence), who shortly thereafter was succeeded by engineer A. I. Petrov – the same Petrov who took part in the fact-finding mission at Petsamon Nikkeli's industrial site in March 1940 (see Chapter 3). There is no documentation confirming that Trofimov's removal was a punishment, but it is likely he did not enjoy the trust of his superiors after the harsh criticism cited above.
68 This time limit is mentioned many places in the correspondence about Jäniskoski. See for example RGAE, f. 9037, op. 1, ed. khr. 319, ll. 52–54, Kleshko's report on Jäniskoski hydroelectric power station, 21 June 1948.
69 Ibid.
70 In a letter from Petrov to Minister of Metallurgical Industry Tevosyan 18 December 1948, Petrov describes Imatran Voima as conscientious (*dobrosovestnyi*) and efficient (*akkuratnyi*). He also credits the firm with

its willingness to accommodate its Soviet customer in all requests. See RGAE, f. 9037, op. 1, ed. khr. 319, ll. 76–77.
71 Ibid., ll. 74–75, letter from Tevosyan to Malenkov, 17 December 1948.
72 Ibid., ll. 80–83, letter from Petrov to Tevosyan, 17 December 1948.
73 Ibid., ll. 67–69, letter from Petrov to Ilin (copied to Kleshko), 22 November 1948. The exception for foreign currency would of course exclude Pechenganikel from many aspects of direct contact with Imatran Voima and other non-Soviet subcontractors involved in the project.
74 All major Communist Party committees in the Soviet Union had sections dealing with agitation and propaganda (agitprop). Their job was to socialize Soviet citizens, that is, workers, into the common project of 'building socialism', which was considered pivotal to the success of the Soviet state. See Richard Sakwa (1989), *Soviet Politics: An Introduction*, London: Routledge, p. 210ff.
75 RGAE, f. 9037, op. 1, ed. khr. 319, l. 62, letter from Verbitskii in Murmansk regional party committee to Zhimerin and Lomako, 17 June 1948.
76 Ibid., l. 63, letter from Petrov to Verbitskii, undated.
77 Ibid., l. 16, letter from Pechenga regional party committee to Lomako, 16 July 1948.
78 Ibid., l. 17, letter from Mironov to Pechenga regional party committee, 28 August 1948.
79 Though very much a central figure in the economic realm of the Soviet dual structure, Malenkov was part of the inner circle surrounding Stalin, which effectively ran the country when the state leader took his many extended leaves after the Second World War. Consequently, Malenkov was not only a very powerful man, but also one of the most feared actors on the top of the Soviet power pyramid. See Donald Rayfield (2005), *Stalin and His Hangmen*, London: Penguin, pp. 421ff.
80 RGAE, f. 9037, op. 1, ed. khr. 319, ll. 80–83, letter from Petrov to Tevosyan, 17 December 1948.
81 Ibid., ll. 93–94, letter from Tevosyan to Malenkov, 27 December 1948.
82 Ibid., ll. 149–150, letter from Petrov to Central Committee of the Communist Party, dept. of heavy industry, 31 August 1948.
83 The Communist Party served the function of what could be termed 'superior moral judge'. Any problem within the sphere of industrial life

could be assessed not only by industrial standards but, more worryingly for those involved, by ideological standards set by the Party. Therefore, maintaining good relations with the Party would always be a priority for any industrialist, or any Soviet citizen for that matter. For examples of the Bolshevik party's influence on Soviet production life, see Kotkin, *Magnetic Mountain*.

84 RGAE, f. 9037, op. 1, ed. khr. 318, ll. 117–120, Lebedev's report from visit to Jäniskoski, 16 March to 27 April 1948, 29 April 1948.
85 The cargo would usually come by boat to Kemi and then be transported further by rail to Rovaniemi, where the train tracks stopped.
86 RGAE, f. 9037, op. 1, ed. khr. 376, ll. 105–111, Kleshko's report to Petrov, 1 November 1949 (l. 108).
87 USI Finland had its offices with the Soviet trade representation (Torgpredstvo) in Helsinki, which was subordinated the Directorate for Soviet Property Abroad (Glavnoe Upravlenie sovetskim imushchestvom za granitsei) and ultimately to the Soviet Ministry of Foreign Trade. In the aftermath of the Second World War, the Soviet Union established companies operating in several countries, among them Austria, Bulgaria, Hungary, Germany, China, Romania, and Yugoslavia as well as Finland. For a list of units, see Jeffrey Burds et al. (eds) (1996), *A Research Guide: 2. Guide to Collections*, Moscow: Russian State Archive of the Economy, pp. 393–5.
88 This, at least, is how Kleshko himself saw things. It was also a perception for which he convincingly argued. See RGAE, f. 9037, op. 1, ed. khr. 376, ll. 105–111, Kleshko's report to Petrov, 1 November 1949.
89 This account is based mostly on the above cited November 1949 report from Kleshko to Petrov, but also on USI Finland's and Vakava's reports on the same matter, found respectively in ibid., ll. 91–95 and ibid., ll. 97–98.
90 RGAE, f. 9037, op. 1, ed. khr. 376, ll. 91–95, memo from Maslov to head of sixth department in the Directorate for Soviet Property Abroad M. I. Ivanov, 3 September 1949 (l. 91).
91 Ibid., l. 95.
92 Ibid., ll. 97–98, memo from Vakava's general director Avanesov and Suomen Petrooli's general director Molchanin to Maslov, undated (l. 98).

93 Ibid., l. 102, telegram from Glavnikelkobalt (Galper) to Kleshko, 15 October 1949 and ibid., l. 101, telegram from Glavnikelkobalt (Galper) to head of sixth department in the Directorate for Soviet Property Abroad M. I. Ivanov, 15 October 1949. Kleshko's recall to Moscow is not directly reflected in these documents. He was, however, in Moscow briefly after the Vakava incident explaining his side of the story. See RGAE, f. 9037, op. 1, ed. khr. 376, ll. 105–111, memo from Kleshko to Petrov, 1 November 1949.

94 This quote and the quotes in the paragraph above are all taken from RGAE, f. 9037, op. 1, ed. khr. 376, ll. 105–111, memo from Kleshko to Petrov, 1 November 1949.

95 Ibid., l. 112, letter from Petrov to Ivanov, 10 November 1949.

96 On several occasions, Kleshko refers to his communication with Lomako and Politburo member Anastas Mikoyan. For the importance of connections in the Soviet economic sphere, see Eugenia Belova (2001), 'Economic Crime and Punishment', in Paul R. Gregory (ed.), *Behind the Façade of Stalin's Command Economy: Evidence from the Soviet State and Party Archives*, Stanford, CA: Hoover Institution Press, pp. 131–58.

97 On the Party Control Commissions and the punitive processes within the economic realm in the Soviet Union, see Belova, 'Economic Crime and Punishment'.

98 RGAE, f. 9037, op. 1, ed. khr. 376, ll. 136–137, draft letter from Minister of Metallurgical Industry Kuzmin to Deputy Chair in the Council of Ministers Tevosyan, undated (1949).

99 Ibid., ed. khr. 430, l. 29, letter from A. I. Petrov to Kuzmin, Prokofyev (secretary of the Murmansk Oblast Party Committee) and Petrov in Glavnikelkobalt, 26 July 1950. Petrov was later allowed to reward the Helsinki-based employees. See ibid., ll. 15–17, protocol from meeting about Soviet takeover of Jäniskoski, 1 May 1950. The governmental commission that oversaw the handover of Jäniskoski power station to the Soviet Union made special mention of Kleshko's Helsinki office and how its task had been carried out successfully 'despite complicated and unusual conditions and difficulties in the fulfillment of the work'. See ibid., ed. khr. 498, ll. 12–18, Kleshko's report on Jäniskoski, 6 March 1951 (l. 14).

100 Ibid., ed. khr. 376, l. 132, letter from Petrov to Head of Border Control Stakhanov, 24 November 1949.

101 Ibid. ed. khr. 430, l. 3, letter from Kuzmin to Tevosyan, 27 February 1950.
102 Ibid., ll. 31–33, Kleshko's report on Jäniskoski, 4 August 1950.
103 Ibid., l. 111, letter from deputy head of Glavtsentrenergo to Petrov, 21 November 1950.
104 Ibid., ll. 108–109, letter from Deputy Minister of Metallurgical Industries Dzhaparidze to Ryaboshapko and Minister of Power Stations Zhimerin, 9 December 1950.
105 This was a reversal of the re-organization two and a half years earlier, in July 1948, when Minstvetmet and the Ministry of Ferrous Metallurgy were merged. See RGAE, f. 9022, op. 31, ll. 6–7, introduction (by V. V. Solovyev) to fond 9022, *Narkomat-Ministerstvo Tsvetnoi Metallurgii SSSR*.
106 RGAE, f. 9037, op. 1, ed. khr. 498, ll. 2–3, letter from Lomako to Tevosyan, 27 January 1951.
107 Ibid., ll. 9–10, letter from Lomako to Tevosyan, 12 March 1951.
108 Ibid., ll. 12–18, Report on the Jäniskoski power plant, signed by the Head of Glavnikelkobalt's energy section Ilinskii, March 1951. The plant was completed and running at full capacity from August 1951. See Potemkin (1965), *U severnoi granitsy*, p. 265.
109 Adam B. Ulam (1974), *Expansion and Coexistence: Soviet Foreign Policy 1917–73*, 2nd ed., New York: Praeger.
110 RGAE, f. 9037, op. 1, ed. khr. 376, ll. 58–60, Telestam's report on the possibility of building hydropower plants on the Pasvik River, 28 December 1948. In this report, Telestam describes several other rapids and their expected power production. All these were later developed by the Soviet Union in collaboration with either Finland or Norway.
111 Ibid., ll. 86–87, letter from Deputy Head of Glavnikelkobalt Mironov to Deputy Head of Gosplan's department for external affairs Podugolnikov, 1 October 1949.
112 Ibid., l. 81, letter from Kuzmin to Tevosyan, 9 September 1949.
113 This point was emphasized several times in the Soviet–Finnish talks about Rajakoski. Telestam had suggested starting preliminary work in the spring 1949, so as not to lose valuable time. However, the project did not get underway until spring 1951. See numerous documents in RGAE, f. 9037, op. 1, ed. khr. 376 and ibid. ed. khr. 430.
114 RGAE, f. 9037, op. 1, ed. khr. 430, l. 58, letter from Minister of Foreign Trade Menshikov and Kuzmin to Tevosyan, 6 September 1950.

115 Ibid., l. 59, Draft resolution from the Council of Ministers (to be signed by Stalin), November 1950.
116 Potemkin, *U severnoi granitsy*, pp. 265–6.
117 For an interesting discussion of 'the honest manager's dilemma', see Belova, 'Economic Crime and Punishment'. Belova shows how the typical Soviet factory manager was squeezed between demands from central planning authorities and law enforcement agencies. On the one hand, supplies were not sufficient to reach the planned target, while on the other the manager was not able to fulfil these demands without breaking the laws that prohibited barter trade.
118 One example is the case of Head Engineer Fedulkin, the newly appointed manager of the Jäniskoski power station. When Fedulkin arrived at Jäniskoski in 1950, he basically found himself in a Finnish enclave on Soviet soil. The canteen catered to the Finns and accepted only Finnish marks, of which he had none. However, in the Soviet system, access to foreign currency could be granted only by the very top level. In Fedulkin's case, several letters had to be sent to the Council of Ministers before permission was granted and he was able to eat legally among his Finnish colleagues. (Obviously, however, Fedulkin was served in the canteen also before this.) See various documents in RGAE, f. 9037, op. 1, ed. khr. 390.

Chapter 6

1 Philip Roth (2005). *The Human Stain,* London: Vintage Books, p. 209.
2 The quoted phrase is taken from Kotkin, *Magnetic Mountain*, p. 363.

Bibliography

1 In addition, there are various units pertaining to individuals, so-called *lichnye fondy*; these I have not examined. For an excellent introduction to RGAE's holdings, history and how to work in the archives, see Chase's (1996) 'Researcher's Introduction to the Russian State Archive

of the Economy', in William Chase, Jeffrey Burds, S. V. Prasolova, A. K. Sokolov and E. A. Tiurina (eds), *A Research Guide I: Guide to Collections*, Moscow: Blagovest, pp. I–XII.

2 For a study that uses documentation from GAMO, see Bruno, *The Nature of Soviet Power*.

Sources

Primary and secondary material

The primary sources reflected in this book stem almost exclusively from Soviet archives, except for a handful of German documents referred to in Chapter 3 (I am grateful to colleagues Rolf Hobson and Mari Olafson Lundemo for alerting me to this information). While my primary goal and original contribution is to bring the Soviet outlook to the reader's attention, perspectives of other states play a subsidiary role. German, Finnish, British and Canadian assessments are generally provided through secondary sources. Thus, this book remains and should be read as an investigation into Soviet interests and motives.

Overall, the one perspective that has been the least accessible to me is that of Finland. Lacking skills in the Finnish language, I have not been able to study collections relating to my subject that are to be found in Helsinki and elsewhere in Finland. Similar problems pertain to Finnish secondary sources. Aside from literature in Swedish and in English on the Winter War and the Moscow parenthesis, most books on Finnish history have been written by Finns in their mother tongue. Thus, this study will inevitably suffer from some gaps, and I can only appeal to those with better knowledge of the Finnish language to fill them in.

In writing this book, I have relied mainly on findings in the Russian State Archive of the Economy (RGAE) in Moscow. Here, I located most of the documents that contain information about the Soviet interest in the nickel resource of Petsamo in the 1940s, and about the rebuilding phase that started after the takeover of the territory in 1944. For insight into how Soviet approaches to Petsamo were expressed at the highest political level, I have consulted various volumes of *Dokumenty vneshnei politiki* (see under 'published document collections and annotations' below). Some additional material, primarily pertaining to the Communist Party structure in Murmansk and Pechenga, was located in the Russian State Archive for Socio-Political History (RGASPI).

The RGAE holdings are immense. They comprise documents relating to the vast Soviet economy and are structured according to the institutions that worked within this system. Thus, Soviet administrative agencies that functioned on the all-union level have their own archival unit (*fond*) in RGAE.[1] The content of each *fond* is divided into *opisi*. Each *opis* is a description (mostly in the form of brief headings) of the documents contained in corresponding subsections, the files or *dela* (alternatively *edinitsy khraneniya*). It is through an examination of the *opisi* that one can narrow down the search for documents. As seen from the list of archives below, I have studied sections of two ministerial *fondy*, which typically contain resolutions, decrees, executive orders and directives. In addition, I have reviewed documents in two *fondy* on the directorate level (*glavnoe upravlenie*). These contain annual reports, correspondence between the enterprise level and the directorate, and communications pertaining to matters of specific interest to central authorities.

Since RGAE sources stem from the all-union level, only occasionally can information on day-to-day activities at the local level be found there. That said, the RGAE holdings frequently do provide an impression of local developments in condensed form, for example, through annual reports from enterprises. In matters deemed important enough for the directorate or the ministry level to be continually informed, lower-level processes are even more accessible. One such episode was the early rebuilding phase at Pechenganikel, and to an even greater extent the Jäniskoski hydroelectric power plant project. That said, if I had aimed at presenting a historical investigation truly committed to the perspective from below, documents in the State Archive of the Murmansk Region (GAMO) should have been consulted. Although investigations there would most certainly have yielded interesting insights,[2] I have – primarily in order to be able to handle the amount of information in a meaningful way – chosen to restrict my archival research to the central level.

Throughout this study, I have translated source quotations from the Russian language. For Russian words and names, the Library of Congress transliteration system has been used, with the exception that diacritical marks for soft signs have been suppressed.

Archives

Rossiiskii Gosudarstvennyi Arkhiv Ekonomiki (RGAE) (the Russian State Archive of the Economy, formerly Tsentralnyi Gosudarstvennyi Arkhiv Narodnogo Khozyaistva, or TsGANKh)

Fond 9039: Glavnoe upravlenie po stroitelstvu predpriyatii alyuminevoi i magnievoi promyshlennosti Mintsvetmeta SSSR (the Soviet directorate for building of enterprises within the aluminum and magnesium industry), 1944–1947

Fond 9022: Narodnyi kommissariat/Ministerstvo tsvetnoi metallurgii (Peoples' Commissariat/Ministry for non-ferrous metallurgy), 1944–1957

Fond 9037: Glavnoe upravlenie nikelevoi i kobaltovoi promyshlennosti Mintsvetmeta SSSR (the Soviet directorate for nickel and cobalt industries), 1939–1957

Rossiiskii Gosudarstvennyi Arkhiv Sotsialnoi i Politicheskoi Istorii (RGASPI) (the Russian State Archive for Socio-Political History, until 1991 the CPSS party archive (TsPA IML) and from 1991 to 1999 Rossiiskii Tsentr Khraneniya i Izucheniya Dokumentov Noveishei Istorii, (RTsKhIDNI))

Fond 88: Murmanskoi Oblastnoi Komitet KPSS (the Murmansk oblast committee of the CPSU), until 1952.

Published document collections and annotations

Adibekiv, G. M., K. M. Anderson and L. A. Rogovaya (eds) (2001). *Politbyuro TsK RKP(b): Povestki dnya zasedanii 1919–1952*. Moscow: Rosspen.

Akten zur Deutschen Auswärtigen Politik (1961). Baden-Baden: P. Keppler Verlag KG.

Burds, Jeffrey, S. V. Pravoslova, A. K. Sokolov and E. A. Tiurina (eds) (1996). *A Research Guide: 2. Guide to Collections*. Moscow: Reform-Press.

Chase, William, Jeffrey Burds, S. V. Prasolova, A. K. Sokolov and E. A. Tiurina (eds) (1996). *A Research Guide I: Guide to Collections*. Moscow: Blagovest.

Dokumenty vneshnei politiki 1940–22 iyunya 1941, vol. 1 (1995). Moscow: Mezhdunarodnye otnoshenya.

Dokumenty vneshnei politiki 1940–22 iyunya 1941, vol. 2 (1995). Moscow: Mezhdunarodnye otnoshenya.

Dokumenty vneshnei politiki 22 iyunya–1 yanvarya 1942 (2000). Moscow: Mezhdunarodnye otnosheniya.

Egge, Åsmund and Vadim Roginskij (eds) (2006). *Komintern og Norge: DNA-perioden 1919–1923. En dokumentasjon*. Oslo: Unipub.

Holtsmark, Sven G. (ed.) (1995). *Norge og Sovjetunionen: En utenrikspolitisk dokumentasjon*. Oslo: J. W. Cappelen.

Slusser, Robert M. and Jan F. Triska (with the assistance of George Ginsburgs and Wilfred O. Reiners) (1959). *A Calendar of Soviet Treaties, 1917–1957*. Stanford, CA: Stanford University Press.

Sovetsko-norvezhskie otnosheniya 1917-1955. Sbornik dokumentov (1997). Moscow: Elia Art-O.

Suomen Ulkoasiainministeriö (The Finnish Ministry of Foreign Affairs) (1941). *Finland Reveals Her Secret Documents on Soviet Foreign Policy: March 1940–June 1941*, with a Preface by Hjalmar J. Procopé. New York: Wilfred Funk.

Bibliography

Aitamäki, A. (2009). 'Linhamar som ett andningshål mot väst – Godstrafiken längs Ishavsvägen under freden mellan vinter- och forsättingskriget', in M. Engman and K. Westerlund (eds), *Petsamo och havet*. Åbo: Uniprint.

Andreen, Per G. (1980). *Finland i brännpunkten: mars 1940 – juni 1941*. Stockholm: Lindfors nya Bokförlag.

Appelbaum, Anne (2003). *Gulag: A History of the Soviet Camps*. London: Allen Lane.

Appelbaum, Anne (2012). *Iron Curtain: The Crushing of Eastern Europe 1944–1956*. London: Allen Lane.

Autere, Eugen and Jaako Liede (eds) (1989). *Petsamon Nikkeli: Taistelu strategisesta metallista*. Helsinki: Vuorimiesyhdistys – Bergsmannaföreningen r.y (with English summary).

Baryshnikov, N. I. (2001). 'Problema Petsamo v sovetsko-finlyandskikh otnosheniyakh (1939–1944gg.)', in M. N. Suprun (ed.), *Voina v Arktike (1939–1944gg.)*. St. Petersburg: Izdatelstvo Pravda Severa.

Beckerman, Gal (2010). *When They Come for Us, We'll Be Gone: The Epic Struggle to Save Soviet Jewry*. Boston, MA: Houghton Mifflin Harcourt.

Belova, Eugenia (2001). 'Economic Crime and Punishment', in Paul R. Gregory (ed.), *Behind the Façade of Stalin's Command Economy: Evidence from the Soviet State and Party Archives*. Stanford, CA: Hoover Institution Press.

Björklund, Eric (1981). *Petsamotrafiken*. Danderyd: Åkeriförlaget.

Bond, Andrew R. (1996). 'The Russian Copper Industry and the Noril'sk Joint-Stock Company in the Mid-1990s', *Post-Soviet Geography and Economics*, Vol. 37, No. 5, pp. 286–329.

Borkin, Joseph (1979). *The Crime and Punishment of I.G. Farben*. New York: Pocket Books.

Bray, Matt (1994). 'INCO's Petsamo Venture, 1933–1945: An Incident in Canadian, British, Finnish and Soviet Relations', *International Journal of Canadian Studies*, Vol. 9 (spring), pp. 173–94.

Bruno, Andy Richard (2011). 'Making Nature Modern: Economic Transformation and the Environment in the Soviet North', Ph.D. dissertation in history, University of Illinois, Urbana, IL.

Bruno, Andy (2016). *The Nature of Soviet Power: An Arctic Environmental History*. Cambridge: Cambridge University Press.

Brusletto, Hanne (1994). 'Forhandlinger mellom Norge og Sovjetunionen om kraftutbygging i Pasvikelven 1945–1963: Norsk–sovjetisk brobygging under den kalde krigen', MA thesis in history, University of Oslo, fall 1994.

Cohen, Yohanan (1989). *Small Nations in Times of Crisis and Confrontation*. Albany, NY: State University of New York Press.

Davies, R. W. (2001). 'Making Economic Policy', in Paul R. Gregory (ed.), *Behind the Façade of Stalin's Command Economy: Evidence from the Soviet State and Party Archives*. Stanford, CA: Hoover Institution Press.

Edele, Mark (2007). 'Soviet Society, Social Structure, and Everyday Life', *Kritika: Explorations in Russian and Eurasian History*, Vol. 8, No. 2, pp. 349–73.

Edwards, Robert (2006). *White Death: Russia's War on Finland, 1939–40*. London: Weidenfeld & Nicolson.

Egge, Åsmund (1993). *Fra Aleksander II til Boris Jeltsin: Russland og Sovjetunionens moderne historie*. Oslo: Universitetsforlaget.

Eloranta, Jari and Ilkka Nummela (2007). 'Finnish Nickel as a Strategic Metal, 1920–1944', *Scandinavian Journal of History*, Vol. 32, No. 4, pp. 322–45.

Engman, Max and Kasper Westerlund (eds) (2009). *Petsamo och havet*. Åbo: Uniprint.

Fredrik Fagertun (ed.) (2016). *Nenne Rachløw Isachsen: Min krigsdagbok*. Stamsund: Orkana forlag.

Galushko, O. Ya. (1985). '40 let trudovoy vakhty gorno-metallurgicheskogo kombinata "Pechenganikel"', *Tsvetnaya Metallurgiya*, No. 9.

Gregory, Paul R. (2004). *The Political Economy of Stalinism: Evidence from the Soviet Secret Archives*. Cambridge: Cambridge University Press.

Gregory, Paul R. and Robert C. Stuart (1981). *Soviet Economic Structure and Performance*, 2nd ed. New York: Harper & Row.

Hanski, Eero J. (1992). *Petrology of the Pechenga Ferropicrites and Cogenetic, Ni-Bearing Gabbro-Wehrlite Intrusions, Kola Peninsula, Russia*. Espoo: Geological Survey of Finland, Bulletin 367.

Harding, Neil (1996). *Leninism*. London: Macmillan.

Hentilä, Seppo (1999). 'From Independence to the End of the Continuation War 1917–1944', in Osmo Jussila, Seppo Hentilä and Jukka Nevakivi (eds), *From Grand Duchy to a Modern State: A Political History of Finland since 1809*. London: Hurst & Company.

Holtsmark, Sven G. (2003). 'Fra periferi til krigsteater. Nordområdene i sovjetisk militær tenkning i mellomkrigstiden', *Forsvarsstudier*, Vol. 4.

Hønneland, Geir and Lars Rowe (2004). *Health as International Politics: Combating Communicable Diseases in the Baltic Sea Region*. Burlington, VT: Ashgate.

Istoriya ordena Lenina. Leningradskoe voennogo okruga (1974). Moscow: Voennoe izdatelstvo Ministerstvo oborony SSSR.

Jacobsen, Alf R. (2006). *Nikkel, jern og blod*. Oslo: Aschehoug.

Jacobson, Max (1961). *The Diplomacy of the Winter War: An Account of the Russo-Finnish War, 1939–1940*. Cambridge, MA: Harvard University Press.

Jacobson, Max (1984). *Finland Survived: An Account of the Finnish–Soviet Winter War 1939–1940*. Helsinki: Otava.

Jussila, Osmo (1999). 'Finland as a Grand Duchy', in Osmo Jussila, Seppo Hentilä and Jukka Nevakivi (eds), *From Grand Duchy to a Modern State: A Political History of Finland since 1809*. London: Hurst & Company.

Kershaw, Ian (2000). *The Nazi Dictatorship: Problems and Perspectives of Interpretation*, 4th edn. London: Bloomsbury Academic.

Kirov, Sergei M. (1957). *Izbrannye stati i rechi*. Moscow: Gosudarstvennoe izadatelstvo politicheskoi literatury.

Kivimäki, Ville (2012). 'Three Wars and Their Epitaphs', in T. Kinnunen and Ville Kivimäki (eds), *Finland in World War II: History, Memory, Interpretations*. Boston: Brill.

Kotkin, Stephen (1995). *Magnetic Mountain: Stalinism as Civilization*. Berkeley, CA: University of California Press.

Krosby, H. Peter (1967). 'Petsamo in the Spotlight: A Study in Finnish–German Relations, 1940–1941', Ph.D. thesis, Columbia University, New York.

Krosby, H. Peter (1968). *Finland, Germany and the Soviet Union 1940–1941: The Petsamo Dispute.* Madison, WI: University of Wisconsin Press.

Lee, Lloyd E. (1991). *World War II: Crucible of the Contemporary World: Commentary and Readings.* Armonk, NY: M. E. Sharpe.

Londen, Magnus, Joakim Enegren and Ant Simons (2008). *Come to Finland.* Helsinki: Edita Publishing.

Manninen, Ohto (2004). 'The Soviet Plans for the North Western Theatre of Operations in 1939–1944', *Finnish Defence Studies.* Helsinki: National Defense College.

Mastny, Vojtech (1979). *Russia's Road to the Cold War: Diplomacy, Warfare and the Politics of Communism, 1941–1945.* New York: Columbia University Press.

Mastny, Vojtech (1996). *The Cold War and Soviet Insecurity: The Stalin Years.* Oxford: Oxford University Press.

Matsak, V. A. (ed.) (2005). *Pechenga. Opyt kraevedcheskioi entsiklopedii.* Murmansk: Prosvetitelskiy tsentr 'Dobrokhot'.

McCannon, John (1998). *Red Arctic: Polar Expedition and the Myth of the North in the Soviet Union, 1932–1939.* Oxford: Oxford University Press.

Meinander, Henrik (2018). 'Finland', in David Stahel (ed.), *Joining Hitler's Crusade.* Cambridge: Cambridge University Press.

Murray Wallace, Carl and Ashley Thomson (1993). *Sudbury: Rail Town to Regional Capital.* Toronto: Dundurn Press.

Nevakivi, Jukka (1999). 'From the Continuation War to the Present 1944–1999', in Osmo Jussila, Seppo Hentilä and Jukka Nevakivi (eds), *From Grand Duchy to a Modern State: A Political History of Finland since 1809.* London: Hurst & Company.

Nove, Alec (1978). *An Economic History of the U.S.S.R.* New York: Penguin Books.

Nove, Alec (1980). *The Soviet Economic System.* London: George Allen & Unwin.

Paasikivi, Juho Kusti (1958). *Minnen: 1939–1940.* Stockholm: Albert Bonniers Förlag.

Paasikivi Juho Kusti (1959). *Minnen II: Mellankrigstiden – som sendebud i Moskva.* Stockholm: Albert Bonniers Förlag.

Papunen, Heikki (1986). 'One Hundred Years of Ore Exploration in Finland', in Heikki Tanskanen (ed.), *The Development of Geological Sciences in Finland.* Espoo: Geological Survey of Finland, Bulletin 336, pp. 165–203.

Pentitilä, Risto E. J. (1994). 'Finland's Security in a Changing Europe: A Historical Perspective', *Finnish Defence Studies*, Vol. 7. Helsinki: National Defence College.

Peterburgskii, Petrogradskii, Leningradskii voennyi okrug 1864–1999 (1999). St. Petersburg: Poligon.

Pipes, Richard (1997). *Three 'Whys' of the Russian Revolution*. New York: Vintage.

Polvinen, Tuomo (1986). *Between East and West: Finland in International Politics, 1944–47*, ed. and trans. D. G. Kirby and Peter Herring. Minneapolis, MN: University of Minnesota Press.

Potemkin, Leonid A. (1965). *U severnoi granitsy: Pechenga sovetskaya*. Murmansk: Murmanskoe knizhnoe izdatelstvo.

Pyatikovskii, Veniamin Petrovich (1974). *Preobrazhennyi Sever*. Murmansk: Murmanskoe knizhnoe izdatelstvo.

Rautio, Vesa (2000). 'Petsamo – "Kaipaukseni maasta" globaalitalouden pyörteisiin', *Terra*, Vol. 112, No. 3, pp. 129–40.

Rayfield, Donald (2005). *Stalin and His Hangmen*. London: Penguin Books.

Roth, Philip (2005). *The Human Stain*. London: Vintage Books.

Rzheshevskii, O. A. (ed.) (1999). *Zimnyaya Voina. Politicheskaya istoriya*. Moscow: Nauka.

Sakwa, Richard (1989). *Soviet Politics: An Introduction*. London: Routledge.

Sakwa, Richard (1998). *Soviet Politics in Perspective*. London: Routledge.

Sandvik, P. T. and J. Scherner (2016). 'Why Did Germany Not Fully Exploit the Norwegian Nickel Industry 1940-45?' in Hans Otto Frøland et al. (eds), *Industrial Collaboration in Nazi-Occupied Europe: Norway in Context*. London: Palgrave Macmillan.

Schwendemann, Heinrich (1993). *Die wirtschaftliche Zusammenarbeit zwischen dem Deutschen Reich und der Sowjetunion von 1939 bis 1941. Alternative zu Hitlers Ostprogramm?* Berlin: Akademie Verlag.

Service, Robert (2001). *Lenin: A Biography*. London: Macmillan.

Service, Robert (2005). *A History of Modern Russia from Nicholas II to Vladimir Putin*. Cambridge, MA: Harvard University Press.

Shulman, Marshall D. (1963). *Stalin's Foreign Policy Reappraised*. Cambridge, MA: Harvard University Press.

Smirnov, M. B. (ed.) (1998). *Sistema ispravitelno-trudovykh lagerei v SSSR*. Moskva: Zvenya.

Solheim, Marianne Neerland (2005). 'Slavene fra øst: Sovjetiske krigsfanger i Norge 1941–45', *Defence Studies*, Vol. 5. Oslo: Institute for Defence Studies.

Stadius, Peter (2016). 'Petsamo: Bringing Modernity to Finland's Arctic Ocean Shore 1920–1039', *Acta Borealia*, Vol. 33, No. 2, pp. 140–65.

Sukharev, M. I. (1979). *Sever industrialnyi: Deyatelnost KPSS po rukovodstvu industrialnym razvitiem Evropeiskogo Severa SSSR na zavershayushchem etape sotsialisticheskogo stroitelstva 1946–1958*. Murmansk: Murmanskoe knizhnoe izdatelstvo.

Thompson, John F. and Norman Beasley (1960). *For the Years to Come: A Story of International Nickel of Canada*. New York and London: G. P. Putnam's Sons and Longmans and Green & Co.

Tucker, Robert C. (1990). *Stalin in Power: The Revolution from Above, 1929–1941*. New York: Norton.

Ulam, Adam B. (1974). *Expansion and Coexistence: Soviet Foreign Policy 1917–73*, 2nd edn. New York: Praeger.

Upton, Anthony F. (1965). *Finland in Crisis 1940–1941: A Study in Small-Power Politics*. Ithaca, NY: Cornell University Press.

Vasilevskii, A. M. (1973). *Delo vsei zhizni*. Moscow: Izdatelstvo politicheskoi literatury.

Väyrynen, Heikki (1938). *Petrologie des Nickelerzfeldes kaulatunturi-kammikivitunturi in Petsamo*. Helsinki: Commission Geologique de Finlande, Bulletin 116.

Wallace, Carl Murray and Ashley Thomson (1993). *Sudbury: Rail Town to Regional Capital*. Toronto: Dundurn Press.

Weiner, Douglas (1988). *Models of Nature: Conservation and Community Ecology in the Soviet Union, 1917–1935*. Bloomington, IN: Indiana University Press.

Weiner, Douglas R. (1999). *A Little Corner of Freedom: Russian Nature Protection from Stalin to Gorbachëv*. Berkeley, CA: University of California Press.

Wuorinen, John H. (1965). *A History of Finland*. New York: Columbia University Press.

Ylikangas, Heikki (1995). *Vägen till Tammerfors: Striden mellan röda och vita i finska inbördeskriget 1918*. Stockholm: Bokförlaget Atlantis.

Zubok, Vladislav and Constantine Pleshakov (1996). *Inside the Kremlin's Cold War: From Stalin to Khrushchev*. Cambridge, MA: Harvard University Press.

Index

References to figures are shown in *italics* and to maps in **bold**. References to endnotes consist of the page number followed by the letter 'n' followed by the number of the note.

Administration for Soviet Property in Finland (USI Finland, Directorate for Soviet Property Abroad)   135, 136, 137, 138
administrative-command system   9–10, 77, 146, 147, 153–6
Aleksandr II, Tsar of Russia   18
Allied Control Commission   109, 189 n.6
Alphons Custodis Chimney Construction Company   82
ammunition, nickel ore for   4, 31, 150
Andrianov, I. A.   114–15, 192 n.37
Antonov, General A. I.   178 n.82
archives, access to Russian archives   8
Arctic Circle   1, 7, *see also* Soviet Arctic
Arctic Highway (Rovaniemi-Liinahamari)   21–2, 23, 81
  Kolosjoki seen from   *34*
armaments, nickel as 'strategic metal'   4, 29, 31–2, 65, 97, 102, 150, 157
armoured plates, nickel ore for   4, 30–1, 150
ASEA (Swedish firm)   131, 140
Avanesov (Vakava general director)   136

Barbarossa, *see* Operation Barbarossa
Barents Sea   1, 3

Baryshnikov, N. I.   59–60
Beasley, Norman   167 n.51
Berdnikov, A. E.   81, 83, 84
Blücher, Wipert von   48
Bolsheviks   1, 14, 15–16, 18, 49, 132, 134, *see also* Communist Party of the Soviet Union
Borisoglebskii area   108
Bray, Matt   59, 167 n.51, 170 n.13
Britain, *see* Great Britain

Canada, *see also* International Company of Canada (INCO)
  declaration of war on Germany (1939)   49
  discovery of nickel ore deposits (1800s)   30
  Finnish scheme to sell Petsamo nickel to Germany   51–2
  industrialists' interest in Petsamo ore   4, 23
  interest in Petsamo through INCO   50
  Soviet takeover of Petsamo and compensation to INCO   69, 70
Churchill, Winston   58
Coframent (French firm)   24
Cold War
  and Soviet nickel industry   97, 152, 157
  tightening of Norwegian-Soviet border   190 n.17
collectivization   6–7, 79, 101
Collier, Lawrence, Sir   40
Comintern, Second Congress   20

command economy 9–10, 77, 146, 147, 153–6
Communist Party of the Soviet Union 91, 93–4, 95, 132–4, 196 n.83, *see also* Bolsheviks
Continuation War 35, 45, 54, *see also under* war and Petsamo
copper
 ore deposits in Petsamo 25, 27
 Outokumpu mines (Finland) 24
Cronstedt, Axel Fredrik 29
culture, *navedenie kultury* (tidiness) 99

dams
 Jäniskoski 32, 71, *92*
 Niskakoski *68*, 107, 111
de-kulakization campaign 7
Dietl, General Eduard 54–5
Directorate for Construction of Aluminum and Magnesium Enterprises (Glavalyuminstroi) 81, 83, 90
Directorate for Main Roads (UShossDor) 130, 146, 194 n.59
directorate for nickel and cobalt industries, *see* Glavnikelkobalt (directorate for nickel and cobalt industries)
Directorate for Soviet Property Abroad, USI Finland (Administration for Soviet Property in Finland) 135, 136, 137, 138

Edele, Mark 160 n.11, 161 n.14
Eden, Anthony 58
electricity, *see* hydroelectric power plants

Eloranta, Jari 28, 166 n.41
environmental issues 99–100, 158

Fedulkin (head engineer) 200 n.118
Finland, *see also* Imatran Voima (Finnish semi-statal power company); Petsamo under Finnish rule; war and Petsamo
 alliance with Hitler's Germany 4–5, 35, 36, 54
 defined as within Soviet sphere of interest (secret protocol) 37, 49, 64
 fishery industry 3
 Soviet 'expansion and coexistence' policy towards 143
 Soviet-Finnish armistice (1944) 35, 57–8, 67, 69, 103, 109, 111
 Soviet-Finnish border (1939 and 1944) **19**
 Soviet-Finnish border commission 117
 Soviet-Finnish Moscow Peace Treaty (1940) 35, 40, 44, 46, 48
 Soviet-Finnish relations after Russian Revolution 3
 Soviet-Finnish treaty on transfer of Jäniskoski 117
 war reparations to Soviet Union 70, 80, 109, 110, 111, 114
Finnish-Soviet Winter War (1939–40), *see under* war and Petsamo
Finnmark (Norwegian county) 1, 61, 64
Fitzpatrick, Sheila 9
five-year plan (1928–32) 86, 88
five-year plan (1946–50) 5, 87–8, 97, 101, 151
Frantsuzov, A. 41, 61–2, 74

Friedrich Krupp AG (German company)   25, 26

Germany, *see also* Molotov-Ribbentrop Non-Aggression pact; war and Petsamo
  Finland's alliance with Hitler's Germany   4–5, 35, 36, 54
  impact on Finnish civil war   17
  industrialists' and *Wehrmacht*'s interest in Pechenga ore   4
  Lebensraum project   36
  Nazi assets in co-belligerent states   110, 111–12, 114
  Operation Barbarossa   4–5, 46, 54
  Operation Renntier   54–5
Gidroenergoproekt   144
Glavalyuminstroi (Directorate for Construction of Aluminum and Magnesium Enterprises)   81, 83, 90
Glavnikelkobalt (Directorate for Nickel and Cobalt Industries)
  inspection of Petsamo mines (1940)   40, 62
  Jäniskoski project
    dissolution of Pechenganikel's Moscow office   132
    Kleshko answerable to   113
    policing and insurance issues   122, 125
    progress report forwarded to Malenkov   133
    response to local Communist Party committees   133
    Soviet border zone permits   119, 145–6
    Soviet takeover of the plant   141
    transport issue   129
    Vakava affair   137, 138

Pechenganikel Mining Combine   77, 83, 84, 87–8, 90
  Rajakoski plant   143–4
Goncharov (engineer)   120, 121, 122
Gosplan (State Planning Commission)   86, 147, 154
Great Britain
  Allied Control Commission   109
  Finnish scheme to sell Petsamo nickel to Germany   51
  Foreign Office and INCO's Petsamo operations during Winter War   38–9, 40
  interest in Petsamo   45–6, 51, 53
  interest in Petsamon Nikkeli OY through Mond Nickel   45–6, 49
  Ministry of Economic Warfare   44
  Soviet takeover of Petsamo and compensation to INCO   67, 69
Great Depression (1929)   24
Great Powers
  and Finnish alliance with Hitler's Germany   4
  and nickel as strategic metal   29
  and Petsamo nickel ore   11, 13, 28, 29, 45
  and small nations' ability to benefit from   28
Great Terror (Soviet Union)   7
Gregory, Paul R.   9–10, 161 n.15
Gribin, Aleksandr   71, 72, 73–4, 75–6, 78, 96
GULag   7, 194 n.59
  Monchegorlag   41

Harding, Neil   15
Hausen, Hans   22
Hevoskoski hydropower plant   148

Hitler, Adolf   4–5, 35, 36, 49, 57, 175 n.63
Holsti, Rudolf   37
Holtsmark, Sven G.   60
housing shortages, Nikel (formerly Kolosjoki)   80, 88–9, 100–1, 154, 185 n.79
hydroelectric power plants, *see also* Jäniskoski hydropower plant (INCO era); Jäniskoski hydropower plant (Pechenganikel era)
    Hevoskoski plant   148
    Kaitakoski plant   106, 144–5, 148
    Niva plant   93, 105
    Pasvik River plants   1, 5–6, 108, 143, 148, 157
    Rajakoski plant   106, 108, 143–4, 145, 148
    Tuloma plant   91, 102, 105, 112

IG Farben (Interessengemeinschaft Farbenindustrie Aktiengesellschaft, German company)   25, 26, 27, 49, 50, 55–6, 78, 172 n.36
Ilin, A. A.   132, 195 n.67
Imatran Voima (Finnish semi-statal power company), *see also* Jäniskoski hydropower plant (Pechenganikel era)
    Jäniskoski hydropower plant contract with Pechenganikel   5–6, 111, 112, 127, 131, 145, 148, 190 n.14
    fire incident (1949) and company's admission of responsibility for security   123–5
    fire incident (1950) and possible settlement with Pechenganikel   125–6
    fire incident (1947) and request for Finnish police force and insurance agency   120–3
    partial solution to insurance problem   125
    request for explosives for construction work   128
    'special border zone' permits issue   117, 118–19
    Vakava affair   134–6
Rajakoski hydropower plant   144, 145, 148
industrialists
    'getting-the-job-done' industrialists *vs.* command structure   146–7, 156
    industrious/industrialization spirit   6, 64
industrialization (Soviet Union, 1930s)   7, 8, 11, 79, 101
International Company of Canada (INCO), *see also* Jäniskoski hydropower plant (INCO era); Kolosjoki; Petsamon Nikkeli OY (PNO)
    archetypical representative of Western capitalism   152
Petsamo
    agreement with IG Farben   27, 49
    assessment of agreement with Finnish government   28–9
    development expenditures   32
    installations   32
    Kolosjoki (company town)   33–4, *33, 34*
    negotiations with Finnish government   25–8
    promotion of nickel for civilian purposes   31
    Petsamo during Winter War (1939–40)

apprehensions about future of
   plant   44–5
inspection of mines by Soviet
   engineers   36, 40–4, 61–2,
   63, 64–5, 102, 151
protection of mines by Soviet
   army   40
reduction in construction/
   development work   38–9,
   44
suggestion of sabotaging
   Kolosjoki   39–40
Petsamo during WWII
Anglo-Canadian concession
   rights issue   49–50, 59
Finnish expropriation of
   Kolosjoki mines   55
Finnish scheme to sell
   Petsamo nickel to
   Germany   50–2
Soviet annexation and
   payment of compensation
   to company   67, 69–70
Soviets' preservation of INCO's
   technology   102
iron, deposits in Norway   22

Jacobsen, Alf R.   170 n.12
Jäniskoski hydropower plant (INCO
   era)
built by INCO/PNO   32, 34,
   106, 107
construction stopped during
   Winter War   39, 56, 106
dam   32, 71, *92*
decreased activity during
   WWII   44
German demolition of   71, 91,
   92, 107
shortly before demolition   *106*
Jäniskoski hydropower plant
   (Pechenganikel era)
acquisition of plant by Soviets
Finland's weak position after
   WWII   109–10

Jäniskoski in Finnish
   territory   103, 106, 107–8,
   107, 109
negotiations about 'Nazi
   assets'   110, 111–12
negotiations with Imatran
   Voima to rebuilt
   plant   111, 112, 145, 148,
   190 n.14
Soviet acquisition of
   concession rights   110
Soviet purchase of whole
   area   111, 112, 145
clash of cultures
complexity of Finnish and
   Soviet interests   113
Kleshko blaming Soviet
   agencies for hindering
   progress   116
Kleshko given a freer rein
   115
Kleshko's negotiations over
   services and equipment
   pricing   113–16
Soviet lack of understanding
   of market economy
   principles   115
construction work   *116*
Kleshko *vs.* Vakava (Soviet
   transport agency)
Imatran Voima's frustration
   with transport
   arrangements   134–5
Kleshko and Imatran Voima's
   criticism of Vakava's
   inflated prices   135–6
Kleshko attacked by Vakava
   and USI Finland   136–7,
   146
Kleshko's successful strategic
   defence   137–9
Soviet agencies' internal
   rivalries   139
security and special border
   zone

establishment and unreliability of system   117–19
Kleshko's criticism of visa arrangements   118
system stricter for Soviet citizens   126–7
tensions between different Soviet agencies   145–6, 147
security problems
 fire incident (1949) and Imatran Voima's admission of responsibility for security   123–5
 fire incident (1947) and Imatran Voima's request for police force and insurance agency   119–23
 fire incident (1950) and possible settlement with Imatran Voima   125–6
 fire truck from Pechenganikel   124, 125
 partial solution to insurance problem   125
 Soviet central authorities' relaxed approach to Jäniskoski security   126
 tensions between different Soviet ministries   146
Soviet supplies
 greater role given to Pechenganikel   132
 involvement of Communist party   132–4
 lack of explosives for construction work   127–8
 Liinahamari-Nikel-Jäniskoski road and transport problems   128–31, 134, 146, 155
 poor quality supplies   131
 postponement of power plant starting date   131–2
Soviet takeover of power station
 lack of Soviet qualified personnel   139–41

Minelektrostantsii and Kolenergo's reluctance to complete takeover   141–3, 146, 147
summary and overview
 benefits of project to Soviet and Finnish sides   145
 Soviet agencies' infighting and rivalries   145–6, 154–5
 Soviet command structure *vs.* 'getting-the-job-done' industrialists   146–7, 156
 Soviet use of Western technology   148
Jewish refugees, Petsamo as outlet for   3

Kaitakoski hydropower plant   106, 144–5, 148
Kammikivi mine (Penchega)   98
Kandalaksha aluminium works   91, 93, 105
Karelian Isthmus   18, 37, 60
Karlstad Mekaniska Verkstad   140
Kaula mine (Pechenga)   97
Kaulatunturi mines   23, 32, 33
Kerensky, Aleksandr   14, 15
Kershaw, Ian   10
King, Mackenzie   51–2
Kirkenes (Norwegian port)   39, 56, 59, 72, 73–4, 108
Kirov, Sergei Mironovich   1, 7, 63–4
Kleshko, Boris Mefodievich
 about the person
  appointed Jäniskoski project Pechenganikel representative   112, 113
  connections in higher echelons of Soviet party-state   138
  as embodiment of apolitical industrious spirit   6
  object of great appreciation   139, 143
 Pechenganikel asked to keep him on tight leash   132

remarkable commitment to
the task 146-7
success defying logics of
totalitarian model 155-6
willingness to criticize
shortcomings within Soviet
system 147
negotiations over services and
equipment pricing 113-16
being given a freer rein 115
blaming Soviet agencies for
hindering progress 116
colleagues' lack of
understanding of market
economy principles 115
security problems
fire incident (1947) 120
fire incident (1949) 124-5
instructed to set up Finnish
fire and watchman
brigade 122
issue and criticism of Soviet
border zone permits 117,
118, 119
Rautelin (Finnish union
leader) incident 192 n.37
Soviet supplies
lack of explosives for
construction work 127-8
poor quality supplies 131
transport problems 130
Soviet takeover of plant, on
lack of qualified Soviet
personnel 140-1
Vakava (Soviet transport agency)
affair
attacked by Vakava and USI
Finland 136-7
criticism of Vakava's inflated
prices 135-6
successful strategic defence
137-9
Kola Peninsula
hydroelectric power needs 105,
143, 144
hydroelectric power plants 108

industrialization (1930s) 7, 11
Kirov on socialist transformation
of 63-4
Northern Fleet 157
Pechenga location 1
post-war high-speed rebuilding
programme 101
'settling of the North' policy 151
Soviet naval bases 48, 60
Kolenergo 105, 141, 144, 147
Kolosjoki, *see also* Nikel (formerly
Kolosjoki); Petsamon
Nikkeli OY (PNO)
Finnish expropriation of the
mines 55
German destruction of 57, *68*
INCO company town 33-4
INCO nickel plant 33, *33*
INCO's reduced activity after
Winter War 44
INCO's suggestion of company-
organized sabotage
(1939) 39-40
production figures under German
rule 56, 57
production problems under
German rule 56
renamed Nikel after Soviet
takeover 71
seen from Arctic Highway *34*
Soviet forces' entry into 58
Soviet interest in 36, 53, 64
Soviet takeover and compensation
to INCO 67, 69-70
Kolosjoki, battle of (1944) 67, 96
Kone (Finnish firm) 114, 115, 116
Korhonen, Arvi 59
Kotkin, Stephen 8, 9, 160 n.11,
161 n.14, 200 n.2
Kotselvaara mine (Penchega) 98
Krosby, H. Peter 54, 55-6, 58-9,
167 n.49, 170 n.14, 171 n.26
Krupps, *see* Friedrich Krupp AG
(German company)
kulaks, de-kulakization campaign 7
Kupfernickel (devil's copper) 29-30

Kursk, battle of (1943)   57
Kuzmin, A.   193 n.50

labour camps, *see* GULag
labour force
   Jäniskoski (Pechenganikel era), lack of Soviet qualified personnel   139–41
   Pechenganikel
      Kirkenes Soviet prisoners of war   73–4
      labour recruitment plan   80
      organized recruitment, high salaries and perks   79–80
      piecework (*sdelshchina*)   88
      'socialist competition' (stakhanovites)   86–8, 94–6, 101, 152
      specialists and party workers   74–5, 85
      workers' disciplinary breaches   88–9
      workforce turnover   86
Lake Inari   1, 22, 106, 109
Lapin Kuletus (Finnish transport firm)   135, 136, 137, 138
Lapland War (1944–45)   35, 36, 58
Lavoisier, Antoine   29
Lebedev (engineer)   129, 134, 139
Lebensraum project   36
Le Nickel (French company)   25–6
Lenin, Vladimir   15–17, 161 n.15, 163 n.5
Leningrad-Murmansk railway line   48, 60
Liinahamari
   Arctic Highway (Rovaniemi-Liinahamari)   21–2, 23, 34, 81
   British efforts to avoid German control of (WWII)   46
   damage assessment after war   72
   Finnish/Swedish access to world markets through   3

   Finnish target in 1918 military expeditions   18
   Liinahamari-Nikel-Jäniskoski transportation line   128–30, 134, 146
   Liinahamari-Nikel transportation line   76, 79
   Pechenganikel's rebuilding of port and dwellings   79
   Soviet control of (WWII)   39
   strategic role in interim peace period (1940–41)   176 n.74
Tartu Peace Treaty   20
Lomako, Petr F.
   career at Mintsvetmet   180 n.9, 193 n.50
   Jäniskoski project   119, 127–8, 132–3, 141–2
   Kleshko's relationship with   198 n.96
   Nikel housing problems   100
   Pechenganikel   71, 74–5, 78, 83, 90
Lvov, Georgi   14, 15

Magnitogorsk   8, 9, 183 n.40
Malenkov, Georgi   133
Mannerheim, Carl Gustav Emil   17, 58
manpower, *see* labour force
Maslov (USI Finland deputy head)   136, 138
Mastny, Vojtech   162 n.18
Matsak, V. A.
   on mass enthusiasm in Nikel   77
   on Western estimates for rebuilding Pechenga factory   96
Mensheviks   15
Mercia, Paul   26
Metallgesellschaft GmbH   25
Mikoyan, Anastas   74, 127–8, 198 n.96
Ministry of Ferrous Metallurgy   180 n.9, 199 n.105

Ministry of Foreign Affairs
    (MID)   117, 121, 122,
    125–6
Ministry of Internal Affairs
    (MVD)   116, 117, 119,
    121, 129, 145
Ministry of Metallurgic Industry
    (Minmetallurgprom)
    125, 133, 140, 141, 145–6,
    180 n.9, 194 n.50
Ministry of Non-ferrous Metallurgy
    (Mintsvetmet)
  Jäniskoski project
    border zone permits   145–6
    Kleshko answerable to   112,
      113, 115
    lack of explosives for
      construction work   127–8
    response to Murmansk
      Communist Party
      committee   132–3
    security issue   117, 120
    takeover of the plant   142–3
    transport problems   155
  Pechenganikel   75, 77, 78, 82, 83,
    84, 95
  re-organization   180 n.9,
    193 n.50, 199 n.105
  scope of responsibilities
    162 n.21
Ministry of Power Stations
    (Minelektrostantsii)   105,
    132–3, 139, 140, 141–3,
    144, 162 n.21
Mironov, A.   128, 133
Molotov, Vyacheslav, *see also*
    Molotov-Ribbentrop Non-
    Aggression pact
  compensation to INCO   69
  conversation with Hitler on
    economic significance of
    Petsamo   175 n.63
  inspection of Petsamo mines
    and return of Petsamo to
    Finland   62
  on military circles against
    returning Petsamo to
    Finland   171 n.30
  Petsamo proposals to
    Finland   46–8, 52, 53,
    57–8, 59, 65, 150–1, 169 n.5
  protocols from his meetings with
    officials   60
  Tartu Peace Treaty   21
Molotov-Ribbentrop Non-
    Aggression pact   35, 36,
    49, 52, 53, 172 n.36
  Finland defined as within Soviet
    sphere of interest (secret
    protocol)   37, 49, 64
Monchegorlag   41
Monchegorsk, *see* Severonikel plant
    (Monchegorsk)
Mond Nickel Company (British
    company)
  Britain's interest in PNO
    through   45–6, 49
  Finnish scheme to sell Petsamo
    nickel to Germany   51
  INCO's takeover of   25–6
  INCO's taking over of its PNO
    shares   32
  Petsamo concession rights
    through PNO   49, 59
  representing INCO in Petsamo
    negotiations with
    Finland   27, 28
  scheme to reduce Petsamo
    production during Winter
    War   38–9
Moscow Peace Treaty (1940)   35, 40,
    44, 46, 48
munitions, nickel ore for   4, 31, 150
Murmansk
  as buffer zone   11
  as crossing point   20
  electricity provided by
    Kolenergo   105
  Leningrad-Murmansk railway
    line   48, 60

Murmansk-Pechenga sea
  voyage 94, **94**
Pechenga location 1
power shortages 91, 93
regional Communist Party
  committee 132–3
Soviet offensive (1944) 57

navedenie kultury (tidiness) 99
'Nazi assets' question 110, 111–12, 114
Nicholls, J. C. 26, 28
nickel
  history of
    difficult to separate 30
    military significance 30–2
    nickel-steel alloys 30
    origin of word 29–30
    production for civilian
      purposes 31
    recognised as element 29
  nickel as 'strategic metal' 4, 29, 31–2, 65, 97, 102, 150, 157
  Soviet nickel industry 40–1, 63, 65, 97, 151–2, 157, 185 n.78
nickel matte (nickel ore concentrate)
  German need for and
    Petsamo 46, 56, 72
  IG Farben's refining
    technology 25, 27, 55, 172 n.36
  INCO's provision of to Soviet
    Union 70
  Pechenganikel's nickel matte 76, 79, 85, 98, 99
  Soviet imports of (1942–43) 63
Nikel (formerly Kolosjoki), *see also*
  Kolosjoki; Pechenganikel
  Mining Combine
  background
    battle and destruction of
      Kolosjoki 67, *68*
    Soviet takeover and
      compensation to
      INCO 67, 69–70
  Soviet takeover and new
    names 71
  damage assessment
    degree of destruction 71–3
    industrial network in
      Pechenga (1944) **72**
    manpower needs 73–5
    supply needs 75
    transport needs 75–6
    vodka supply 76
  resurrection
    challenges and mass
      enthusiasm 76–7
    climatic conditions and
      remoteness 80–1
    construction workers' high
      workforce turnover 86
    decree making Nikel
      Penchega's administration
      centre 82
    housing shortages 80, 88–9, 100–1, 154, 185 n.79
    Mintsvetmet and
      Glavalyuminstroi dual
      structure 83
    new town infrastructure 78, 82
    Nikel-Liinahamari
      transportation line 76, 79
    rapidity of resurrection 96, 101–2
    resurrected by people
      who wanted to rebuild
      socialism 155
    sealing off of 113
    transport and supply
      problems 83–4, 89, 154
    sulphur dioxide emissions 159
Nikel transportation lines
  Liinahamari-Nikel 76, 79
  Liinahamari-Nikel-
    Jäniskoski 128–30, 134, 146
Nikitin, A. I. 129–30, 139

Index

Nikolay II, Tsar of Russia 14
Niskakoski dam *68*, 107, 111
Niva hydropower plant 93, 105
Norilsk Nikel 151
Norway
  hydroelectric power plants 1, 157
  iron ore deposits 22
  Pasvik River 1, **2**, 105–6, 108
  Soviet 'expansion and coexistence' policy towards 143
  tightening of Norwegian-Soviet border 190 n.17
  work on Soviet power stations 5, 148
Nosal, V. I. 90
Nummela, Ilkka 28, 166 n.41
Nykopp (head of trade department, Finnish Ministry of Foreign Affairs) 114, 115

Operation Barbarossa 4–5, 46, 54
Operation Renntier 54–5
organized recruitment of labour (*orgnabor*) 79
Outokumpu (Finnish state-owned company) 24

Paasikivi, Juho Kusti
  biography 169 n.4
  Finnish-Soviet talks (1938) 37
  Jäniskoski as compensation for other territories 189 n.8
  Soviet claims on Petsamo 46–8, 52, 57–8, 61, 65, 150–1, 171 n.30
  on Soviet demands after WWII 109
  Tartu Peace Treaty 20
Pam, Edgar 28
Pasvik (*Paz*) River, *see also* International Company of Canada (INCO); Kolosjoki; Nikel (formerly Kolosjoki); Pechenganikel Mining Combine; Petsamon Nikkeli OY (PNO); Petsamo under Finnish rule (1920–44); war and Petsamo
  geographical details 1, **2**
  hydroelectric power plants 1, 5–6, 108, 143, 148, 157
  Jäniskoski area 32, 107–8
  national border with Norway 105–6
  Pasvik valley and border controls 113
  Pasvik valley and Soviet 'expansion and coexistence' policy 143, 145
Pechenga (overview)
  geo-economic details 1–3
  Petsamo (Pechenga), significance of 3–6
  Soviet 'settling of the North' and Stalinist totalitarianism 6–11
  summary (1921-late 1970s) 156–8
Pechenga Communist Party committee 91, 93–4, 133
Pechenga mines, *see* Petsamo mines
Pechenganikel Mining Combine, *see also* Jäniskoski hydropower plant (Pechenganikel era); Nikel (formerly Kolosjoki); Petsamon Nikkeli OY (PNO)
  combine
    building of combine impeded by climatic conditions 81
    building of Liinahamari port and dwellings 79
    Glavnikelkobalt nickel-producing plant 82–3, 90–1
  Pechenga Communist Party's role 91, 93–4

Petsamon Nikkeli OY (PNO)
   replaced by 71
   preservation of Western
      technology 78, 102
   rapid development and nickel
      as strategic metal 96-7
   smelting plant 76, 82, 85,
      89-90
electricity
   power needs and Pasvik
      River 1, 144-5
   power shortages 91, 93,
      102-3, 105-6
environmental/health issues
   silicosis investigation 100
   sulphur dioxide
      emissions 158
   tidiness (*navedenie kultury*)
      99
   ventilation problems 99-100
labour force
   Kirkenes Soviet prisoners of
      war 73-4
   labour productivity
      and piecework
      (*sdelshchina*) 88
   labour productivity and
      'socialist competition'
      (stakhanovites) 86-8,
      94-6, 101, 152
   labour recruitment plan 80
   organized recruitment, high
      salaries and perks 79-80
   shortage of qualified
      engineers 85
   specialists and party
      workers 74-5
   workers' disciplinary
      breaches 88-9
   workforce turnover 86
nickel production
   discovery of new ore deposits
      and expansion 96
   first batch of nickel matte 85
   first metallurgical figures 81,
      84
   low nickel percentage
      problem 84, 98
   mechanization 97-8
   nickel enrichment plant 98
   production of nickel ore
      (1944-45) 81-2
   production of nickel ore and
      nickel matte (1948-53)
      98
   Soyuznikelolovoproekt's
      plan 77-8, 97-8
transport
   renewal of transport fleet
      (1948) 99
   sea voyage Murmansk-
      Pechenga 94, **94**
   transport problems 93-4,
      154
Pekkala, Mauno 189 n.8
permit (*propusk*) system (Jäniskoski,
   Pechenganikel era)
   117-19, 126-7
Petrov, A. I.
   industrialization spirit 64
   inspection of Petsamo mines
      41, 42-4, 61-2, 170 n.16
   Pechenganikel posting 74, 139,
      195 n.67
Petrov, Semyon
   Jäniskoski plant
      border zone permits 119
      dissolution of Pechenganikel's
         Moscow office 132
      lack of explosives for
         construction work
         127-8
      policing and insurance
         issues 122, 124, 125-6
      positive view of Imatran
         Voima 195 n.70
      progress report forwarded to
         Malenkov 133

remarkable commitment to
the task 146
response to Murmansk
Communist Party
committee 133
transport issue 129
Vakava affair 138–9
Rajakoski plant 143–4
Petsamo (Finnish for Pechenga), *see*
International Company of
Canada (INCO); Kolosjoki;
Pechenga (overview);
Petsamon Nikkeli OY
(PNO); Petsamo under
Finnish rule (1920–44);
war and Petsamo
Petsamo mines, Soviet inspection
of 36, 40–4, 61–2, 63,
64–5, 74, 78, 102, 151
Petsamon Nikkeli OY (PNO), *see also*
International Company of
Canada (INCO); Kolosjoki;
Pechenganikel Mining
Combine
Anglo-Canadian concession
rights 49, 59
Britain's interest in through
Mond Nickel Company
45–6, 49
Finnish scheme to sell Petsamo
nickel to Germany 51
INCO's Finnish subsidiary 29,
32, 35
Jäniskoski hydropower plant 106
power supply 105–6
reduced operations during Winter
War 38–9
Robert Stanley on PNO's value
44–5
Soviet inspection of Petsamo
mines 36, 40–4, 61–2, 63,
64–5, 74, 78, 102, 151
Soviet takeover and replacement
with Pechenganikel 71

Petsamo under Finnish rule
(1920–44)
Finnish independence
declaration of
independence 16–17
independence and civil
war 17
Lenin's views on national self-
determination 15–17
'Reds' *vs*. 'Whites' in
Finland 16, 17
under Russia's provisional
government 14–15
under Tsarist rule 13–14
Western powers' recognition
of independence 17
Petsamo becoming Finnish
'Greater Finland' project 18,
21
Liinahamari port issue 18,
20
'pork barrel revolt' (1922) 21
post-Treaty Finnish-Russian
border disputes 21
Repola issue 18, 20–1
summer 1918 failed talks
18–20
Tartu Peace Treaty (1920)
13, 20–1, 36–7, 38, 60,
149–50, 169 n.4
Petsamo explored
Arctic Highway (Rovaniemi-
Liinahamari) 21–2, 23
discovery of nickel ore
deposits 22–3, 150
North-South axis (from Lake
Inari) 22
tourism 22
Petsamo industrialized
Finnish ownership and
foreign investments
24–5, 26–7
INCO and Mond Nickel,
negotiations with 25–8

INCO deal, assessment of
  28–9
Petsamon Nikkeli OY as
  operational unit 29
strategic metal
  history of nickel 29–30
  INCO's focus on production
    for civilian purposes 31
  INCO's level of development
    expenditures 32
  increasing military
    significance 30–2
  installations and living quarters
    built by INCO 32–4
  Kolosjoki (company
    town) 33–4, *33*, *34*
piecework system (*sdelshchina*) 88
Pipes, Richard 163 n.5
Pleshakov, Constantine 162 n.18
PNO, *see* Petsamon Nikkeli OY (PNO)
Pohjolan Likkenen (Finnish
  transport firm) 135
Porajärvi, cessation from Finland
  (Tartu Peace Treaty,
  1920) 20–1
'pork barrel revolt' (1922) 21
Potsdam Conference (1945) 110,
  114
prisoners of war (Kirkenes) 73–4
propusk (permit) system (Jäniskoski,
  Pechenganikel era)
  117–19, 126–7
Putinism 10

Rajakoski hydropower plant 106,
  108, 143–4, 145, 148
Rautelin (chairman of Finnish
  construction workers'
  union) 192 n.37
Renntier, *see* Operation Renntier
Repola
  cessation from Finland (Tartu
    Peace Treaty, 1920) 20–1
  Finnish Repola expedition
    (1918) 18

revisionist critique, of Stalinism 8–9
'revolution from above' (1930s) 6–7,
  79
Ribbentrop, Joachim von, *see*
  Molotov-Ribbentrop
  Non-Aggression pact
Roosevelt, Franklin D. 58
Roth, Philip 149
Rovaniemi 56, 118, 134
  Arctic Highway (Rovaniemi-
    Liinahamari) 21–2, 23,
    34, 81
Russia, *see also* Soviet Union
  access to Russian archives 8
  Finnish independence from
    13–17
Russian Review, Stalinism
  debate 160 n.12
Rutshtein, Sh. N. 41, 61–2,
  170 n.16, 170 n.18
Ryaboshapko (head of
  Kolenergo) 141
Ryti, Risto 54, 58, 173 n.44

Saami
  reindeer herders 13
  sovietization of 179 n.1
  winter dwelling of Kolosjoki *33*
Sakwa, Richard 10
Sederholm, Jakob Johannes 23
Serov, Ivan 117, 119
'settling of the North' policy 7, 63,
  151
Severonikel plant (Monchegorsk)
  engineers' inspection of Petsamo
    mines 36, 40–4, 61–2, 63,
    64–5, 74, 78, 102, 151
  nickel content analyses for
    Pechenganikel 84
  power needs 91, 144
  report on Pechenganikel's
    progress 90
  start date 151
  transport of Pechenganikel nickel
    to 76, 79, 99

workers from moving to
    Nikel   80
Shchelkunov, Yevgenii   71, 72, 73,
    75, 76, 78, 83, 96
'shock worker' (*udarnik*)   86–7, 95,
    152, *see also* stakhanovite
    movement
Siberia
  nickel plants   80, 151
  'settling of the North' policy
    151
silicosis   100
Simcox, I. J.   39–40
Smirnov, Aleksandr   75
'socialist competition' (between
    workers)   86–8, 94–6,
    101, 152
Socialist Revolutionaries   15
Söderhjelm, Johan   51, 170 n.13,
    170 n.14
Soviet Arctic, 'settling of the North'
    policy   7, 63, 151
sovietization of Petsamo, *see* Nikel
    (formerly Kolosjoki);
    Pechenganikel Mining
    Combine
Soviet Union, *see also* Communist
    Party of the Soviet Union;
    Molotov-Ribbentrop Non-
    Aggression pact; Russia;
    Stalinism; war and Petsamo
  administrative-command
    system   9–10, 77, 146,
    147, 153–6
  Cold War and nickel
    industry   97, 152, 157
  Cold War and tightening of
    borders   190 n.17
  collectivization   6–7, 79, 101
  de-kulakization campaign   7
  Finland's war reparations   70, 80,
    109, 110, 111, 114
  Finnish-Soviet armistice
    (1944)   35, 57–8, 67, 69,
    103, 109, 111
  Finnish-Soviet border (1939 and
    1944)   **19**
  Finnish-Soviet border
    commission   117
  Finnish-Soviet Moscow Peace
    Treaty (1940)   35, 40, 44,
    46, 48
  Finnish-Soviet relations after
    Russian Revolution   3
  Finnish-Soviet treaty on transfer
    of Jäniskoski   117
  five-year plan (1928–32)
    86, 88
  five-year plan (1946–50)   5,
    87–8, 97, 101, 151
  foreign policy (expansion and
    coexistence)   143
  foreign policy under Stalin   10
  Gosplan (State Planning
    Commission)   86, 147,
    154
  Great Terror   7
  GULag   7, 41, 194 n.59
  industrialization (1930s)   7, 8,
    11, 79, 101
  ministerial structure   11
  ministries/agencies' infighting
    and rivalries   139, 145–6,
    147, 154–5
  'Nazi assets' question   110,
    111–12, 114
  nickel industry   40–1, 63, 65, 97,
    151–2, 157, 185 n.78
  organized recruitment of labour
    (*orgnabor*)   79
  piecework system
    (*sdelshchina*)   88
  post-WWII years and rebuilding
    socialism   152
  prisoners of war punished for
    'treason'   74
  'revolution from above'
    (1930s)   6–7, 79
  'settling of the North' policy   7,
    63, 151

'shock worker' (*udarnik*) 86–7, 95, 152
'socialist competition' (stakhanovite movement) 86–8, 94–6, 101, 152
Soyuznikelolovoproekt 77–8, 97–8
Spanish-American War (1898) 31
Ståhlberg, Karlo Juho 165 n.24
Stakhanov, Aleksei G. 184 n.65
stakhanovite movement 86–8, 94–6, 101, 152
Stalin, Josef, *see also* Stalinism
   on Arctic and northern regions' wealth 178 n.87
   claim on Petsamo 41, 58, 69
   degree of involvement in matters of state 8–9, 10–11, 153, 161 n.17, 162 n.18
   demands for border revisions with Finland 37–8
   on 'foster[ing] utopian industrial schemes' 101
   post-WWII rebuilding effort 5
   'revolution from above' (1930s) 7, 79
   Tartu Peace Treaty, dismissal of 21
   transformation of Soviet Union in 1930s 6–7
Stalingrad, battle of (1943) 57
Stalinism, *see also* Stalin, Josef
   chieftain as omniscient 9
   neither omniscient nor omnipotent 153
   Russian Review debate 160 n.12
   'smaller Stalins' and Soviet command economy 9–10, 153–4, 155, 156
   Stalinist civilization 8, 161 n.14
   Stalinist foreign policy 10
   totalitarian intent *vs.* achievement of total control 10–11
   totalitarian model *vs.* work ethics and professional pride (e.g. Kleshko) 155–6
   as totalitarian paradigm 8, 153, 156, 161 n.14
   as viewed by revisionist scholars 8–9
Stanley, Robert C. 29, 44–5, 51, 69
steel, nickel-steel alloys 30, 97
Strömberg (Finnish firm) 114–15, 116
Studebaker trucks 75
sulphur dioxide emissions 158
Suomen Petrooli (Soviet firm) 137
Svanvik (Norway) 22, 39
Svinhufvud, Pehr Eivind 16

Talvia, Alppi 22, 150
Tampella (Finnish firm) 114, 115, 116
Tanner, Väinö (geologist) 23
Tanner, Väinö (politician) 20
Tartu Peace Treaty (1920) 13, 20–1, 36–7, 38, 60, 149–50, 169 n.4
Teheran conference (1943) 58, 69
Telestam, Gustav 117, 123, 124–5, 134–5, 136, 139, 143–4
Tevosyan, I. F. 133, 193 n.50
Thompson, John F. 167 n.51
tidiness (*navedenie kultury*) 99
Törnquist, Hugo 22, 150, 158
totalitarianism, *see also* Stalinism
   chieftain as omniscient 9
   Stalinism as paradigm of 8, 153, 156, 161 n.14
   totalitarian intent *vs.* achievement of total control 10–11
   totalitarian model *vs.* work ethics and professional pride (e.g. Kleshko) 155–6
tourism (in Petsamo) 3, 22
Tracy, B. F. 30–1
transport, *see also* Vakava (Soviet transport agency)

Arctic Highway (Rovaniemi-
  Liinahamari) 21–2, 23,
  34, 81
Leningrad-Murmansk railway
  line 48, 60
Liinahamari-Nikel transportation
  line 76, 79
Liinahamari-Nikel-Jäniskoski
  transportation line
  128–30, 134, 146
Murmansk-Pechenga sea
  voyage 94, **94**
transport problems
  Jäniskoski (Pechenganikel era)
    128–31, 134, 146, 155
  Nikel (formerly
    Kolosjoki) 75–6, 83–4,
    89, 154
  Pechenganikel 93–4, 99,
    154
Treaty of Brest-Litovsk (1918) 18
Treaty of Versailles (1919) 21
Trifon (monk) 108
Trofimov, V. I. 129, 130–1, 132, 133,
  190 n.16
Trustivapaa Bensini (Finnish
  firm) 137
Tuloma hydropower plant 91, 102,
  105, 112

Ubarov, I. G. 179 n.2
Ulam, Adam B. 143
United States
  military potential of nickel
    30–1
  Spanish-American War (1898)
    31
Upton, Anthony F. 59, 63
UShossDor (Directorate for Main
  Roads) 130, 146,
  194 n.59
USI Finland (Administration for
  Soviet Property in Finland,
  Directorate for Soviet
  Property Abroad) 135,
  136, 137, 138

Vakava (Soviet transport agency)
  Kleshko and Imatran Voima's
    criticism of Vakava's
    inflated prices 135–6
  Kleshko attacked by Vakava and
    USI Finland 136–7, 146
  Kleshko's successful strategic
    defence 137–9
Vasilevskii, Marshall Aleksandr M. 48
Verbitskii (Murmansk Communist
  Party committee
  secretary) 132–3
Virtaniemi 106, 117, 123
vodka supply 76
Voionmaa, Väinö 39, 165 n.24
Vyshinskii, Andrei 47, 53, 117, 127,
  174 n.48

war and Petsamo
  Finnish-Soviet Winter War
    (1939–40)
  Finish-Soviet peace
    agreement (Moscow Peace
    Treaty) 35, 40, 44, 46, 48
  INCO's apprehensions about
    future of Petsamo 44–5
  INCO's reduced activity at
    Petsamo 38–9, 44
  INCO's suggestion of sabotaging
    Kolosjoki 39–40
  Soviet control of Petsamo area
    39
  Soviet criticism of Tartu Peace
    Treaty 36–7, 38
  Soviet demands for border
    revisions 37–8
  Soviet inspection of Petsamo
    mines 36, 40–4, 61–2, 63,
    64–5, 74, 78, 102, 151
  Soviet protection of Petsamo
    mines 40

Soviet return of Petsamo to
  Finland   44, 46, 48–9,
  58–60, 61, 62
 war events   35, 38, 39
Moscow parenthesis (March
  1940-June 1941)
 British interest in
   Petsamo   45–6, 51, 53
 Finland's aim to maximize its
   security   45, 53–4
 Finnish scheme to sell
   Petsamo nickel to
   Germany   50–2
 Finnish-Soviet commission
   (1940–41)   53
 German interest in Petsamo
   46, 48, 49–51, 52–3,
   172 n.36
 Soviet new interest in
   Petsamo   46–9, 52, 53, 54,
   59–65, 102, 150–1
WWII (Continuation War)
 Finland's alliance with
   Hitler's Germany   35,
   36, 54
 Finland's separate armistice
   with Soviet Union   35,
   57–8
 Finnish expropriation of
   Kolosjoki mines   55
 Finnish refusal to transfer
   concession rights to IG
   Farben   55–6
 German occupation of
   Petsamo (Operation
   Renntier)   54–5
 production and transportation
   problems under German
   rule   56
 production for German war
   effort   56–7
 protection of Petsamo by
   German forces   175 n.63

 Soviet advance and
   German destruction of
   Kolosjoki   57, *68*
 Soviet annexation of
   Petsamo   58, 62
WWII-Lapland War (1944–45),
  German-Finnish hostilities
  west of Petsamo   35, 36, 58
war material, nickel as 'strategic
  metal'   4, 29, 31–2, 65, 97,
  102, 150, 157
Western technology   42, 78, 102,
  148, 157
Wingate, Henry S.   69
Winter War (1939–40), *see under*
  war and Petsamo
World War II, *see also* Molotov-
  Ribbentrop Non-
  Aggression pact; war and
  Petsamo
 battle of Kursk (1943)   57
 battle of Stalingrad (1943)   57
 Canada's declaration of war on
   Germany   49
 Finland's alliance with Hitler's
   Germany   4–5, 35, 36,
   54
 German advances (April/May
   1940)   50
 German attack on Poland   38,
   172 n.36
 'Nazi assets' question   110,
   111–12, 114
 Operation Barbarossa   4–5, 46,
   54

Yartsev, Boris   37
Yuzhuralnikel combine   80, 151

Zapolyarnyi   157
Zhdanov, Andrei   109
Zhimerin, D. G.   132–3, 142
Zubok, Vladislav   162 n.18

www.ingramcontent.com/pod-product-compliance
Lightning Source LLC
Chambersburg PA
CBHW072107010526
44111CB00037B/2019